Cup of Salvation

A Powerful Journey Through King David's Psalms of Praise

RABBI PESACH WOLICKI

THE CENTER FOR JEWISH-CHRISTIAN UNDERSTANDING & COOPERATION

CJCUC

CJCUC PUBLISHING HOUSE

In January of 2008, the first Orthodox Jewish institution was established in the world dedicated to religious dialogue, mutual understanding and active cooperation with Christians – the Center for Jewish-Christian Understanding & Cooperation (CJCUC). Since then, CJCUC has moved to the forefront of theological advancements in Jewish-Christian relations. It has changed the Jewish-Christian relational paradigm by engaging tens of thousands of Christians through Bible studies, developing Jewish theology with a positive understanding of Christianity and Christians, organizing faith-based events that bring Jews and Christians together, and coordinating humanitarian aid for the persecuted Christian community in the Middle East.

Cup of Salvation: A Powerful Journey Through King David's Psalms of Praise authored by Rabbi Pesach Wolicki is published by the Center for Jewish-Christian Understanding and Cooperation, located at:

Bible Lands Museum Jerusalem
21 Shmuel Stephan Weisz Street
Jerusalem, Israel 9104601
972-50-200-4733
516-882-3220 (calling from the United States)

Library of Congress Cataloging-in-Publication Data

Names: Wolicki, Pesach, author.
Title: Cup of salvation : a powerful journey through King David's Psalms of
    praise / Rabbi Pesach Wolicki.
Description: [Jerusalem] ; [Springfield], New Jersey : Gefen Publishing
    House, [2017]
Identifiers: LCCN 2017039962 | ISBN 9789652299352
Subjects: LCSH: Hallel. | Bible. Psalms, CXIII–CXVIII—Commentaries. | Bible.
    Psalms—Devotional use. | Pilgrim Festivals (Judaism)—Liturgy.
Classification: LCC BM670.H35 W65 2017 | DDC 223/.207—dc23
LC record available at https://lccn.loc.gov/2017039962

ISBN-978-965-229-935-2

CONTENTS

WHO AM I AND WHY DID I WRITE
THIS BOOK?

Since I began telling people that I am writing a book about Psalms 113 through 118, inevitably they are curious as to why I would write an entire book about these six chapters of the Bible.

Whether the person I was speaking to was Jewish or Christian would determine the motivation behind their curiosity. For Christians, they wanted to know how I chose these six psalms. A book on Psalms makes sense. There are commentaries on many books of the Bible. But why specifically Psalms 113 through 118? What is special about these particular chapters? For Christians, these psalms are not on the top ten list of most famous psalms. Had I been writing a book about Psalm 23, for example, my Christian friends wouldn't have batted an eyelash.

The answer to the curiosity of my Christian friends will explain why Jews would never wonder about this. For Jews, the question came from a different place.

Psalms 113 through 118 hold a very special place in Jewish worship. Collectively, they are called *Hallel* – praise. These six *Hallel* psalms are recited joyously on all of the major festivals; Passover, Pentecost, Tabernacles, Hannukah, as well as on the day of the beginning of each new month, the new moon.

The Talmud records that "the early prophets established for Israel the recitation of *Hallel* to be said upon every season and upon redemption from every danger." This means that in addition to the Biblical feasts, any redemptive event that happens to the Nation of Israel collectively calls for the *Hallel* to be said. In modern times, the Chief Rabbinate of the State of Israel saw the return of Jewish sovereignty to the land of Israel in 1948

1

as an event that meets these qualifications. So today we recite *Hallel*, in addition to the festivals mentioned above, on Israel's Independence Day as well as Jerusalem Day, the anniversary of the unification of Jerusalem under Israel's sovereignty in 1967.

So Jews don't wonder why I would choose to write about these specific psalms. They are fully aware of the special place that these six chapters occupy in Jewish life. Many of them – perhaps most of them – even know these psalms by heart. For them, the curiosity was not about the choice of these psalms. My Jewish friends were generally puzzled by the decision to devote an entire book to the subject. You see, in Jewish circles nobody writes entire books explaining just six chapters of Scripture. To many Jews my plan to write so much about six chapters just seemed excessive.

Beyond this curiosity, there was another question that I got from both Christians and Jews. *Why this?* Everyone who knows me knows that I am involved full time in Jewish-Christian relations. What does a commentary on *Hallel* have to do with this work? I guess that everyone's expectation was that my first full length book would relate directly to my work. What do Psalms 113 through 118 have to do with Jewish-Christian dialogue and cooperation?

The truth is that this is precisely why I chose to write this book. Psalms 113 through 118, the *Hallel*, has *everything* to do with the bridge building work that I am involved in every day.

My first real contact with Christians came about in the early 1990s. At the time, I was Executive Director of the International Coalition for Missing Israeli Soldiers located in Jerusalem. Our purpose was to raise a voice and raise awareness on behalf of Israeli soldiers who were being held captive or whose whereabouts were not known. We represented the families of these men to governments, media, and whoever would listen.

In the course of looking for allies and partners in other Israel related organizations, I met various groups of Christian Zionists. At first I was hesitant. Like most Jews, I thought that Christian Zionists were all just missionaries who were trying to get all Jews to stop being Jewish. I had the same distrust of their love for Israel as most Jews did at the time. But we needed allies so we got involved with them.

As we got to know each other I discovered that my preconceived notions about these Christians were completely wrong. Their love and support for Israel did not derive from some sinister desire to change us. It was not a tactic to make inroads for some ulterior motive. It became abundantly clear to me that the love of these Christians for Israel and the Jewish people was an expression of their faith in God and the Bible. Simple as that.

What I found were people who quite simply saw the State of Israel and the events of our times exactly the way I did; exactly the way I had been taught to see them at home and in school in the Jewish community. I was taught that the modern ingathering of the Jewish people to our homeland after thousands of years of exile was the beginning of the long awaited fulfillment of the prophecies in Deuteronomy 30:

> "Even if your scattered ones shall be at the end of the heavens, from there the Lord your God will gather you and from there He will take you. Then the Lord your God will bring you to the land which your fathers possessed, and you shall possess it. He will prosper you and multiply you more than your fathers."

Simply put, after many centuries of dispersion and exile we will come back and become more numerous and more prosperous than ever before. These words have become the reality of our times. The Christians that I met took these words as literally and as seriously as I did. They believed, as I did, that the words of Zechariah, Isaiah, and Zephaniah are real. They are prophetic.

I grew up in a fiercely religious Zionist home. I was raised to embrace the processes of history as an expression of God's presence on earth. I was raised to see the events of the last century as the footsteps of the beginning of the redemption.

There are two tenets that, I believe, underlie the world view of any religious Zionist.

1. The redemption of Israel, like other historical processes, happens in stages.
2. As servants of God we are supposed to play an active role in the unfolding of the redemption.

Like the religious Zionist community that I was raised in, the Christians that I met understood that we live in the time of the beginning of the redemption. They understood that the story has begun and is by no means over. My new friends also understood that as people of faith in God we must be involved in moving the redemption of Israel forward.

What amazed me most about the Christian Zionists that I met over twenty years ago was their sincere love for Israel. These activists were engaged in support of Israel despite sharp criticism from within their own communities. Not only were they not trying to convert Jews to Christianity - despite Jewish suspicion and accusations to the contrary - one of the chief criticisms that they faced from the rest of the Christian world was that they were *not* trying to convert Jews! They were attacked from all sides. And yet, they were steadfast in their love and support for our people and our land. Understand, in the early nineties Christian Zionism was not quite as mainstream as it is today. These people were paying a price for their love *for us*!

Today, Christians United For Israel has over three million members and regularly has thousands attending its summit in Washington DC. But back then the gatherings of Christian Zionists in the American capitol were made up of a few dozen people at best. I recall being at one of the first such gatherings. The ad hoc organization that hosted the event was called Voices United for Israel. Over the course of a few days various experts on security, mid-East affairs, and the like gave talks while everyone networked and got to know each other's organizations and causes.

I'll never forget this. After one of the security briefings, Richard Hellman, head of CIPAC – the Christian Israel Public Affairs Committee – got up and asked everyone in the room to rise. When all were standing he asked everyone to join him in praying for Israel. After a brief prayer has asked everyone to join him in reciting Deuteronomy 6:4 *Shema Yisrael Adonai Eloheinu Adonai Echad*. Hear O Israel, the Lord is our God, the Lord is One. I was stunned. *What just happened?* He then introduced the next speaker for the next briefing.

There are many other stories that I can tell but I have made this too long already. Suffice it to say that I understood that something was happening. The world was changing. God's promises to His people were being fulfilled and there was a growing number of Christians who saw this the way that I did.

It was not long after that experience in Washington that I was in synagogue reciting the *Hallel* and the words of Psalm 117 hit me like never before.

Praise the Lord all nations; exalt Him all peoples; For His kindness has been great upon us; and the truth of the Lord is forever, Hallelujah.

All nations? All peoples? Praising the Lord for being so good to *the Jews?* I began to wonder how impossible these words must have sounded to my ancestors over the centuries of the exile. Other nations praising God for bestowing blessings on the Jewish people must have seemed just as absurd as the splitting of sea or the plague of frogs in Egypt. But I had seen it with my own eyes. I knew these people. And their numbers were growing by the day.

To make a long story short, my world view was profoundly impacted by these experiences. After leaving the world of political activism behind I continued to retain a strong interest in the changes that were taking place in the Christian world with regard to Israel and Judaism. A few years later, when I entered the pulpit as a rabbi of a synagogue in Newport News, Virginia I invited local Christians to join in the various classes that I offered. I was even a guest speaker at Sunday school at one of the local churches. It was clear to me that the love of God and Scripture that I saw in Christians was a point of commonality that manifested itself in a wide range of shared values. In the cultural battles that were being waged in Western society, Christians and Jews who believed in the living word of God in the Bible were partners in so many ways whether they realized it or not.

In 2003 I returned to Israel and, together with my close friend Rabbi Scott Kahn, opened Yeshivat Yesodei HaTorah, a post secondary institute of higher Torah study in Israel. Together Rabbi Kahn and I led this institution until 2015, when I took my current position as Associate Director of the Center for Jewish - Christian Understanding and Cooperation (CJCUC).

While during the years of Yesodei HaTorah I was not involved in Jewish - Christian relations, the topic was never far from my mind or my lips. When friends and acquaintances wonder aloud about my transition a few years ago from Jewish education to Jewish - Christian relations, I always respond that the only people who are not at all surprised are my students. My discourses and teachings during those years inevitably were built on an understanding of Judaism as a religion with a universal vision; to bring all the peoples of the earth to service of the one God. In any discussion of the goals or theology of Judaism, of the monumental events of our times, or even of mundane political opinions, my recognition of the role being played by modern Christians was included.

In the spring of 2015, as a result of a conversation with Rabbi Shlomo Riskin, Chief Rabbi of the city of Efrat, I picked up the phone and made a call that would change my life. I called David Nekrutman, Executive Director of the Center for Jewish-Christian Understanding and Cooperation. I told him that I wanted to get involved in the work of the center. We got together. We spoke about theology, about God, and about the goals of CJCUC. I knew that I had found my next calling. The inspiration and passion that I had originally felt back in the 1990s was reawakened. I knew that I had to get involved in a big way.

Later that spring, David invited me to be one of the speakers at a unique event to be held on Israel's Independence Day. The concept was pretty simple. Just as Jews recite *Hallel* every year on Independence Day, we were going to host an event for Christians to join us in reciting these Psalms as well. It made perfect sense.

Think about it. We Jews recite *Hallel* in praise and thanks to God for the founding of State of Israel because we understand that this historical development is the fulfillment of Biblical prophecy and a major step in the process of the redemption of Israel. Well, Christian Zionists share these exact beliefs. Shouldn't they be thanking God for the State of Israel as well? What could be more appropriate – and prophetic - than members of the nations of the world reciting Psalm 117, the *one passage in the entire Bible* that describes the nations praising and exalting the Lord for His kindnesses to Israel?

Praise the Lord all nations; exalt Him all peoples; For His kindness has been great upon us; and the truth of the Lord is forever, Hallelujah.

What makes more sense than an event that fulfills this Scripture exactly?

The event was called Day to Praise. It was held in a synagogue in Jerusalem. I was one of three rabbis honored with the opportunity to share words between the readings of the *Hallel* psalms. There were interludes of beautiful music. The event went as planned.

Everyone in the room that day knew that something incredible had begun. This was not merely an Israel Independence Day celebration with a few Scriptural readings. The feeling in that synagogue in Jerusalem when Psalm 117 was read was uplifting and prophetic.

Something that felt simultaneously very new and very ancient was taking place. There we were, Jews and Christians praising and thanking God in Jerusalem, on the same day, with the same words, for the same reason; a reason that was described by the very words that we were saying; words that were written thousands of years ago prophetically describing a time in the distant future. And here we were.

Since that day, CJCUC has hosted *Hallel* – Day to Praise events on Feast of Tabernacles as well as Israel Independence Day every year. It is from the inspiration drawn from my participation in these powerful gatherings that this book was born.

To make a long story short, I left the world of Jewish education and joined CJCUC as its Associate Director. My work takes me to many corners of the Christian world. I continue to learn and be inspired by the people that I meet; by their love of God, love of Scripture, and love of Israel.

Through my work with CJCUC I have the opportunity to break down walls of fear and misunderstanding between our communities. Most Jews and Christians do not realize just how much we share with each other. It is far easier to focus on our differences. Make no mistake about it, our differences are significant. The differences between us are important and not to be compromised. For many Jews and Christians the dual barrier of theological difference and historical animosity is too difficult to overcome. But we are making a terrible mistake - both politically and theologically - if we allow those differences to blind us to the opportunities for cooperation and to the many values and beliefs that we do share.

As Dr. Brad Young of Oral Roberts University said at that very first Day to Praise event in Jerusalem, "We can not ignore the wrongs in the history of the Church towards Judaism; but we are not bound by that history." We must seize every opportunity to create a new and lasting relationship between our faiths.

Our battles – both culturally and spiritually – are increasingly the same. Our challenges are shared whether we acknowledge that fact or not.

At CJCUC, we seek to connect our communities around all that is shared while respecting and acknowledging the differences between our communities of faith. Every day, I wake up proud and honored to play a role in such sacred work.

In the course of my many talks to Christians I discovered something that makes their eyes light up with excitement every single time. Whenever I quote the Bible in Hebrew and share a nuance of meaning that they were not aware of from translation, I see smiles and joy throughout the room. They have a genuine love of the word of God and a thirst for the authentic understanding that can only come from the original text.

I hope that at this point I have answered the original question. Namely, why did I choose to write precisely this book? I hope that it is now clear that this book is both the direct result and the highest expression of my work with the Center for Jewish-Christian Understanding and Cooperation.

The primary goal of this project from the beginning was to expose the Christian reader to the poetic beauty and layers of meaning that lie beneath the surface of Biblical text. I try to demonstrate how the lessons that Scripture has in store for us can often be found only by asking the right questions. *Why was this word used? Why was the verse written is exactly this way? Where else does this unusual phrase appear and what does that tell me about the passage that I am reading?* These are the questions that are at the forefront of my mind as I explore Scripture. I wanted to bring the Christian audience into this experience.

But as I worked on the book, as I progressed through the verses of these *Hallel* psalms, I discovered something that I did not expect. I discovered that although I knew these psalms by heart – after all, they are a prominent part of our liturgy – I had no idea what they were actually saying? Oh, I knew the words alright. But the fact that there was a progression of ideas from verse to verse and from psalm to psalm was something that I had never known was there.

I started asking Jewish friends of mine, some of them serious scholars, if they knew what *Hallel* was saying? It became clear to me that I had discovered something that has been there all along but had never been uncovered.

I read through every available commentary on psalms going back two thousand years. Almost without exception, the approach of these classic commentaries is either to explain verses or words in a vacuum or at best, to explain a single psalm standing alone. Poetic repetitions, unusual word choices, and, most of all, the progression of ideas – the narrative – that runs through these six *Hallel* psalms were almost completely absent from the content of any prior writing on these psalms. Here and there I would discover an occasional solitary comment in one of the commentaries alluding to a broader idea. Rarely would these ideas be elaborated or followed up on later in the text.

But the more I studied, the more I wrote, the more I asked the questions that come from reading carefully, the more I discovered the structure of Psalms 113 through 118. I discovered the "story" of *Hallel*. This story is told in the pages of this book. But I will sum it up here.

Psalm 113 begins by introducing the total mastery and control that God employs in His governance of the world both on a macro-historical level as well as on the individual level. 113 describes God's power to manipulate and even completely disregard the both the laws that govern human affairs as well as the laws of nature. Most importantly, God does all of this out of love and mercy for the righteous and neglected.

After this introductory paragraph which makes no mention of specific people or events, Psalm 114 applies the lessons of Psalm 113 to Israel. The Exodus from Egypt, the revelation at Sinai, the water from a rock, and the miraculous crossing of the Jordan are all examples of God's mastery over nature for the benefit of His chosen people.

But lest we begin to think that God does all of this for the sake of Israel's glory, lest Israel begin to believe that they are the be all and end all, along comes Psalm 115. *Not to us, but to You shall be the glory*. The psalm continues with a discourse on the folly and error of idol worship followed by an explanation of God's blessings upon those who embrace His mission. In this way, Psalm 115 responds to and informs the miracles described in Psalm 114 before it.

Psalm 116 at first seems to break the series. It is written as a first person singular account. It tells the story of someone who suffers and is in danger, is redeemed by God, and uses this experience as a springboard for the spreading of God's glory to others; ultimately, in Psalm 117 to *all nations and all peoples*.

While initially appearing out of place, Psalm 116 is the key to understanding the mission laid out in Psalm 115 before it. Psalm 116 provides the road map for the transition that any person of faith must go through to move from a personal relationship with the Lord to the embrace of the larger mission to create His kingdom over all the earth.

At the end of Psalm 116, the psalmist committed himself to bring a sacrifice of thanksgiving. In Psalm 118 we figuratively find ourselves present at the temple attending this event. Speaking on behalf of the People of Israel, the singular psalmist tells the story of persecution, redemption and praise in which we are all participants.

This is the story of *Hallel*. If you want to know more, well, keep reading.

At this point I would like to explain something about the process of writing this book. First, I read each verse carefully. I thought about it in the context of the verses immediately preceding and following. I made note of anomalous choices of words and syntax. I frequently thought about an individual verse for a few days or even an entire week. And then I read prominent commentaries from Jewish tradition.

The commentaries that I looked at on every verse were Rashi (11th cent. France), Radak (12th cent. France), Ibn Ezra (12th cent. Spain), Meiri (13th cent. France), Seforno (16th cent. Italy), Malbim (19th cent. Eastern Europe), and R. S.R. Hirsch (19th cent. Germany)

After reading through all that they wrote I would think about the verse again and come to my own conclusions about how to answer my questions. Although, I made use of these commentaries in the process, you will notice that there are no footnotes in this book. I made this choice primarily because I very rarely based what I wrote on what I saw in these commentaries. They rarely addressed the most basic textual questions that I had. On the occasions when I did use them, I inevitably took their ideas in a different direction from what they intended. That said, I am sure that knowledgeable readers will find echoes of these great rabbis' ideas in what I have written. This leads me to the second reason for my avoidance of footnotes. Since these commentaries are almost completely inaccessible to the Christian reader I felt that footnotes would not serve their primary purpose in a work like this.

In sum, if you discover that something that I wrote bears some similarity to what you find in one of the great commentaries listed above, you can feel free to assume that I was inspired by what I saw there. Apologies again for a lack of citations.

A number of people made significant helpful contributions to the writing of this book. My good friend Lisa Nehring, a true lover of the Lord and Scripture, read through the draft and made many invaluable comments that led to significant changes. Lisa's Christian eyes were essential in helping me see how certain ideas would be understood by the Christian segment of my audience. On the Jewish side, Rabbi Avraham Fischer served a similar role. Rabbi Fischer's expertise in grammar saved me from a number of missteps and his poetic feel for Scripture and theology enriched the text and refined my message. Thank you.

But my true mentor and guide throughout this project has been CJCUC's Executive Director, David Nekrutman. It has been David's vision and planning that has made this book a reality. Without his efforts, it simply would never have been written. From the moment we came up with the idea for the book David has been my chief editor, critic, coach, enabler, publicist, podcast host, and friend. The Jewish – Christian relational work that I am so passionate about and so grateful to be a part of would simply not be possible without everything that David does. David, my debt of gratitude to you grows by the day. I may be listed on the cover as the author but this work is as much yours as it is mine.

The work that I do entails a great deal of travel. I am away from my family much more than most dads and husbands. This is a sacrifice that is made not only by me but by my family as well. I owe a great debt of gratitude to my wife Kate and to my children Sarah, Meir, Rina, Nechama, Ezra, David, Asaf, and Ayelet for appreciating the importance of my work and for managing without me around so much of the time.

Most of all, I am grateful to HASHEM, God Almighty for giving me the strength and opportunity, not only to write this book but to serve Him through the work that I am privileged to do. I go to bed every night and awake every morning with gratitude for the journey that He is leading me through.

Give thanks to the Lord for He is good; for His kindness is eternal.

PSALM 113

HOW GOD RUNS OUR WORLD

Psalm 113, the opening of the *Hallel* psalms of Praise serves as an introduction to the five other psalms that follow.

The theme of this psalm is the extent of God's total control and mastery over all of human affairs.

In the first three verses the psalmist makes a general call to praise and bless the Lord.

Verses 4 and 5 then describe God's dominance over the fates and wills of nations. This is the theme of psalms 114 and 115. This is hinted at by the reference to God as ELOHENU - *our God* - in verse 5. This name of God, as opposed to *the Lord*, appears later in these psalms only in reference to God's special relationship to Israel; see 114:7 and 115:2-3.

The final four verses of psalm 113 tell of the Lord's concern, involvement, and willingness to perform miracles even with regard to the lives of individuals who are in need no matter how insignificant those people may seem in the grand scheme of history.

Each of these themes will be expanded upon in later psalms in the *Hallel* series. The Lord's dominion over the fates of nations, and Israel in particular, will be expanded upon in Psalms 114, 115, and 117; the Lord's redemptive concern for the individual who is suffering in Psalms 116 and 118. And as we will see, these two themes are synthesized as the *Hallel* reaches its conclusion.

God is master of nations, of history, and at the same time He shows compassion for the poor person or the childless mother suffering quietly at home. He is as lofty as He is humble.

Psalm 113

הַלְלוּיָהּ: הַלְלוּ, עַבְדֵי יְהוָה; הַלְלוּ, אֶת שֵׁם יְהוָה.	א	1.	*Praise the Lord. Praise, O servants of the Lord; praise the Name of the Lord*
יְהִי שֵׁם יְהוָה מְבֹרָךְ מֵעַתָּה, וְעַד עוֹלָם.	ב	2.	*May the Lord's name be blessed from this time to Eternity.*
מִמִּזְרַח שֶׁמֶשׁ עַד מְבוֹאוֹ מְהֻלָּל, שֵׁם יְהוָה.	ג	3.	*From the rising of the sun until its setting, may the Name of the Lord be praised.*
רָם עַל כָּל גּוֹיִם יְהוָה; עַל הַשָּׁמַיִם כְּבוֹדוֹ.	ד	4.	*Raised up high over all nations is the Lord, upon the heavens is His glory.*
מִי, כַּיהוָה אֱלֹהֵינוּ הַמַּגְבִּיהִי לָשָׁבֶת.	ה	5.	*Who is like the Lord our God who causes Himself to sit most high*
הַמַּשְׁפִּילִי לִרְאוֹת בַּשָּׁמַיִם וּבָאָרֶץ.	ו	6.	*Who brings Himself down low to look upon the Heavens and the Earth*
מְקִימִי מֵעָפָר דָּל; מֵאַשְׁפֹּת, יָרִים אֶבְיוֹן.	ז	7.	*He raises up the poor from the dust; from the trash-heap he elevates the needy.*
לְהוֹשִׁיבִי עִם נְדִיבִים; עִם, נְדִיבֵי עַמּוֹ.	ח	8.	*He seats them with nobles, with the nobles of His people.*
מוֹשִׁיבִי, עֲקֶרֶת הַבַּיִת אֵם-הַבָּנִים שְׂמֵחָה: הַלְלוּיָהּ	ט	9.	*He makes a barren woman who dwells in a home into a joyful mother of children Praise God! (Halleluyah)*

113:1 *What's in a name?*

Praise the Lord. Praise,
O servants of the Lord; praise
the Name of the Lord

Why praise a name?

What does it mean to praise the *Name of the Lord*? Why not just say that we must praise God and leave it at that? What does it even mean to praise a *name*? Would I care that much if a friend of mine or an admirer told me that they admire me not only as person but they admire *my name* as well? "You're a great guy. And you know what? You've got a great *name* too!"

And yet, frequently Scripture refers to the *Name* of God as though God's Name has importance over and above God Himself. To cite just one example among many,

The Lord will be king over all the earth; on that day the Lord will be One and *His Name* will be One. (Zachariah 14:9)

I understand what it means that the Lord will be One. There is only one God. Power must not be attributed to anything else, that God alone will be recognized as the supreme being. Well, here's our question. What is added by saying that "His *Name* will be One"?

It can't possibly mean that God only has one name because we know that that is not true. God has many names that appear throughout Scripture.

A name means that people know me

Think about what a name is. If you lived alone on a desert island you would have no need for a name. In fact, you wouldn't really have a name at all. I mean, you'd *have* a name but only in theory. It would never get used. A *name* is a means by which we are known and addressed by others. To have a *name* means that someone is interacting with me and recognizes me. More specifically, it means that my identity - what makes me who I am and what defines me is *known*. This is what makes a *name* different from an *attribute*.

An *attribute* is one aspect of who I am. For example, my kids call me *Dad*. Lots of people are called *Dad*. *Dad* is not a unique name to me. Moreover, it is only *one aspect of my identity*. *Dad* is not who I am to my wife or to my students. The title *Dad* refers to *one attribute* of my total self. My *name* is a different story. My *name* is who I am. My *name* encompasses the fullness of my persona. *Pesach Wolicki* is my name. Pesach Wolicki is a Dad, a husband, a Rabbi, an excellent scrambled egg maker (according to my kids), etc. *Dad* and *Rabbi* are *attributes*; Pesach Wolicki, on the other hand, is not an attribute; it's my *name*. It is the fullness of my self.

To sum up, a *name* means two things:
1. It means that others see me and are interacting with me. (Think of the desert island).
2. It means that the *fullness of who I am* is perceived and not merely a single attribute.

Praise God vs. Praise His Name
Now we can understand the difference between praising God and praising *His Name*. When I praise God I am praising the creator and ruler of heaven and earth – *whether I see Him or not*. When I praise *God's Name* I take it a step further. I am saying, in effect,

1. *God is perceptible*, I see Him in the world and in my life. I am interacting with Him.
2. *All of His attributes are One*. I am praising the totality of who God is. All of the different aspects of His creation, of life, and of the complicated reality around me are One. They are all contained within Him. They are all parts of the same ultimate Will, plan, and purpose. They are all expressions of the same Living God.

Why <u>servants</u> of the Lord?

With this in mind, we can understand why our verse begins by calling on the *servants of the Lord* to praise Him. *Servants*, by definition, are subservient to the will of their master. Servants do not follow their own will. They are *servants*. It is not their understanding or free will that determines their behavior. They subordinate their own will to the will of their master. In other words, referring to people of faith as *servants of the Lord* focuses on the fact that part of faith in God is the willingness to negate ones own understanding and will in favor of the will of God – even though it is beyond our understanding.

To accept and praise the fullness of who God is, one must relate to God as a servant and be willing to embrace what is unknowable to limited human beings.

Praise, O servants of the Lord. Praise the Name of the Lord. When we accept and praise the fullness of the Lord as servants; when we express our faith in the fact that all attributes of God are One; it is then that through us *His Name*; i.e. *the fullness of the Lord* is praised.

As a servant of the Lord I praise and worship the fullness of God – His Name – even beyond the limits of my human perception.

113:2 *Does God need our blessings?*

**May the Lord's name be blessed
from this time to Eternity.**

What blessings does God need?

Does God need to be blessed by us? What are we actually doing when we bless God? I understand what it means to *bless* another person. It usually means either that I am bestowing gifts upon them or that I am offering a prayer for their success and well-being. When we speak of *blessing* someone we mean that we have something to offer them that will benefit them. Colloquially, someone is *blessed* with wealth or with a particular talent.

For example, when Isaac blessed his sons, Jacob and Esau, he bestowed gifts upon them both in terms of material wealth as well as in the spiritual arena. In this context the word *blessing* indicates material wealth, spiritual gifts, or loftiness of status and power.

For example, the phrase *And He will bless your bread and your water* (Exodus 23:25) likewise refers to the granting of something beneficial by the blesser to the one being blessed.

So what does it mean to bless God? Are we to understand that when we bless God we are bestowing something upon Him? The implication that there is some good that we could give God makes no sense. God is complete and perfect in every way. To say that we could bestow anything upon Him implies that there is some way in which He could be improved. Furthermore, as God's creations, we cannot possibly possess anything to give God that does not come from Him to begin with. Obviously, when we talk about *blessing God* we mean something other than the conventional use of the term.

Blessing = Abundance

In the previous verse we spoke of *praising* God. This makes sense. Praise of God publicizes Him in the world and reinforces our sense of awe of Him. But what is the difference between *praising* Him and *blessing* Him?

The Hebrew word for blessing is BERACHA. The first time that this word - or its verb root - appears in the Torah is on the fifth day of creation.

> God] *blessed* them [the fish] saying, 'Be fruitful and multiply and fill the water in the seas.' (Gen. 1:22)

God told the fish that there would be many of them. BERACHA - *blessing* – refers to *abundance*. God blessed the fish by saying, "May there be a lot of you." More broadly, *blessing* is the actualization of hidden potential for good. For example, two fish, or two people, may have the *potential* to reproduce. This is not a blessing. The *blessing* is the realization of this potential when a child is actually produced.

When we *bless* God we are not bestowing anything on God. We are attempting to draw out the hidden potential for *more Godliness* in the world. In Judaism every blessing, whether it is over food, prior to the performance of a commandment, or as part of the prayer liturgy, begins with the words *Blessed are You, Lord*. When we say *Blessed are You, Lord...*, we are saying to God, "Let there be *more of You* revealed in this world."

Seeing the Godliness in Everything

Everything that God created can be used to reveal Him. Every one of God's creations contains latent Godliness. Allow me to explain. Anything created by anybody is an expression of that person's personality and will. A piece of music, art, or writing reveals the identity and personality of the artist. We learn about the creator by looking at his creations. The same is true of the Lord. Everything in creation; every person, every natural phenomenon, every event is an expression of who God is. There is Godliness in everything because God is the creator. But often, this Godliness is hidden and exists only in potential. When we see it ourselves and allow other to see it we reveal the hidden potential for awareness of God.

For example, if I take an apple and eat it without recognizing the Godliness within it - that it is one of God's creations - I have not revealed the hidden Godliness in the apple. There is less perception of God in the world.

If, on the other hand, I recite a blessing and praise God before eating and thus declare my awareness of the Godliness in the apple, I have revealed the potential of this apple to be a vehicle for knowledge of God in the world. As a result, there is more awareness and glory of God.

With this perspective we can understand our verse as saying, *May God's name* – i.e. awareness of Him – *be blessed* – i.e. increased and multiplied - *from this time forward to Eternity*.

By blessing God's name we reveal the Godliness that is hidden in His creation.

113:3 *Praise by Day*

---

*From the rising of the sun until
its setting, may the Name
of the Lord be praised.*

Until Sunset?

One traditional interpretation of this verse sees *the rising of the sun* as referring to the Easternmost place in Earth and *its setting* to the Westernmost. And yet, the precise wording and imagery in this verse refers not to directions but to the times of day, *sunrise and sunset*.

At first glance, this verse seems to be saying simply that God's name is praised *all the time*; i.e. from sunrise to sunset – i.e. all day long.

However, look closely at the verse. It specifically states that God's name is praised *until the setting of the sun*. The implication is that God's name is not praised at night. If this is an accurate reading of the verse then the obvious question is, *Why? What about night time?* Why not praise God's name at all times, both day and night? Is He worthy of our praise only during the day and not at night time as well?

The spiritual meaning of Night

Throughout the book of Psalms, the imagery of *night* is used to indicate times of difficulty or struggle.

For example:

I am worn out from my groaning. All night long I flood my bed with weeping and drench my couch with tears. (Psalm 6:7; see also Psalms 17:3 and 77:3 among others)

Night time is the time of darkness. It is the time when we don't have clarity of vision. Universally, the expression *dark times* indicates times of suffering; times when evil seems to be prevailing in our lives and in the world.

In those trying moments, we call out to God in prayer. We seek His help, His strength, and His salvation.

Praise is for God Revealed.

And that is exactly the point. These psalms of praise are not about seeking God in dark times. Psalms 113 through 118 are songs of *praise*. These psalms are about praising God as *He reveals Himself to us* in times of overt – even miraculous – kindness and salvation.

As I explained in verse 1, the *Name* of God indicates Godliness that I can see. The God we can point to and say, as the People of Israel said as they crossed the Red Sea, "THIS IS MY GOD!"

Night is for Prayer; Daytime is for Praise

If times of trial and struggle are what Psalms refers to as *night*, then the experience of God's revealed miracles and abundant kindness is, figuratively speaking, what the psalmist refers to as *day*. During difficult dark times, the *night* of our lives, we are certainly called upon to *seek* God, to *pray* to Him, and even to be thankful to Him for whatever He has given us. But to *praise Him* during those times as though He has supernaturally revealed Himself is wrong. If there is no difference between God's concealment in dark times and the revelation of Him in times of light, then what is the point of God's miracles?

Consider this verse:

To declare Your *loving-kindness* in the morning And Your *faith* by night, (Psalm 92:3)

Notice that God's *loving-kindness* is associated with *morning* and *faith* with the *night*. When we experience God revealed openly and miraculously we would not call that *faith*; just as I don't have *faith* that I am sitting at my desk and writing these words. I *know* this to be true. Here I am. *Faith* is what I experience when I believe something to be true when it is *not* perceptible to my five senses. *Faith at night* – during the dark times when I can not see Him clearly. *Kindness by day* – when He shows Himself.

So why is it wrong to praise God in dark times as well as when I experience His open kindness? Think about it. The ultimate goal of Biblical faith is to bring about knowledge of God. In the words of Isaiah:

> The wolf will live with the lamb, the leopard will lie down with the goat, the calf and the lion and the yearling together; and a little child will lead them. The cow will feed with the bear, their young will lie down together, and the lion will eat straw like the ox. The infant will play near the cobra's den, and the young child will put its hand into the viper's nest. They will neither harm nor destroy on all my holy mountain, *for the earth will be filled with the knowledge of the Lord as the waters cover the sea.* (Isaiah 11:6-9)

These verses describe a series of overt miracles; a complete overturning of the laws of nature. These miracles lead to *knowledge* of the Lord; not *faith*. If we treat every situation as though God has revealed Himself miraculously, then how are we to distinguish when God truly reveals Himself?

Our human experiences of God, the natural instinctive feelings that well up inside of us in response to what we are seeing, are meant to be used as tools and doorways that allow us to relate to the Almighty. Of course, God is equally present in times of both dark and light – but it *doesn't feel that way to us.* God wants us to use our experiences and our natural feelings in every situation as a way to reach out to Him. To pretend that God has performed great miracles for us when we don't feel that way would be disingenuous and would cheapen the kindness and blessing – and gratitude that we feel - when He does explicitly reveal Himself.

[handwritten: Praise comes from confidence in God's in hand for your good]

[handwritten: Knowing vs Believing]

Psalms 113 through 118 are included in Jewish liturgy only on days that commemorate great miracles; the Exodus, the giving of the Torah, the founding of the State of Israel. We do not say Hallel every day. To do so would belittle and cheapen those awe-inspiring moments when God *overtly* makes His presence – His *name* – known; moments that change our lives and the course of history forever.

So right at the beginning of these psalms of praise, the psalmist sets this tone.

From the rising of the sun <u>until</u> its setting, the name of God is praised.

While we worship and seek the Lord at all times in our lives, Praise is reserved for those times when we see Him clearly.

113:4 *God's Plan and Human Free Will*

*Raised up high over all nations
is the Lord, upon the heavens is
His glory.*

Free will vs. God's Will

One of the most confusing theological issues – one that has bothered great religious thinkers for centuries – is the problem of Free Will vs. predetermination. On one hand, we know that God has ordained a plan for the world. Scripture describes the future and it is axiomatic to any Bible believing person that God's Will must be done. In other words, God's will trumps human free will. But if this is so, *human* free will must be limited.

On the other hand, God granted free will to human beings. Without free will, there is no meaning to our choices. God wants us to be able to make choices. He wants us to choose Good and to reject Evil. Without free will we are neither deserving of reward for the good that we do nor are we responsible for our deviances. Without free will, we can not *choose* to have a relationship to God and our lives are rendered meaningless.

To sum up: God's Will and plan for the world overrides any decisions that humans can make and therefore human free will must be limited. On the other hand, humans must have complete free will so that our lives have purpose and meaning; so that we are responsible and worthy of reward and punishment. This appears to be a paradox. Do humans have free will or don't they?

The limits of human free will

While there is a wide range of opinions to deal with this question, one conclusion remains certain regardless of the approach one chooses. Free will must exist; *however,* Free will must be limited. Where different theologians disagree is in regard to the extent of the limitations.

So what are the limitations? Well, as I mentioned above God clearly has a plan for the world. The story of history has a beginning and an end. Scripture tells us about the ancient past beginning with creation as well as giving us an outline of the distant future up to the end of time. How this story ends is predetermined.

For example, Deuteronomy 30 describes the miraculous return of the People of Israel to the Land of Israel after a lengthy and difficult exile scattered to all corners of the earth. So here's the question: Do we have the freedom to prevent this from happening? Can the miraculous ingathering of the exiles of the People of Israel to their land that we have witnessed in our days be undone? What if the leaders of the nations of the world decided to reverse this process? What about all of the other prophecies that foretell the future?

The answer is that while we are free to make certain choices, we are not free to negate God's plan for the world. Political leaders of nations all too often think that history is in their hands. They feel themselves so powerful that they think that it is their plans rather than God's that will come to pass. They are obviously mistaken. This is where their free will is limited. Only God has the power to govern history; to determine the fate of nations.

God's Will is Higher

The Hebrew word for *raised up high* – RAM – appears twice in the book of Psalms. Once in this verse and once in Psalm 99:

> *The Lord is great in Zion, and He is raised up high over all peoples.*
> (Psalm 99:2)

In both instances, this description of God as *raised up high* is in reference to *all peoples* or *all nations*.

If the point of this verse is merely that God is more powerful than the nations of the world, well, that is obvious to any person of faith. Presumably, this is not a point that must be made here in Psalms. Nations are made up of human beings of flesh and blood. God is certainly more powerful than them. Furthermore, there are other adjectives that are better used to describe power than *raised up high.* What exactly does *raised up high* say about God and His relationship to the nations of the world?

A number of verses in Psalms refer to God controlling the fate of the nations. For example, Psalm 2:

> Why do the nations conspire and the peoples plot in vain?
> The kings of the earth rise up and the rulers band together against the Lord and against his anointed, saying, "Let us break their chains and throw off their shackles."
> The One enthroned in heaven laughs; the Lord scoffs at them.
> (Psalm 2:1-4)

Arrogance and power are universally seen as *high*. Just think of the standard way to address a king, "Your *High*ness". When God's will for history overwhelms and overrules the plans of arrogant rulers, the word RAM is used. In the story of the Exodus from Egypt, Exodus 14:8 refers to the Children of Israel leaving Egypt *with a high hand*. The word for *high* there is RAM as well.

There are many people who claim to believe in God but don't really see Him as governing history. Maybe they profess a faith in Him that is limited to the wonders of natural creation, but not as ruler over the decisions of men. They are willing to believe in God in a general vague sense but they do not see themselves as created beings subservient to the will of their creator.

And then there are times when history clearly takes a miraculous turn and we see with our own eyes that it is God's Will and not the will of men that governs historical events. At times like these we open our mouths and declare,

Raised up high over all nations is the Lord! It is He and He alone who moves history forward, *upon the heavens is His glory* beyond where human eyes can see and the human mind can comprehend, all of creation glorifies His great plan.

While humans have free will, that freedom does not include the ability to change the course of God's plan for the world. God's will overrides and overrules the will of men.

113:5 *God Sits*

Who is like the Lord our God
who causes Himself to sit
most high

While at first glance this verse is simply stating the theological fact that God dwells in a most high place, a closer look at the precise word choice reveals much more.

God sits

Many verses in scripture refer to God *sitting*. (e.g. Psalm 2:4, 91:1) Considering the obvious fact that God neither possesses a physical body with which to sit nor does He need to get off his feet and relax in a comfortable chair, the imagery of *God sitting* needs to be understood.

Isaiah 66:1 states, *The heavens are my throne and the earth is my foot-stool*. God *sits* in the sense that a king sits on his throne. The throne is the location of sovereignty. It is from the position of *sitting on the throne* that the king renders his rulings and decides the fate of the king-dom. *Sitting* indicates a settled relaxed position from which to render a decision.

Think about it. When we are in motion - walking, running, driving our cars - and something very important is on our minds that we need to think about, we feel the need to sit down. Sitting down allows us to think clearly and calmly. When we get excited or angry we have trouble sitting. If someone is overreacting and we want them to calm down we tell them to take a seat.

In other words, *sitting* implies *reason, lack of impulsiveness,* and *sovereignty*.

Additionally, sitting is quite literally a lowering of the body towards the ground. To say that God *sits* implies that He is governing, He is deciding, and He is not distant. He has lowered Himself – so to speak – towards us.

The King's Thoughts are Most High

The king is not a legislature of many. He is not a House of Representatives. The sole forum for deliberation and decision making is the mind of the King as He sits on His throne. We, the subjects, are not privy to or partners in His thinking.

The fact that God's choices are distant from our understanding is indicated by the verb "HaMaGBIHI" – *who causes to be most high* in this verse. The same verb root GBH – *high*, or *raised* - is used in Isaiah 55:9 and Isaiah 5:16 to indicate how *God's thoughts and decisions* are beyond our comprehension and purview.

As the heavens are higher – GaBHU - than the earth, so are my ways higher – GaBHU - than your ways, and my thoughts than your thoughts. (Isaiah 55:9)

The Lord of hosts shall be exalted – VaYiGBaH - in judgment, and God that is holy shall be sanctified in righteousness. (Isaiah 5:16)

To sum up, God *sitting* indicates that He is concerned with what is happening in our world below, that He is governing, that He is making wise deliberate decisions from the throne. Saying that *He causes Himself to sit most high* tells us that His decisions, while relating to our earthly world, originate from a place that is far beyond any wisdom that we could ever conceive of.

Sitting	=	Governing, wise, deliberate, concerned
Most high	=	His thoughts are beyond our understanding

He Causes Himself to Sit

There is one more linguistic oddity in this verse that is worth noting. The verse does not say: *Who is like the Lord our God who sits most high*. It says *Who is like the Lord our God who causes Himself to sit most high*. Unlike English, Hebrew verbs can be conjugated in a way to imply causing someone else to do something. For example, *I stand* can mean that I stand up myself or that I help someone or something else stand, as in "The bookcase fell so *I will stand it back up*." The first is direct. The second is *causative*. I am *causing* the bookcase to stand. In our verse the causative conjugation *He causes Himself to sit* seems pointless. Why doesn't the psalm simply state that God *sits most high*? Of course He *causes* His own sitting. Who else would be *causing* it?

I'd like to suggest that there is a deep lesson that the psalmist poetically implies by this choice of words.

God's decisions are beyond our comprehension. They come from the throne that is *most high*. A person might think that perhaps if only we were smart enough we could figure out God's mind. Perhaps our lack of understanding is merely due to our limited intellects. In other words, maybe we don't understand God's decisions because of our own failing, but if we really thought about it we could figure it out. If God's decisions were beyond us because He *is most high* this might be correct. However, with the causative wording we see that this is not so. God <u>causes</u> *His throne to be most high.* Our inability to understand God's sovereign rulings is not the circumstantial result of our human failing. It is a premeditated decision by God; part of His plan. It is axiomatic. *God causes His decisions to be beyond us.*

In other words, God's sovereign decisions are not merely unknown; they are unknowable.

Part of the very definition of God is that He is unknowable. His decisions are beyond us; not because of our failure but because He has set it up this way.

113:6 *Great and Humble God*

*Who brings Himself down low
to look upon the Heavens
and the Earth*

God cares about the "little" things

This verse forms a matched couplet with the previous verse. After stating that God sits and governs from a throne that is so lofty that it is fundamentally beyond us, the psalm now tells us that despite this loftiness, God *brings Himself down low to look upon the Heavens and the Earth.*

God is most high. His divine wisdom with which He governs our world is inaccessible to us. And yet, this distance and the incomprehensible nature of God do not mean that He is concerned only with what seems like the big things in the world below. In the previous verses we discussed that God alone governs history despite what arrogant human rulers may think. Now we take this providential concern one step further. Not only does God govern history. Not only is He in full control of the seemingly important things. His providence extends to every detail of creation no matter how lowly it may be.

God sees

Two verbs are used here to describe this all encompassing Providence. *Brings Himself down low* and *to look.*

Once again, taking into account that God is not physical, when we encounter verbs describing God in physical spatial terms, we must consider precisely what each of these descriptions implies.

God *seeing* or *looking* seems simple enough. He is aware. He is watching. But what, then is the difference between God *hearing* as an indication of awareness (e.g. Exodus 2:24) and God *seeing*? If both *hearing* and *seeing* imply *awareness*, how would we explain Exodus 2:25?

And God *saw* the Children of Israel, and God *knew.*

If *seeing* indicates awareness, how is it different from *knowing*?

Hearing vs Seeing vs Knowing

The difference is actually quite simple. Hearing means that there is a sound to be heard. Something is making that sound. Something is being expressed. Because I can hear sounds that are around me in any direction regardless of the direction I am facing, hearing is more *passive* than seeing. Seeing implies a more active concentration; a choice to see and be aware. To see I must be facing that which I am seeing. Therefore, I often have to turn my head towards something in order to see it. *Knowing* – as opposed to both seeing and hearing - is an *internal* experience. It is a cognitive experience that comes after the sensory data – that which is *seen* or *heard* - has been taken in.

Inasmuch as these terms are all metaphors for God's awareness of the human condition, it's valuable to sum up what each term implies.

Hearing = passive awareness; *reactive* rather than proactive
Seeing = more *proactive* than hearing; facing or turning towards; concerned
Knowing = mental; internal, *cognitive* reaction to sensory data

To say that God *looks* or *sees* indicates that He is *proactively* seeking out His creation and *paying attention* to it. He is not merely *hearing*, i.e. reactively responding to a call to Him. God *sees*, therefore, means that God is *proactively aware*. He cares. In other words, even without someone crying out, He is there.

God Humbles Himself

The Hebrew verb *brings Himself down low* is not the usual verb used in scripture for descending. Here, the verb is a causative conjugation of the Hebrew root ShFL, meaning *lowly, humble,* or *meek.* The causative form of this Hebrew verb - *brings down low* – appears some seventeen times in Scripture. Every single time this word appears it is used to describe a person or thing that is arrogant or seemingly strong that is being *cut down to size* or *humbled.* The only exception is our verse in which this verb is used in reference to God. Obviously, God is not arrogant. He is not being cut down to size.

In other words, from all of the other appearances of this word throughout the Bible we see that the *bringing low* described by this word does not indicate mere *descent* from up to down. Rather, this word indicates *being forced down* from a place of arrogance to a place of humble lowly status.

Contrast this to the scene in Genesis when God *descends* to inspect the evil ways of Sodom and Gomorrah.

> Then the Lord said, "The outcry against Sodom and Gomorrah
> is so great and their sin so grievous that I will *go down* and *see*
> if what they have done is as bad as the outcry that has reached
> me. If not, I will know." (Genesis 18:20-21)

The verb root for *go down* is not ShFL as in our verse in Psalms. Here in Genesis it is RDH meaning *to descend*, spatially, plain and simple. This verb would be used to describe any physical move downward. Two typical examples are the angels in Jacob's dream *descending* the ladder as well as Moses *descending* from Mount Sinai with the Tablets in Exodus. Similarly, in the Sodom and Gomorrah scene I just cited, God was *descending* as judge and ruler to assess the misbehavior of his subjects and decide on a fitting punishment. RDH is the root used in all of these. It is always the word that describes God *going down*; except for here in our verse.

Here in our verse in Psalms, the verb root and its connotation are completely different. In this verse God is not merely descending, so to speak, *He is humbling Himself.* The image is both powerful and beautiful. The Lord is lowering Himself from His lofty distant status to concern Himself with matters that one would think are beyond His concern.

To put it all together, **Who _brings Himself down low_ to _look_ upon the Heavens and the Earth** means that God is *proactive* in concerning Himself with even what seem to us to be minutia and trivialities. Nothing – no person, no event, no decision - is too lowly for God's Providential care and concern. *He is humble just as He is Most High.*

The Lord is actively concerned with our individual lives. He is not an aloof and distant King.

113:7 *The Two Sides of Poverty*

He raises up the poor from the dust; from the trash-heap he elevates the needy.

No repetition in Scripture

There is a tendency to read verses such as this and see them as simply stating the same idea twice. After all, psalms are poetic. It seems natural to repeat an idea with different words to convey the poetic idea. *He raises up the poor from the dust* followed by *from the trash-heap he elevates the needy.* Indeed, at first glance this looks like a simple example of poetic repetition.

However, a deeper look reveals much, much more.

Poor vs Needy

There are two different Hebrew words used here for *poor* and *needy*.

DaL   poor
EVYON   needy

The word for *poor* – DaL - is used throughout scripture to refer to something or someone that is *lacking what they need*. While it is used elsewhere to refer to a poor person (e.g. Ruth 3:10), it is also used to describe the lean, ugly cows in Pharaoh's dream:

> After them, seven other cows came up *scrawny* – DaL - and very ugly and lean. (Genesis 41:19)

In other words, DaL refers to the simple fact that a poor person is *lacking*. What he has is insufficient.

EVYON – *needy* – has a different connotation. It comes from the root AVaH – *to want, desire,* or *crave*. Two examples of the use of AVaH are:

1. In Genesis, Abraham tells his servant to go find a wife for Isaac. When the servant asks Abraham what to do if the woman that he finds does not want to go with him he says, *Maybe this woman will not want to come back with me to this land* (Genesis 24:5).
2. In Deuteronomy, Moses retells the story of Israel's sin with the Golden Calf. When Moses describes how he prayed successfully to prevent God from destroying the Children of Israel due to the sin he says, *and the Lord listened to me this time also. He did not want to destroy you.* (Deuteronomy 10:10)

When this verb root – AVaH – *need* - becomes a noun for a *needy person*, the word is EVYON. Think about the meaning of this root as we have seen it. Desire. Want. Need. With this in mind we can see that EVYON - *needy person* - refers to something beyond the simple fact that this person lives in poverty and has insufficient funds. EVYON describes his emotional state, *how he feels* as a result of being poor. He is preoccupied with his many unfulfilled needs and basic wants. In other words, as opposed to the first word – *poor* – this second term sees the plight of the poor person in terms of the *experience* of suffering and anguish in being poor.

To sum up: The first word – *poor* – describes *the fact* that the poor person is poor. The second word – *needy* – describes how *he feels* about it.

DaL	=	poor, lacking	=	the *fact* of poverty
EVYON	=	needy, wanting	=	the *experience* of poverty

Poor from the Dust

Dust is lowly. It is cheap. It is trampled. In the hierarchy of earthly things there is nothing lower. This is not a bad thing. It is a fact. Actually, if you think about it, if dust didn't exist then something else would be the lowliest thing on earth. Dust is not the lowliest thing on earth because of something wrong with it. It just is. Something has to be. In this sense, dust is similar to poverty.

It is impossible for everyone to have the same amount of wealth. It is unnatural and unsustainable. Even if everyone started out with the same amount of money and possessions it wouldn't take long for differences in wealth to emerge. People have different goals and priorities. Some people would want to use their time and money to make more money. Others would choose to live simply and do less lucrative work in favor of something that they find more meaningful. Some people would be blessed with many children and the expenses that come along with a family. Others may never marry. The ideal that many people espouse that everyone should have the same amount of money is absurd.

My point is this. In any economic system somebody will be on the bottom. In some societies the people on the bottom are starving and have never owned a pair of shoes. In others, the poorest people may be homeless but have clothing and food on a daily basis. Regardless of how the poorest people in our society compare to the poorest in a different time or place, those who are able to help the poor must do so. This natural fact of poverty is stated explicitly in Deuteronomy 15:11 "For *the poor will never cease from the land;* therefore I command you, saying, 'You shall open your hand wide to your brother, to your poor and your needy, in your land.'"

In other words, in the hierarchy of socio-economics just as in the hierarchy of nature, unfortunately someone has to be on the bottom. There will always be *poor people* just as there is always *dust.*

Needy from the Trash

Trash is, by definition, rejected. It is the stuff that was thrown away. Trash is trash because someone decided that it is worth so little that it is not worth keeping, selling, or even giving away. It is not only valueless because nature has deemed it so. It has been *declared* worthless.

In addition to the fact that they occupy the lowest rung on the socio-economic ladder, poor people *feel rejected.* They feel that society has *deemed them worthless* – just like trash.

Once again, in the second half of the verse, the psalmist describes the *experience of being poor.* The EVYON – the *needy person* who suffers and does not have the luxury to think beyond his basic unfulfilled needs, *feels rejected.* He feels worthless not only because he happens to be poor but because society has no use for him.

Our verse teaches that God tends to the poor man's needs not only economically but *emotionally* and *existentially* as well. Not only does He raise him up from the basic fact of his poverty, He supports him and provides for the emotional trauma that poverty brings with it.

He raises up the poor from the dust;	=	God provides the poor what they lack
from the trash-heap he elevates the needy	=	He helps them emotionally as well

A Call to Action

In Deuteronomy 8:6 we are told *to walk in His ways*. This is repeated in Deuteronomy 19:9, 26:17, 28:9, and 30:16. We are to live as God lives. *We must do as He does.*

There are many needy people. They need our help. We must do as God does. We must see this verse not only as a praise of God but as a *call to action*. We must care for the needy. We must fill their needs for basic necessities. *For the poor will never cease from the land*. At the same time, we must be conscious and sensitive to the other side of poverty. We must be sensitive to the emotional and spiritual trauma of poverty, the sense of worthlessness and rejection.

He raises up the poor from the dust; from the trash-heap he elevates the needy. So must we.

113:8 *Sitting with Nobles*

**He seats them with nobles,
with the nobles of His people.**

Noble, Generous, & Wise

The word for *nobles* used here - NaDIV - literally means *generous ones* as in,

Many seek the favor of the *generous*, - NaDIV - and everyone is a friend to a giver of gifts. (Proverbs 19:6)

Or

Take a sacred offering for the Lord. Let those with *generous* – NaDIV - hearts present the following gifts to the Lord: gold, silver, and bronze; (Exodus 35:5)

And yet in numerous other verses in Scripture the word NaDIV refers to *rulers* and *nobles*.

The well that the leaders sank, that the *nobles* of the people dug, with the scepter, with the staff. (Numbers 21:18)

Or

For you say, 'Where is the house of the *noble* (prince)? And where is the tent, the dwelling place of the wicked?' (Job 21:28)

In yet another meaning, NaDIV is also used as the opposite of either *evil* or *foolishness* such as,

No longer will the fool be called *noble*, nor the scoundrel be highly respected. (Isaiah 32:5)

To sum up all of these verses, the word NaDIV refers to *nobility, power, wealth* and *wisdom*, being used *for the good*.

NaDIV means...
Noble   (Numbers 21:18, Job 21:28)
Generous   (Exodus 35:5, Proverbs 19:6)
Wise   (Isaiah 32:5)

The Common Denominator: Expanded Free Will
In Hebrew, when one word is used to express multiple different concepts what this means is that the various meanings have a shared essential quality. At some level they are the same. If I was forced to give one single definition for the word NaDIV, I would suggest that a NaDIV is one who is completely *free* to use his God given powers – be they *money, power*, or *intelligence* – for *generous* and good purposes.

In a related use of the same Hebrew root, a *free-will offering* in the Temple as in Leviticus 7:16 is called a *NeDaVa*, or literally, a *generosity offering*.

Wisdom, wealth, and power are types of freedom. The more money that one has, the more that one is *free* to do in the material world. The more wisdom one has, the more one is *free* to think beyond what is commonly thought and known. The more power one has, the more one is *free* to act and influence. All of these gifts result in an expansion of a person's free will; of the ability to act and influence.

Poverty Limits Free Will

A person who is impoverished has extremely limited free will. He may dream big but his ability to act out what he wants to do is limited. In fact, he probably doesn't even have the luxury to dream big all that often. He certainly does not have the luxury of being generous. Generosity means that I am thinking and expressing concern outside of myself. Worrying about one's daily bread narrows a person's vision. Basic temporal needs make it difficult to think about larger influence. Simply put, he is a slave to his basic needs.

In *raising up the poor and the needy from the dust and the trash*, God does more than provide them with their needs. He brings them into the company of the *noble*. Notice that the verse does not say that He brings them *to the nobles*. Rather, *He seats them with nobles*.

By elevating the poor from the dust of their basic poverty, by healing their broken hearts and their natural sense of worthlessness and rejection, God brings them to a higher state of being. They are now *with the nobles*. They are among them. Having been given dignity and self worth, they too are now free to think outside of their own private worldly concerns.

God's salvation on a grand scale, what these psalms praise and celebrate, elevates even the lowest rung of God's people to the level of *nobility*. Every single one of us is valuable, powerful, and willful participants in God's great plan.

He seats them with nobles, with the nobles of His people.

History is not the story only of the famous, wealthy, and powerful. It is the story of every single person who puts his trust in God.

113:9 *The Barren Woman of the Home*

> *He makes a barren woman who*
> *dwells in a home into a joyful*
> *mother of children Praise God!*
> *(Halleluyah)*

Psalm 113 at a Glance

After the first three verses spoke of the importance of praising God, our psalm has described how God controls the seemingly powerful (verse 4); how His will overrides theirs (verse 5). It went on to speak of how God compassionately raises up the poor and hopeless to a higher status of freedom and prosperity (verses 7 & 8).

It is in the nature of human socio-economic power structures that the rich and powerful become more rich and powerful and that the poor and powerless remain so. God turns this state of affairs on its head. He controls the will of the powerful. He elevates the poor. This is Psalm 113 up to this point.

God's Salvation Breaks all the Rules

In the closing verse of the psalm God's loving control over human affairs is taken to another level. Not only does God control history (4-5); not only does He change the status and fortunes of the needy (7-8); He even goes so far as to violate the rules of natural physical reality to show His love for those who are suffering.

A *barren woman* is not merely a woman who has *not yet* had children. She is a woman who can not have children. She is incapable. The Hebrew word AKaRaH – barren woman – is from the root AKaR meaning *uprooted* or *destroyed*. The implication is that not only does this woman lack offspring, she lacks the *capability of fertility* altogether.

For such a woman to bear children requires a reversal of the physical reality, a violation of nature. She is biologically incapable of having children. Yet, miraculously, God makes her into a joyful mother of children.

Barren Woman of the Home

Why does the verse describe the *barren woman* as one *who dwells in a home*? What does this add? Wouldn't the idea be complete if the verse had said, *He makes a barren woman into a joyful mother of children Praise God!* without the phrase *who dwells in a home*?

The verse says:	It could have said:
He makes a barren woman <u>*who dwells in a home*</u> *into a joyful mother of children*	*He makes a barren woman into a joyful mother of children*

Moreover, despite the standard translation that appears above, *a barren woman who dwells in a home*, the actual etymologically precise translation is *a barren woman of the home*. The word *dwell* actually is not there at all. The Hebrew AKeReT literally means *barren woman of....* Consequently, the word HABAYIT - *the home* - that follows it functions grammatically as a modifier of the word *barren woman*. To simplify things, the most precise translation of the verse is *He makes a barren woman of the home into a joyful mother of children Praise God!*

Standard translation:	Actual exact Hebrew translation:
He makes a barren woman <u>*who dwells in a home*</u> *into a joyful mother of children*	*He makes a barren woman* <u>*of the home*</u> *into a joyful mother of children*

Based on this understanding, I'd like to suggest that the seemingly extra and unusual term *of the home* serves to deepen our awareness of the pain of the barren woman. Appreciating what she is feeling helps us to fully appreciate God's kindness. The barren woman described here has not resigned herself to her state of barrenness. She has not made peace with her situation. She is a barren woman *of the home*. Family life is her focus and priority. It is where she *lives*. She wants a *home*; it is her identity. This phrase serves to emphasize her yearning and, consequently, the depth of her suffering in her state of barrenness.

God responds to her silent pain and violates the biological scientific reality to give her children. He breaks the rules of the natural order that He created not only to move nations across the playing field of history but to give joy to a childless woman.

The Meaning of the Barren Woman

Barren women are common in the Bible. The matriarchs in Genesis, Sarah (Genesis 11:30), Rebecca (Genesis 25:21), and Rachel (Genesis 29:31) all are described as *barren*; i.e. incapable of bearing children. None of them could have children naturally. Each of them became pregnant only after Divine intervention.

> And the Lord did unto Sarah as he had spoken. For Sarah conceived, and bare Abraham a son in his old age, at the set time of which God had spoken to him. (Genesis 21:1-2)

> Now Isaac pleaded with the Lord for his wife, because she was barren; and the Lord granted his plea, and Rebekah his wife conceived. (Genesis 25:21)

> Then God remembered Rachel, and God listened to her and opened her womb. (Genesis 30:22)

While we praise God for miraculously giving children to barren women, we have no choice but to wonder why God made them barren in the first place.

While the matriarchs were all barren, the paradigm of the *barren woman of the home* who ceaselessly yearns to be a mother is Hannah.

I Samuel chapter 1 tells of Elkanah, a man who had two wives; Peninah and Hannah. Peninah had children and Hannah was childless. To appease Hannah, Elkanah would give her extra portions and gifts.

Seeing that Hannah was unhappy, Elkanah tried to further cheer her up with what would appear to be beautiful words of empathy.

> Then said Elkanah her husband to her, 'Hannah, why are you weeping? And why do you not eat? Why is your heart grieved? Am I not better to you than ten sons?' (I Samuel 1:8)

Not only do these words not make Hannah feel any better, they send her a clear and inescapable message. Hannah realizes that she is alone.

While she may have believed all along that Elkanah shared her pain in her childlessness, this well intentioned statement by her husband tells Hannah that he does not understand. He has children. He does not feel her need. Immediately following this comment, Hannah stands up from the feast at the Temple and, "In her deep anguish Hannah prayed to the Lord, weeping bitterly."(1:10)

So long as Hannah believed that her husband shared her suffering, she believed that he too was equally pleading with the Almighty for her to have a child. It is when she is alone in her barrenness that she prays to God differently. When no one else is there, He is there.

Perhaps we have, in Hannah, a glimpse of the purpose of the barrenness of great biblical women. Perhaps – although who can know God's thoughts? – it is the prayers of the righteous in their loneliness that arouses God's mercy and brings great children into the world. Perhaps the barrenness, suffering, and subsequent prayer all produce a heightened awareness by these great mothers of the heavenly gift of fertility. Perhaps the greatness of these children – Samuel to Hannah; Isaac, Jacob, and Joseph to the matriarchs - was fostered precisely by this heightened awareness of the supernatural gift that children are.

God disregards nature and performs miracles. God listens to prayer. When we feel alone God is there. All of these messages come to mind in the image that closes Psalm 113.

He makes a barren woman who dwells in a home into a joyful mother of children Praise God! (Halleluyah)

A final thought for Psalm 113

A life of faith calls on us to live in two dimensions. Anyone who believes and trusts in God feels this.

On one hand, each of us nurtures our own personal relationship to God. We feel His presence in our day to day lives. When we are hurting we cry to Him. When we experience gifts in our lives, we thank and praise Him.

At the same time, as people of faith, we yearn to build God's kingdom on this earth. We are pained when we see humanity sliding away from God's values. Our faith in God and His love drives us to be compassionate and moral in our dealings with others.

A life of faith is a life of personal relationship with God as well as universal concern for His world.

Around the time I started writing this book I was reading a book titled The Intellectual Adventure of Ancient Man. This classic work on Ancient Near Eastern society describes in detail the belief systems of Mesopotamian, Egyptian, and Hebrew societies of thousands of years ago.

One day after I was reading about Mesopotamian religious beliefs, I put down the book and sat at my computer to work on this commentary to Psalm 113. And it hit me. Mesopotamian pagans also believed in higher forces. They also believed that the gods controlled the fates of nations; that humans could not understand their wisdom. They probably would not disagree with the first few verses of Psalm 113.

What those ancient pagans *did not believe* and is beautifully described in Psalm 113 is that God cares for each and every one of us. That he looks after the weak, the poor, the barren woman who suffers in silence.

A loving God who is lovingly concerned with the hardships of downtrodden individuals was alien to the pagan belief system.

As this thought crossed my mind I was filled with a sense of purpose in writing this book. Exploring these *Hallel* Psalms of Praise of the Almighty was not going to be merely an exercise in linguistic exegesis. Through careful reading I was engaged in a personal journey of praise and recognition of the unique greatness of the Lord, our God; how He governs His world and how He cares for each and every one of us.

PSALM 114

THE MIRACLES OF ISRAEL

Psalm 113 introduced us to the fact that God governs the world both on the historical scale as well as the personal individual level. Psalm 114 turns our attention to two new themes. The People of Israel and God's miracles.

In the first two verses of this psalm we will be introduced to Israel's dual identity as both a separate people set apart and distinct as well as a nation charged with the universal mission to bring knowledge of God to all humanity.

The psalm then turns to the subject of God's miraculous upending of the natural order in order to save His people. The splitting of the Reed Sea, the revelation at Sinai, and Moses' bringing forth water from stone serve as examples of nature bowing to the will of God.

No human being was alive to witness the God's creation of the universe in Genesis. From Genesis alone we would only know God as creator by faith in His word. The Exodus from Egypt and the wholesale upending of the natural order demonstrated unequivocally to all humanity that God, and God alone, is Master and Creator of all.

Psalm 114

בְּצֵאת יִשְׂרָאֵל, מִמִּצְרָיִם; בֵּית יַעֲקֹב, מֵעַם לֹעֵז.	א	1.	*When Israel came out of Egypt, the house of Jacob from a people of foreign tongue*
הָיְתָה יְהוּדָה לְקָדְשׁוֹ; יִשְׂרָאֵל, מַמְשְׁלוֹתָיו.	ב	2.	*Judah was His holy one, Israel His dominions.*
הַיָּם רָאָה, וַיָּנֹס; הַיַּרְדֵּן, יִסֹּב לְאָחוֹר.	ג	3.	*The sea looked and fled, the Jordan turned back;*

47

הֶהָרִים, רָקְדוּ כְאֵילִים; גְּבָעוֹת, כִּבְנֵי צֹאן.	ד	4. **The mountains danced like rams, the hills like young sheep**
מַה לְּךָ הַיָּם, כִּי תָנוּס; הַיַּרְדֵּן, תִּסֹּב לְאָחוֹר.	ה	5. **What is there to you, O sea that you fled; O Jordan that you turned backward;**
הֶהָרִים, תִּרְקְדוּ כְאֵילִים; גְּבָעוֹת, כִּבְנֵי צֹאן.	ו	6. **O mountains that you dance like rams; O hills like young sheep?**
מִלִּפְנֵי אָדוֹן, חוּלִי אָרֶץ; מִלִּפְנֵי, אֱלוֹהַּ יַעֲקֹב.	ז	7. **Tremble, O earth, at the presence of the Lord, at the presence of the God of Jacob**
הַהֹפְכִי הַצּוּר אֲגַם מָיִם; חַלָּמִישׁ, לְמַעְיְנוֹ מָיִם.	ח	8. **Who transforms the rock into a pool of water, the hard rock into springs of water.**

114:1 *Israel and the House of Jacob*

---

*When Israel came out of Egypt,
the house of Jacob from a
people of foreign tongue,*

Psalm 114 is made up entirely of verses that appear to repeat themselves, with each verse composed of two phrases that seem to be simply poetic redundancy.

Notice that this verse is actually an incomplete sentence. In other words, it will be completed with the verse that comes next. This is particularly interesting because of the three terms used for the people of Israel in these verses. Her, in our verse we have *Israel* as well as the *House of Jacob.* In the next verse we see the term *Judah* and then *Israel* again. We will deal with *Judah* in the comments to verse 2. For now we will deal with the two titles for God's chosen people that appear in verse 1.

Israel vs House of Jacob

Israel. House of Jacob. These two titles for the chosen people appear throughout scripture. In fact, there are two verses that describe the nation of Israel during their sojourn in the Sinai desert that use both of these names in the same verse.

The first is right after the exodus from Egypt when the nation arrives at Mount Sinai to receive the Torah.

> Then Moses went up to God, and the Lord called to him from the mountain and said, 'This is what you are to say to the *House of Jacob* and what you are to tell the *People of Israel:*' (Exodus 19:3)

These two names appear a second time when Bilaam the wicked prophet is overcome by the spirit of God and, despite his original evil intent to curse Israel, he blesses Israel:

> How beautiful are your tents, *Jacob*; your tabernacles, *Israel!* (Numbers 24:5)

Tents vs. Tabernacles

Notice that Bilaam refers to *tents* in relation to *Jacob* and *tabernacles* in relation to *Israel*.

> How beautiful are <u>your tents, Jacob; your tabernacles, Israel</u>! (Numbers 24:5)

These words bring to mind the words of Genesis 25:27 where, as youngsters, Jacob is described as *a dweller of tents* in contrast to his brother Esau; *a hunter and a man of the field*.

Tents are homes. They are private places. A *tabernacle*, on the other hand, is very public. The entire purpose of a tabernacle is the glory of God. It is open to all to come to worship and be inspired.

Tent   = Private dwelling
Tabernacle   = Public place of worship

The *public covenantal relationship with God* is implied by *the taber-nacle*. Anyone who has faith in God and devotes their life to serving Him understands that the focus of that service is to bring knowledge of God to the entire earth. *Israel* is a name that implies this grand mission. It is derived from two words. SaR – meaning *prince* or *minister*, and EL – *God*. *Israel* connotes the *ministering, influencing* role of God's people.

The <u>House</u> of *Jacob;... your <u>tents</u> Jacob. Jacob* describes the *private relationship to God*. Any devoted servant of God confronts challenges on a daily basis. It is true that the primary task in serving God is to influence, to lead, and to help others get close to Him. But there can be no influence without interaction. It is impossible to repair the world without engaging in it. And with that engagement, people of faith often find themselves in the position of being influenced by the darker parts of society, even as they try to make the world a better place.

To face this challenge we need to be like Jacob; *dwellers of tents*. To stay strong in one's religious values; to have the strength to continue to influence the world for the good, we must sometimes *retreat from it*. We must travel inward to our homes; to our families; to our *tents*.

Israel = Public, ministering role   = Tabernacle
Jacob = Private relationship to God; retreat = Tents
          from the outside influences

When Israel came out of Egypt,

Israel the strong. Israel the influential. Israel who sings the song at the sea and testifies to the world about the glory of God, emerges from Egypt, land of slavery and bondage to humans who declare themselves to be gods. This is the leadership role that all who call on God and have faith in Him are called upon to play. To wrestle the forces of evil and to win. To be princes and ministers and a light to the world. To be *Israel*.

the house of Jacob from a people of foreign tongue

How do we survive when the society that surrounds us seems to be speaking a *foreign tongue*? How do we stay strong in our convictions and faith when the culture in which we live is driven by values that threaten us? This verse provides a guide for any person of faith who wants to impact the world without losing himself in the process. We retreat into the *house of Jacob*.

The external redemption – our ability to influence and inspire others – must be built on the foundation of the private redemption. The redemption of the family; of the home.

114:2 *The Kingdom of Priests*

*Judah was His holy one, Israel
His dominions.*

Here, as in the previous verse, two different names are used for the Jewish people. While it is true that Judah is only one tribe of the twelve tribes of Israel, the name *Judah* can sometimes refer to the entire nation due to the fact that the royal lineage comes from Judah. Since a king represents the entire nation and makes decisions for the entire nation it is fair to refer to the whole nation as *Judah*.

The name *Judah* in this verse refers to the entire people. This is clear from the context. The previous verse used two names for the entire people; *Israel* and the *House of Jacob*. In this verse the name *Israel* appears again in the second phrase of the verse. As I pointed out at the beginning of Psalm 114, the verses of this entire psalm are made up of poetically repetitive couplets describing the same idea in different words with different nuances of meaning. So clearly *Judah* in this verse refers to the entire nation.

So what does this name for the people of Israel imply? What makes it different than the name *Israel*? Furthermore, why does the verse state that *Judah* was God's *holy one* and *Israel* His *dominions*?

What are His Dominions?

The Hebrew word for *His dominions* is MaMSHeLOTaV. While every English translation that I have seen translates this word in the singular – *dominion*, the word is unmistakably plural. MaMSHeLOT is a plural of the word MeMSHALaH – *dominion* – the *"AV"* at the end of the word is the possessive suffix *His* when the object that is possessed *is a plural*. If it were singular - *His dominion* - the word here would be MeMSHaLTO.

If that confused you, here's a chart to keep it simple: *the word in our verse is in italics*

MEMSHALAH	MAMSHEL<u>OT</u>	*MAMSHELOT<u>AV</u>*
Dominion	Dominion<u>s</u>	*<u>His</u> Dominions*

To sum up our questions:

1. What is the significance of calling the people of Israel by the name *Judah*?
2. Why is *Judah* paired with *holy one* and *Israel* with *dominions*?
3. What does this plural – *His dominions* - mean?

Dominions & Holy Ones

The root of the word MEMSHALAH meaning *dominion* or *government* appears twenty times in scripture. In many places it is used as a synonym for *kingdom*. For example, Psalm 145:13,

> *Your kingdom is an everlasting kingdom, and Your dominion –* MEMSHALAH *-endures through all generations.* (see also Micah 4:8, Jeremiah 34:1, I Kings 9:19)

The juxtaposition of *holiness* and *dominion* in our verse describing the People of Israel brings to mind the description that God Himself gives to the people immediately prior to the giving of the Torah on Mount Sinai.

And you shall be for me a *kingdom* of priests and a *holy nation*. (Exodus 19:6)

What is a kingdom of priests? What is a holy nation?

The word for *priest* – *Kohen* in Hebrew – is used throughout scripture to refer to a religious official or leader; someone who ministers spiritually. For example I Samuel 5:4 refers to the *priests of Dagon*, a pagan god. In other words, a *kingdom of priests* is an entire society of religious leaders. What does this mean?

Think back to the original blessing to Abraham, *And all the families of the Earth will be blessed through you,* (Genesis 12:3). This is the goal and purpose of Abrahams' offspring, the People of Israel. The entire world is to be influenced by Israel. The entire world is to be brought to God through Israel, specifically through fulfillment of the covenant of Mount Sinai. The Torah, the word of God that will guide all the families of the earth to a loftier more Godly existence, will be brought to the world by the People of Israel. *This is a priestly kingdom.* A kingdom whose mission is to spiritually influence the entire world.

I'd like to suggest that the reason that *dominions* is written in the plural is precisely because the mission of Israel as a *kingdom of priests* is to expand God's kingdom to include all the peoples of the earth. The ultimate goal of Israel's mission is summed up by Zechariah:

And the Lord shall be king over all the earth: on that day the Lord will be one and His name will be one. (Zechariah 14:9)

In other words, perhaps the phrase *Israel His dominions* is in the plural to indicate the goal of expanding God's kingdom to include not only Israel but all the peoples of the earth.

How about *holy nation*? The Hebrew word for holy – KaDOSH – connotes not only holiness but *different* or *set apart*. When we refer to God as *holy* we are describing how distant, lofty, and different He is from us.

When an animal or money is *set aside* for use in the Temple it is called KaDOSH referring not only to its sanctified spiritual status but also to the mere fact that it was *separated* from the pack. For example,

> Yet you know me, Lord; you see me and test my thoughts about you. Drag them off like sheep to be butchered! *Set them apart* for the day of slaughter. (Jeremiah 12:3)

The Hebrew here for *set them apart* is a conjugation of this same word, KaDOSH.

"And you shall be for Me a kingdom of priests and a holy nation"(Exodus 19)

Kingdom of priests	=	ministering role to others	=	Universal mission to bring the world closer to God
Holy nation	=	separate, distinct	=	retain your distinct identity

Calling Israel a *holy nation* refers to the *separateness* and *distinctness* of the People of Israel. They are different. If you think about it, in order to be a *kingdom of priests* – to be a nation that is called by God to influence the world – the chosen nation must remain *distinct*. If they lose their distinct quality they have lost their identity. If they lose their identity, they lose their ability to influence the world.

In other words, when God told the People of Israel that they will be *a kingdom of priests and a holy nation* He was telling them as follows: "You have a job to do. You will be the *priests* of the world. Your mission is to draw everyone on earth closer to me. In order to continue to carry out that mission you will need to be *holy* – to have a distinct and different identity from the rest of the world."

Judah as a name for Israel

Judah as a name for the People of Israel rarely appears in Scripture. However, there is one book of the Bible in which *Judah* is the *only* name given to the nation. In the Scroll of Esther the name for the People of Israel is YeHUDIM – the plural of *Judah*. This is the origin of the word *Jew*. This is significant as the Scroll of Esther is the only book of the Bible whose narrative takes place entirely outside of the Land of Israel – *in exile.*

Esther is a story of persecution and survival. It is a great story. It has a wonderful plot and compelling characters. It is also typical of the Jewish experience in the exile. Haman's argument for the destruction of the Jews to Ahasuerus is telling,

> There is a certain people dispersed among the peoples in all the provinces of your kingdom who keep themselves *separate*. Their customs are *different* from those of all other people, and they do not obey the king's laws; it is not in the king's best interest to tolerate them. (Esther 3:8)

They are different and separate. KaDOSH. *A holy nation.*

To be a *kingdom of priests* is to lead, to influence, to inspire. To be a *holy nation* is to be separate and different.

Judah was His holy one,: Only by remaining *distinct* and by guarding their unique identity do God's chosen people realize their ultimate goal; to minister and lead the world to the kingdom of God on earth –

Israel His dominions. Dominions is plural because it doesn't refer to the People of Israel. *It refers to everyone else.* The full realization of Israel occurs only when they have fulfilled their mission; when they have brought God's dominion to all the nations. (see commentary to 114:1 for discussion of the name *Israel*)

To be in covenant with God calls on us to simultaneously bring others closer to Him while at times retreating from the world strengthens our private relationship with Him.

114:3 *Two Types of Miracles*

The sea looked and fled, the Jordan turned back;

Back in verse 1, Psalm 114 opened by making reference to the Exodus from Egypt. Now, verse 3 mentions two specific miracles that God performed for the People of Israel;

1. The splitting of the Reed Sea* in Exodus 14
2. The stoppage of the flow of the Jordan River that allowed Israel to cross it on dry land in Joshua 3

Why is the Jordan here?

It's strange that the crossing of the Jordan is mentioned here. Look back at verse 1.

1. *When Israel came out of Egypt, the house of Jacob from a people of foreign tongue;*
2. *Judah was His holy one, Israel His dominions.*
3. *The sea looked and fled, the Jordan turned back;*

The Jordan was not crossed *When Israel came out of Egypt* as the psalm seems to be saying. Actually, the Jordan was crossed forty years later by a generation who, for the most part, were not even born at the time of the Exodus from Egypt. Why is the miraculous crossing of the Jordan mentioned here at all?

At first glance there is the obvious similarity between the two events. Both involved a body of water receding or splitting to allow the nation of Israel to cross on dry land. However, the similarity ends there. In fact, the greatest difference between the two events is directly relevant to our verse in Psalm 114.

---

*Although many call it the _Red Sea_, this translation is incorrect. The Hebrew name is *Yam Suf. Yam* is the Hebrew word for *Sea* and the translation of *Suf* is *Reeds. Reed Sea*, not *Red Sea*

Splitting the Sea to Save their Lives

The splitting of the Reed Sea had a very obvious purpose. The People of Israel were under attack from the rapidly approaching Egyptian army.

> As Pharaoh approached, the Israelites looked up, and there were the Egyptians, marching after them. They were terrified and cried out to the Lord. They said to Moses, "Was it because there were no graves in Egypt that you brought us to the desert to die? What have you done to us by bringing us out of Egypt" (Exodus 14:10-11)

The danger of annihilation was imminent – or so it seemed to the people of Israel. They were in need of salvation.

> Moses answered the people, 'Do not be afraid. Stand firm and you will see the deliverance the Lord will bring you today.' (Exodus 14:13)

Danger. Fear. Crying out. The miraculous salvation of the Lord. That's what the splitting of the Reed Sea was about.

Why Stop the Jordan?

Now look at the miracle at the Jordan. In Joshua 3, Israel was not in any kind of danger. They had no immediate need of salvation. Furthermore, had the miracle not been performed at all, they probably would not have had too much trouble getting across the river. The Jordan River is between 3 and 10 feet deep depending on where in the river one measures it. It's not a very wide river either, ranging from 30 to 50 feet across in most places. Sure, the miracle was nice; but was it necessary? More to the point, as opposed to the splitting of the Reed Sea, the miracle of the Jordan did not provide the People of Israel with salvation from danger. No enemy army was chasing them. Why include this miracle in psalms of praise and thanks? After all, there are many miracles recorded in Scripture that did *not* save the people. For example, the ten plagues that God brought upon the Egyptians did not have the effect of saving Israel from imminent danger. There are many other examples as well. They, too, aren't mentioned here in Psalm 114.

Perhaps that is exactly the point of this verse. The splitting of the Reed Sea saved Israel from danger. The crossing of the Jordan did not.

Two Reasons for Miracles

As people of faith, we tend to pray for miracles when we need help. More to the point, we pray for miracles when we are in danger and the situation looks hopeless - just like the People of Israel on the banks of the Reed Sea. By all natural methods or by the efforts of our own hands there seems to be no hope. We need God. *We need a miracle.* We want and pray for the Almighty to intervene and miraculously alter the situation.

But why should God save us? Why should He tamper with the rules of nature for our benefit? Why? Because the forces of nature are His. They are subordinate to His will. If it is His will that we should be saved, He demonstrates this to us by circumventing the natural order – *His natural order* - because *His will* is supreme.

Well, we certainly want miracles when we *need* them. What about when we feel like we have it all under control? What about those times when we are confident that *we ourselves* can accomplish whatever we set out to do? *Do we still pray?* Do we still appreciate the miraculous hand of God in our lives and successes? Do we want Him involved only when we have exhausted our own resources and have nothing but hope?

The People of Israel were sent a powerful message at the Jordan River. They were entering to land to engage in years of war to conquer the land from the pagan peoples who inhabited it. The wars for the land of Israel were simultaneously an all-out war on paganism. Paganism is – first and foremost – the worship of natural forces. So, just as Israel is about to begin this chapter of their history God sends them a clear message. Do not put your trust in natural forces. Do not say *my power and the strength of my hand performed all this success.* (Deut. 8:17)

In effect, God was telling them, "Just as I was there when you left Egypt and were powerless and in danger, so too I am there when you are strong and confident in your military might."

God's control of the natural order is not merely some kind of last resort when all else fails – a God for times of crisis. God's manipulation of nature provides miraculous assistance equally when we are strong and entering the promised land.

The sea looked	=	miracle in time of crisis
and fled,		and danger
the Jordan turned	=	miracle when we feel strong
back;		and confident

We must recognize, praise, and thank God for His supernatural intervention not only when we are in overt danger and have no other hope. We must see Him equally when times are good and we are marching to victory.

114:4 *Rejoice with Trembling*

The mountains danced like rams, the hills like young sheep

The Trembling of Sinai

As we have already noted, the context of this Psalm is the Exodus from Egypt. With this in mind, we can assume that the dancing mountains and hills is a direct reference to covenantal revelation at Sinai.

And Mount Sinai was completely covered in smoke because the Lord had descended upon it in fire; the smoke rose like the smoke of a furnace and the entire mountain *trembled.* (Exodus 19:18)

The giving of the Torah to the People of Israel at Mount Sinai was accompanied by lightning, fire, smoke, a thick cloud, great noise, and – as we see from this verse – *the trembling of the mountain.*

God sent a message to the People of Israel. The divine law does not exist in the context of the laws of nature. God's law does not respond to the earth. Nature is moved by the divine law. The earth responds to God's law. This is a fundamental principle of Biblical faith. The fire, smoke, earthquake, etc. displayed the fact that when the divine law enters the world the natural order must bow to it. Nature is weak in the face of the power of God's law.

This message is expressed most profoundly by the Hebrew word for *trembled* that we just quoted in Exodus 19:18. VaYeCHeRaD. Everywhere in the Bible that the root CHRD appears it refers to something more than the *physical* state of trembling. This root CHRD always describes trembling that is *caused by fear.*

Here are a few typical examples of this root:
for his heart <u>trembled</u> from the ark of God (I Samuel 4:13)

When a trumpet sounds in a city, do not the people <u>tremble</u>?
(Amos 3:6)

In other words, the implication is that the mountain was not only *quaking* but in a personified manner the mountain is described as *afraid.* So to speak, the most stable and solid aspects of the natural world – mountains – are revealed to be weak and malleable in the face of God's law. They are not as independently secure and stable as they seem.

Appropriately, it was not only Mount Sinai that was trembling when the Torah was given.

> Then it came to pass on the third day, in the morning, that there were thunderings and lightnings, and a thick cloud on the mountain; and the sound of the trumpet was very loud, *and the entire people that was in the camp trembled.*(Exodus 19:16)

Trembling vs. Dancing

So if Exodus describes the mountain as terrified and *trembling*, why does our verse in Psalm 114 describe the mountain *dancing*? *Dancing* is certainly not an image that conjures up emotions of fear and *trembling*.

I'd like to suggest that these two descriptions of the quaking of the mountain, *trembling* and *dancing* are actually complementary. Each one presents a different aspect of the experience of God's law and the covenant at Sinai.

From the description in Exodus one gets the impression that God's law is terrifying and unsettling. It is true that the revelation at Sinai was scary. Numerous verses in Exodus point to the fear that the People of Israel experienced. God's covenant can be frightening. It demands of us to live lives of holiness and self sacrifice. The stakes are high if we violate His word.

However, at the same time as God's word is serious business, it is also true that *The law of the Lord is perfect, refreshing the soul.* (Psalm 19:8) and *The precepts of the Lord are right, giving joy to the heart.* (Psalm 19:9)

Serving God brings a sense of purpose, happiness, and meaning to our lives. Only as servants of God do we experience true freedom. We are free from human bondage and the restrictions of selfish, temporal, and worldly concerns.

The mountains do not only *tremble* at the revelation of God's word. They also *dance*. With the revelation of God's word at Sinai, the entire natural order was given meaning, purpose, and new life. The response is rejoicing and a sense of youth and promise - like young sheep.

Our sense of awe and fear – our awareness that the stakes are high – in the face of God's Will does not contradict or even mitigate our simultaneous feelings of elation and joy in being granted the opportunity to serve Him.

Here in Psalm 114 where we are celebrating our God given freedom we focus on the joyous aspect of God's law – the higher freedom that we realize in serving Him. We dance even as we tremble.

Serve the Lord with fear, and rejoice with trembling. (Psalm 2:11)

*Living in covenant with God's Will is often challenging and even
frightening while it is simultaneously a life of joyful purpose.*

114:5-6 *The Purpose of Freedom*

---

*What is there to you, O sea that
you fled; O Jordan that you turned
backward; O mountains that you dance
like rams; O hills like young sheep?*

MAH LE – questions in Scripture

The opening words of this verse, *What is there to you*, are difficult to
translate. Published English translations of the Bible render it variously
as, *What ails you*, *Why was it*, and *What happened to you*. The Hebrew here
is MAH LeCHA, literally translated,

MAH	=	*What (is)*
LeCHA	=	*to you.*

This form of question *What is to…* appears dozens of times in Scripture.
It certainly does not always have a negative implication. Often it is sim-
ply an inquiry such as "Why did you do that?" or "What do you want."
However, what is consistent in every context is that MAH Le… – *What
to…* - is always a question of *will* or *motive*. In other words, when MAH
Le is asked it always means *"Why did that person choose to do that?"*

Asking Questions to Inanimate Objects

Obviously, in our context the concept of *will* is not meant to be taken
literally. After all, the subject of the question is *the sea, the Jordan river, the
mountains,* and *the hills*. Obviously these things do not possess consciousness or free will.

I believe that the question being posed to the sea, the Jordan, and the
hills is meant to make an important theological point. God's creation is in

tune with His will. The poetic imagery of posing a question to bodies of water and mountains is meant to paint the picture of a conscious willful creation *choosing* to bow to the will of its master.

Nature Cooperates with God

There are those that would explain supernatural miraculous events as fortunate coincidences; happy accidents of perfect timing. Such a line of thinking not only minimizes the sense of gratitude that we ought to feel to the Creator for His works on our behalf, it also denies the integral role that all of creation plays in God's great plan.

To those addicted to impersonal scientific cause and effect explanations of the relationship of events to their timing and context the Psalmist replies, "No!" When nature assists in the great historical plan of the Almighty God it is not an accident or some fortunate coincidence. It is the submission of all of creation to the supreme will of God who created everything for His purposes.

Achieving Real Freedom

There is an additional point worth noting regarding these verses. Psalm 114 began with the words *When Israel left Egypt*. This Psalm is a praise of God for granting freedom to His chosen people from bondage and slavery. The splitting of the Reed Sea was certainly critical to this process of emancipation from Egypt. With the Egyptian army fast approaching, if there had been no splitting of the sea, Israel would not have been free.

On the face of it, it would seem that the same can not be said of either the giving of the Torah on Sinai or the crossing of the Jordan. After all, with the Exodus already an established fact, freedom had been achieved. And yet the wording of the opening verses of Psalm 114 certainly places the revelation at Sinai and the crossing of the Jordan forty years later into the same context and under the same heading: *When Israel left Egypt, the house of Jacob from a people of foreign tongue*. The verses that follow describe events that occurred at this time or as parts of this event.

The message is clear and decisive. The Exodus was not complete with Israel's freedom from slavery. It was not complete with their departure from Egypt. The Exodus was about the birth of the Nation of Israel – the Kingdom of Priests and Holy Nation whose mission is to bring knowledge of God to all the families of the Earth. This would be accomplished by establishing a society governed by *God's law* in the *land of Israel*.

In other words, the Exodus didn't end with the crossing of the Reed Sea. It ended when the People of Israel *crossed the Jordan* and entered the promised land and began to build their own society; a society that would actualize the kingdom of God on this earth.

Only when they were serving God as free men in their own land would the Exodus – the freedom from slavery to Pharaoh Egypt – be complete.

Freedom from bondage is not an end in itself. The Lord grants us freedom so that we can build His kingdom.

114:7 *God of Jacob*

Tremble, O earth, at the presence of the Lord, at the presence of the God of Jacob

---

God of Jacob

At the end of this verse God is called *God of Jacob*. Nine times in the book of Psalms God is referred to this way. In the book of Exodus God of Jacob appears four times but in all four instances it is as the third part of the phrase *God of Abraham, God of Isaac, and God of Jacob*. The use of *God of Jacob* by itself is unique to David, author of Psalms. In fact, there is only one verse outside of Psalms in all of Scripture which uses God of Jacob.

Now these are the last words of David. So says David the son of Jesse; So says the man raised up on high, The anointed of the *God of Jacob*, And the sweet psalmist of Israel: (II Samuel 23:1)

The only time God of Jacob appears that is not in Psalms these words are spoken by none other than David when referring to him as the author of Psalms! What does this particular description of God indicate?

The name Jacob is used collectively for the people of Israel on many occasions. In my comments on verse 1 of this psalm I pointed out a difference in connotation between the two names, *Jacob* and *Israel*. To understand our verse we will need to know more about the particular meaning of this name.

Deeper Meaning of Jacob

The meaning of Jacob's name is explained twice. First, when Jacob is born his name is explained as referring to his grasping of the heel of his brother Esau (Gen. 25:26). The Hebrew word for *heel* is AKeV. The word for *follow* is AKaV from the same root. Jacob – YaAKoV – <u>followed</u> his brother out of the womb grasping his heel.

The second time that Jacob's name is explained is after he and his mother Rebecca deceived his father Isaac so that Jacob would receive his father's blessings. Esau unjustly accuses Jacob of cheating him despite the fact that Jacob had earlier purchased the birthright from Esau. Esau then refers to another meaning of Jacob's name.

> Esau said, "Is he not rightly named Jacob? For he has *cheated me (alt. deceived / supplanted / tripped)* these two times. He took away my birthright, and behold, now he has taken away my blessing." (Gen. 27:36)

The Hebrew word for *cheated* here is AKaV from the same root as Jacob's name. It implies *lying in wait, ambushing,* or *acting with deception.*

Simply put, the name *Jacob* does not have positive connotations. It variously implies *following, being on the heel, deception,* and *trickery.* In fact, if we look at Jacob's own life we see that he often was compelled to live by his wits and outsmart others - whether it was Laban, Esau, or even his own father.

Not so as *Israel*. This second, nobler name was given to him when he wrestled with and defeated the angel who attacked him. (Gen. 32:29) That was a battle he won without deception but with might. For this victory he was told that he was now capable of truly triumphing. He was no longer *Jacob*. He was now *Israel*.

And yet he retained both of his names. Scripture continues to use both. Sometimes he would need to be *Jacob*, living by cunning and careful tactics in a hostile environment. At other times he would be able to behave as *Israel* – triumphant, influential, and strong.

What is true of Jacob as an individual is true of his offspring – the People of Israel. This is why they are sometimes referred to as *Jacob*. The People of Israel, like their forefather and namesake are sometimes forced to live in exile as subordinates and second class citizens – the *follower*, the *heel* - in a hostile environment. Like Jacob their father, Jews have repeatedly been forced to flee after being unjustly accused and targeted. When the Bible refers to the People of Israel as *Jacob*, it is this weakened, exile identity that is being described.

> For the Lord will deliver *Jacob* and redeem them from the hand
> of *those stronger than they*. (Jeremiah 31:11)

God of Jacob = God who protects in exile

The phrase *God of Jacob* must be understood in light of this deeper meaning of the name. God, who cares for, *protects*, and *redeems* His exiled and subjugated chosen people from exile; from the hands of hostile enemies who are physically stronger and more powerful than themselves.

And in fact, when we look at the other verses where this name is used we see exactly that. For example,

> May the Lord answer you in the *day of trouble*! May the name of
> the *God of Jacob protect* you! (Psalm 20:2)

Or

The *nations rage*, the kingdoms totter; He utters His voice, the earth melts. The Lord of hosts is with us; the *God of Jacob is our fortress*. (Psalm 46:6-7)

Day of trouble? Rage? He is the fortress; the protection. This is the *God of Jacob*. (See also Psalms 76:7, 84:9, 94:7, 75:10, 81:2,5)

To illustrate the point further, contrast this with the one instance where God is referred to as *God of Abraham* in Psalms.

For God is the *King of all the earth*; sing praises with a psalm! God reigns over the nations; God sits on His holy throne. The princes of the peoples gather as the people of the *God of Abraham*. For the shields of the earth belong to God; He is highly exalted! (Psalm 47:8-10)

This is not the *God of Jacob*, protecting and defending his embattled people. Abraham never had to flee a powerful foe. Abraham was never subjugated beneath a hostile master. Abraham did not have to resort to wiles and deceptive tactics in order to survive. Abraham, the *father of the multitude of nations* (Gen. 17:4) through whom *all the families of the earth* would be blessed (Gen.12:3) was given the universalistic world mission to bring knowledge of the one God to all. *God of Abraham* is God as described by this mission.

Jacob from the Hebrew root AKV implies:

following, secondary status, deception, or wiles.

*These traits describe a weakened Israel trying to survive in exile.

The meaning of our verse, then, is as follows. The *earth trembles*, the *mountains dance,* and the seas split - the natural order, no matter how stable and powerful it may seem is completely subordinated to the will of

God to save and protect His chosen people, the children of *Jacob*, fighting as Jacob did, for their survival.

Tremble, O earth, at the presence of the Lord, at the presence of the God of Jacob

The Lord upends the natural order to protect His people when they are in a weakened position.

114:8 *Water from a Rock*

Who transforms the rock into a pool of water, the hard rock into springs of water.

In this final verse, the theme of Psalm 114 is brought to even greater heights. Up until this point the sea has fled, the Jordan has turned backward, the mountains and hills have danced, and the earth has trembled. Powerful natural forces have been brought to their knees. The most solid and stable features of creation have been shaken. All of this has happened in reaction to God's salvation of his oppressed and enslaved chosen nation. God's plan overrides the natural order.

And then, as a closing statement in this message of God's willingness to disregard and manipulate the natural order on behalf of his people, our verse takes this theme to a new level.

A Different Kind of Miracle
The miracles described up until this point in this psalm differ fundamentally from what occurs in the final verse.

The splitting of the sea, reversal of the Jordan, and the various earthquakes described in the earlier verses all involve forces and substances in nature *altering their behavior*. Water does not split; it flows to a point of equilibrium. Rivers do not change direction. Mountains and earth do not shake and quiver. And yet, none of them changed their basic substance. Until now.

> *Who transforms the rock into a pool of water, the hard rock into springs of water.*

Like the splitting of the Reed Sea and the trembling of Mount Sinai, this miracle is part of the Exodus narrative as well. The water that sated the People of Israel throughout the forty years of sojourn in the desert flowed miraculously from the rock that Moses struck with his staff at God's command.

Comparing it to what is mentioned earlier in this psalm, this is a miracle of a completely different kind. Here, creation is not only behaving supernaturally. Creation is being *transformed* from one substance to another. What's more, the transformation is from the hardest and driest of substances – rocks - to water. The earlier miracles in the psalm are *manipulations* of nature. The turning of rocks into abundant sources of water is a *complete transformation* of the substance of nature.

> *Splitting the Sea and shaking the mountain are*
> **miracles that change the <u>behavior</u> of nature**

> *Water flowing from a rock is a*
> **miracle that changes the <u>substance</u> of nature**

Only the Creator

At a deeper level, an important theological point is being made as well. Causing the sea to split or the mountains to quake could be seen as the work of *a force more powerful than* the sea or the mountains – but not necessarily the creator. Just as one force of nature can disrupt another less powerful one, a mighty god like the gods of the ancient pagans could possibly split the sea and cause an earthquake.

The transformation of nature into something fundamentally different is a miracle on an entirely different level. Only the creator, the master of all, can *alter the very substance of creation.*

Seen this way, our verse is not only the final item in the list of miracles in our psalm. It is the capstone of the psalm. It is saying in effect, that not only does the Lord Almighty *manipulate* nature for the redemption of His people; He *completely transforms* it and alters it in their service as well.

Was it Really Necessary?

There is a larger question that one might ask about the miracle of Moses' bringing water from the rock. What was the point? Why go to such supernatural extremes when it wasn't entirely necessary? Wouldn't it have made more sense to simply tell Moses to dig a well anywhere they camped and miraculously assist in making every well yield a successful discovery of water? Why the extreme miracle of water from a rock, of all things?

Let's look back at the original scene.

> The Lord answered Moses, "Go out in front of the people. Take with you some of the elders of Israel and take in your hand the staff with which you struck the Nile, and go. I will stand there before you by the rock at Horeb. *Strike the rock, and water will come out of it for the people to drink.*" So Moses did this in the sight of the elders of Israel. And he called the place Massah and Meribah because the Israelites quarreled and because they tested the Lord saying, *"Is the Lord among us or not?"* (Exodus 17:5-7, italics added)

The conclusion is inescapable. This was not just about water. After God split the sea and brought ten plagues upon Egypt, there is still *a flaw in the faith* of the people. Causing strange storms and manipulating nature is one thing. Producing water in a barren desert is a different matter. Perhaps this was the meaning of the lack of faith expressed here, *Is the Lord among us or not?* In other words, perhaps they were thinking, "Yes. We have seen great miracles and obviously this God is a great force who can move nature around as He pleases. But is He truly the *creator* and master of all? We see that He can split the water that is already there, but can He produce water where there is only dry stone?"

This is the theme of Psalm 114. God is Master of nature. He manipulates it to serve His historical plan; to redeem His chosen people. And when you witness these great miracles; upon seeing that God does with nature as He chooses, do not be mistaken. God is not *merely a force more powerful than nature*, moving mountains and rivers for the children of Jacob. *God is the creator, Master of all.*

The earth is the Lord's and everything in it; the world and all who live in it. (Psalm 24:1)

Only God, the creator, has the ability to not only manipulate nature but to completely transform it to serve His will. Nothing is beyond Him.

A final thought for Psalm 114

Why does God perform miracles? God created the world with a natural order that He chose. Why would he create such a system only to completely upend that system in order to fulfill His will?

Psalm 114, more than any other in the Hallel series, is about miracles. The splitting of the sea, the revelation at Sinai, water flowing from a stone; God's suspension of the rules of nature is on display.

When I was a child I remember reading the Bible and being jealous. It seemed that the people who lived in Biblical times experienced all the cool miracles. Why couldn't I ever see something like the plague of frogs or the splitting of the Reed Sea? It seemed to me that I was living in a world without miracles. Miracles were only for them, not for us.

But I think I was mistaken. Think about it. The simple definition of a divine miracle is a violation of the laws of nature that facilitates God's plan. We do have miracles. We just don't always see them.

For example, I often wonder what the People of Israel thought when Moses told them that after being exiled and scattered to the four corners of the earth they would be gathered back in to the land of their forefathers and become more numerous and more prosperous than their ancestors. (Deuteronomy 30)

Did they believe him? Did they think he was exaggerating? I mean, this just does not happen. Many nations in ancient times were conquered and scattered into exile. They generally did not come back. How much more so if the people in question were going to be small in number to begin with (Deuteronomy 7)? Add in the fact that this exile of a tiny people was to last for many generations (Deuteronomy 29). If you add it all up, the survival and return of the People of Israel to their homeland in our times is a complete violation of the laws of history. Naturally speaking, it is a miracle as great as any that ever happened on this earth. When Moses told them about this great ingathering at the end of times he might as well have told them that water was going to start running uphill!

Psalm 114 began with the Exodus from Egypt and ended with water flowing from a rock. Just as there are laws of nature, there are laws of history. Just as there are miracles in nature, there are miracles of history. For God is master of all.

PSALM 115

THE MISSION TO DESTROY FALSE GODS

The previous psalm described how God upended the laws of nature and performed great miracles for the benefit of His people Israel.

Now in Psalm 115 the psalmist opens with the emphatic statement, *Not to us!* With this the tone and theme are set for this entire psalm; that the goal of God's blessings upon those who serve Him is the increase in knowledge of Him on earth.

The first eight verses of the psalm serve as a kind of polemic arguing against pagan beliefs in and worship of the forces of nature. The psalmist attacks both the futility of worship of these forces as well as the spiritual damage done to those who engage in such worship.

Beginning in verse 9 the psalm focuses on those who serve God and carry out the mission of bringing knowledge and glory of Him to all humanity. They trust in Him. He assists and protects them. Beyond protecting them, He increases them and blesses them thus enabling them to be even more successful in their mission.

The final two verses conclude by circling back to where Psalm 115 began. Those who put their faith in the mortal, finite, natural system are doomed. They can not appreciate, praise, or connect to the infinite God, Master of past, present and future.

Psalm 113

א	לֹא לָנוּ יְהוָה, לֹא לָנוּ: כִּי לְשִׁמְךָ, תֵּן כָּבוֹד עַל חַסְדְּךָ, עַל אֲמִתֶּךָ.	1. *Not to us, O Lord, not to us, but to Your name give glory, for the sake of your kindness; for the sake of your truth.*
ב	לָמָּה, יֹאמְרוּ הַגּוֹיִם: אַיֵּה נָא, אֱלֹהֵיהֶם.	2. *Why will the nations say, 'Where now is their God?'*
ג	וֵאלֹהֵינוּ בַשָּׁמָיִם כֹּל אֲשֶׁר חָפֵץ עָשָׂה.	3. *And our God is in heaven; all that He wills He has done.*
ד	עֲצַבֵּיהֶם, כֶּסֶף וְזָהָב; מַעֲשֵׂה, יְדֵי אָדָם.	4. *Their idols are silver and gold; the work of human hands.*
ה	פֶּה לָהֶם, וְלֹא יְדַבֵּרוּ; עֵינַיִם לָהֶם, וְלֹא יִרְאוּ.	5. *They have a mouth but they do not speak; they have eyes but they do not see.*
ו	אָזְנַיִם לָהֶם, וְלֹא יִשְׁמָעוּ; אַף לָהֶם, וְלֹא יְרִיחוּן.	6. *They have ears but do not hear; they have a nose but do not smell.*
ז	יְדֵיהֶם, וְלֹא יְמִישׁוּן רַגְלֵיהֶם, וְלֹא יְהַלֵּכוּ לֹא יֶהְגּוּ, בִּגְרוֹנָם.	7. *They have hands, but cannot feel. They have feet, but cannot walk. No sounds come from their throats*
ח	כְּמוֹהֶם, יִהְיוּ עֹשֵׂיהֶם כֹּל אֲשֶׁר-בֹּטֵחַ בָּהֶם.	8. *Like them shall be those who make them; all who trust in them.*
ט	יִשְׂרָאֵל, בְּטַח בַּיהוָה; עֶזְרָם וּמָגִנָּם הוּא.	9. *O Israel, trust in the Lord; He is their helper and their shield.*

בֵּית אַהֲרֹן, בִּטְחוּ בַיהוָה; עֶזְרָם וּמָגִנָּם הוּא.	י	10. *O house of Aaron, trust in the Lord; He is their helper and their shield.*
יִרְאֵי יְהוָה, בִּטְחוּ בַיהוָה; עֶזְרָם וּמָגִנָּם הוּא.	אי	11. *O fearers of the Lord trust in the Lord; he is their helper and their shield.*
יְהוָה זְכָרָנוּ יְבָרֵךְ: יְבָרֵךְ אֶת בֵּית יִשְׂרָאֵל; יְבָרֵךְ אֶת בֵּית אַהֲרֹן.	בי	12. *The Lord who remembered us will bless; He will bless the house of Israel; He will bless the house of Aaron.*
יְבָרֵךְ יִרְאֵי יְהוָה הַקְּטַנִּים, עִם הַגְּדֹלִים.	גי	13. *He will bless the fearers of the Lord; the young with the old.*
יֹסֵף יְהוָה עֲלֵיכֶם; עֲלֵיכֶם, וְעַל בְּנֵיכֶם.	די	14. *May the Lord add upon you; upon you and your children.*
בְּרוּכִים אַתֶּם, לַיהוָה עֹשֵׂה, שָׁמַיִם וָאָרֶץ.	וט	15. *Blessed are you of the Lord, maker of heaven and earth.*
הַשָּׁמַיִם שָׁמַיִם, לַיהוָה; וְהָאָרֶץ, נָתַן לִבְנֵי אָדָם.	זט	16. *The heavens are the heavens for the Lord; and the earth He gave to humanity.*
לֹא הַמֵּתִים, יְהַלְלוּ יָהּ; וְלֹא, כָּל יֹרְדֵי דוּמָה.	זי	17. *It is not the dead who will praise the Lord; nor all who descend into silence*
וַאֲנַחְנוּ, נְבָרֵךְ יָהּ מֵעַתָּה וְעַד עוֹלָם: הַלְלוּ יָהּ.	חי	18. *And we will bless the Lord from now and until eternity; Halleluyah.*

115:1 *Why the Exodus was a Certainty*

---

*Not to us, O Lord, not to us,
but to Your name give glory, for
the sake of your kindness; for
the sake of your truth.*

Literally… it's NOT about us!

The previous psalm described the many great miracles that God performs for the redemption of His chosen nation. Now, in Psalm 115, the psalmist wants to make it clear that the purpose of all of this miraculous dominance over the natural order is not the chosen nation at all. The victory and survival of His people is actually not an end in itself. In truth, the supernatural survival and victory of God's people over their enemies is a means to the higher goal – the glory of God over all the earth. This is actually an obvious point. Think about it.

The purpose of the Exodus is the establishment of the Nation of Israel. The purpose of the Nation of Israel is the establishment of God's kingdom over all the earth, i.e. the recognition and glorification of the one God. If A = B and B = C then A = C. The purpose of the Exodus is the glory of God over all the earth.

The Redemption of Israel is not about Israel

Exodus (A) → Creation of Nation of Israel (B)
Creation of Nation of Israel (B) → God's Kingdom on Earth (C)

Therefore:
Exodus (A) → God's Kingdom on Earth (C)

The people of Israel are identified as the bearers of God's covenant – the messengers who brought His word to the world. With this in mind, this psalm makes the following statement: "Whatever happens to the people of Israel happens to God's glory on this earth." If the people of Israel are persecuted, weak, and exiled there is a diminishing of God's glory in the world. When they are victorious and restored to strength in their land, God's glory is increased.

Ezekiel actually states this explicitly:

> So I scattered them among the nations, and they were dispersed throughout the countries; I judged them according to their ways and their deeds. When they came to the nations, wherever they went, *they profaned My holy name—when they said of them, 'These are the people of the Lord, and yet they have gone out of His land.'* But I had concern for My holy name, which the house of Israel had profaned among the nations wherever they went. Therefore say to the house of Israel, 'Thus says the Lord God: *"I do not do this for your sake, O house of Israel, but for My holy name's sake,* which you have profaned among the nations wherever you went. *And I will sanctify My great name,* which has been profaned among the nations, which you have profaned in their midst; and the nations shall know that I am the Lord," says the Lord God, "when I am hallowed in you before their eyes. *For I will take you from among the nations, gather you out of all countries, and bring you into your own land."* (Ezekiel 36:19-24)

There it is. The exile of the Nation of Israel profanes the name of the Lord. He restores Israel to their land in order to sanctify His great name – <u>not</u> *for the sake of Israel!*

What if there had been no promises?

This actually makes a lot of sense. God made numerous covenantal promises to Israel. For example, God told Abraham that his descendents would suffer and be enslaved in a foreign land and would then emerge wealthy and strong (Genesis 15:12-14). This is precisely what happened.

Now, just imagine if God had saved Israel from Egypt and the Exodus story had played out exactly the same way but *without the prior promise to Abraham*. Would the message be any different?

It certainly would. Had the Exodus happened without the prior promise to Abraham we easily would think that God saved Israel from Egypt because they merited it or because of God's mercy upon them. In other words, without a prior promise we could make the mistake of thinking that the Exodus was a *possibility* but not a *certainty*. If it's not a certainty it must depend on circumstances. If it depends on circumstances, it stands to reason that Israel's merit or lack thereof would determine if the Exodus would happen or not.

Since God *promised* that after subjugation and slavery He would redeem Israel from Egypt, *the Exodus was a certainty*. God does not break a promise. If the Exodus is a certainty it does not depend on Israel. It has nothing to do with whether or not they are deserving.

It's about God

But why? Why should the redemption of Israel be a sure thing? Shouldn't they be able to break the covenant?

The answer is no. Not if it isn't about Israel. And it isn't. It's about God. And because it's about God, the covenant can not be broken. Let me explain.

Let's say that God makes a promise that may or may not be fulfilled depending on the merit of the people. Let's say that the promise is then not fulfilled. There are two possible conclusions that can be drawn from this. One conclusion, of course, is that the people with whom covenant was made were not deserving of the fulfillment of the promise. The second conclusion one might draw is that God does not keep His promises or – even worse – that God is *not capable* of keeping His promises.

And this is precisely the point of Psalm 115. *Not to us!* The miraculous salvation described in the previous psalm is not for the sake of God's people. *Whether or not they are deserving is irrelevant*. It is not in their merit. It is not for them or about them. In fact, this makes a lot of sense. After all, the purpose of Israel is to be *a kingdom of priests* (Exodus 19:6) – in other words, a nation that helps the rest of the world enter into a relationship with God. *Their entire raison d'etre is not about them*, it's about the glory of God.

Let me sum up what we have said up to this point:
- The Exodus from Egypt was a promise of God.
- Therefore it had to happen.
- Why?
- Because if God promises and then does not deliver on his promise He seems weak and not all-powerful.
- AND The entire purpose of Israel is to give glory to God.
- Conclusion: The Exodus was not for Israel's sake but for the sake of the glory of God.

Your Kindness, Your Truth

This is the meaning of the end of the verse, *for the sake of your kindness; for the sake of your truth*. The Hebrew words HeSeD – *kindness*, and EMeT – *truth* are used here. HeSeD – *kindness* is not merely kindness in the sense of politeness. HeSeD – *kindness* always implies something *that is given*. Specifically, something that is *not earned or deserved*. If I work and get paid my agreed upon wage, we would not call that *kindness*. If I receive a nice tip over and above my salary, - something not necessarily earned or deserved – it would be an expression of *kindness*. Simply, HeSeD means *kindness that is not earned*.

The verse is saying that God's supernatural redemption of His people displays *His kindness* precisely *because the redemption is undeserved*. In addition, because the redemption is undeserved it shows God's *truth* – His commitment to keep His promises unconditionally.

God keeps His promises and bestows kindness upon those who serve Him not as an end in itself. It is not about us. It is about the glory of His name.

115:2 *"Where Now is Their God?"*

Why will the nations say,
'Where now is their God?'

God keeps His word

In my commentary to verse 1 I discussed the importance of God's promise to Israel prior to the redemption. I explained that had God taken His chosen people from slavery to freedom exactly as He did *without a prior promise*, the message of the Exodus story would have been very different. While God's *might and power* would have been equally as evident in the ten plagues, the splitting of the sea, and everything else that occurred, His *truthfulness* – that He keeps His word unconditionally – would not. I also pointed out that had God not promised redemption, one could easily have been led to believe that Israel was saved because they deserved to be saved. The fact that God *promised* protects against both of these issues. Fulfilling a stated promise shows God's *truthfulness* and the fact that God made the promise *unconditionally* makes it clear that it had nothing to do with merit.

In verse 2 the psalm introduces another dimension to of God's unconditional promise of redemption.

Why will the nations say, 'Where now is their God?'

At first glance, the question asked by the nations could be understood as, "See! Israel's God is not as strong as ours. He *can't* save them." Alternatively, it could mean, "See! Israel *does not merit* the keeping of the promise." However, the context of the psalm leading up to this verse as well as what follows it in the following verses indicates that there is much more to this question.

It's all about the miracles

The previous psalm that led up to this verse was not praising God only for redeeming Israel from Egypt. Psalm 114 praised God for His miracles and overt displays of supernatural power throughout the redemption process. In other words, Psalm 114 praised God for *how* He *did the Exodus* more than for the fact *that* He *did the Exodus*. Furthermore, the answer to the question given in the verse that follows this one would not make sense as a response if the question was saying, "Where is their God? *Why isn't He saving them*?" How would the answer, *Our God is in Heaven* be a response to this?

A more precise understanding of the question is this. "God, even if You do in fact redeem us, if You *don't* carry out great miracles in the process that show Your dominance over nature, Your glory will not be fully realized."

Imagine the Exodus without all the miracles. No ten plagues. No splitting of the sea. The story could have gone something like this: The People of Israel rebel, fight a war, and escape. Certainly they would have been aided by divine assistance in their victory, but not with the *explicit* upending of the laws of nature that occurred in the Exodus story. What would people say?

To some, the entire story would have seemed like a natural process. Skeptical people would have been able to say, "Where is their God? Sure; we see Israel leaving Egypt. But who says there is anything *Godly* about it?" In effect, the verse is saying, "God, if the goal is only to save us from slavery in Egypt it is sufficient to do it through seemingly natural means. But *for Your glory's sake* please make it supernatural. Show them that You are God! Don't let them think that it was just a happy coincidence or a natural process."

In the contexts of both ancient polytheistic paganism as well as modern atheism, there is another dimension to this question. Ancient pagans and modern atheists share one theological principle in common. They both have a difficult time believing in a God that they can not see. For the ancients, this meant that a God that is not housed in a physical object is not real. For modern atheists, if I can't see it under a microscope or measure it with the instruments in the lab, it doesn't exist. Both ask the question, "Where is their God?" Where is this God that can't be seen or measured?

Where now is their God?

I'd like to suggest that this is the meaning of the word *now* in this verse. The God of Israel is the God of history. While at any given moment in time in the present tense – with only the narrow perspective of *now* - one could ask "Where is God?", it is much harder to doubt God when looking at the long term. The broader one's view of history, the more one looks at the incredible supernatural journey of Israel throughout the centuries, the more one sees clearly that God is present and revealed.

Why will the nations say, 'Where _now_ is their God?'

God reveals Himself in the unfolding of history. The more we broaden our historical perspective the more we see Him.

115:3 *His Will is Done*

And our God is in heaven; all
that He wills He has done.

In response to the challenge of the enemies of Israel, "Where now is their God?" our verse responds with a two part answer. *First our God is in Heaven.* Second, *all that He wills He has done.* In the commentary to the previous verse I suggested that the answer, *our God is in Heaven* expresses the fact that there is no need for God to be seen in a physical object. But for both ancient pagans and modern atheists alike, a God that is not physically perceptible does not exist.

I would like to suggest another dimension to this answer. *And our God is in heaven; all that He wills He has done* could be paraphrased as follows:

A skeptic might think, "Okay. You want to believe in a non-physical God, a purely spiritual being? Go ahead. But don't try to tell me that your non-physical God can act and have influence in the physical material world." To this line of thinking the verse responds, that even though our God is not physical; i.e. He does not have a body and He dwells not on this earth but in heaven; despite this distance from the earthly realm He is in total control of nature.

All that He wills He has done

How does a spiritual being with no body or physical properties carry out His will in the concrete physical world? He does this by using His will and His will alone. In order to create or manipulate the material world below all God needs to do is to *will it*. Whatever He wills *is done!*

This point is actually subtly stated by the peculiar grammar of the second half of the verse. The two verbs in the second phrase of this verse are in two different tenses. *All that He wills He has done*. Every single English translation that I could find changed the tense of either one or the other of these verbs in order to make the two verbs consistent. In every translation either the verse is rendered, *all that He wills He does* making them both present tense, or *all that He willed, He has done*, changing the first to past tense. Furthermore, the present perfect *has done* that I – and all the translations that used past tense - used here is not even completely accurate. *A more precise* but admittedly clumsy translation would be, *All that He wills, He did*.

The translators' dilemma of 115:3

Choice #1	Actual Hebrew	Choice # 2
All that	All that	All that
He wills	He wills (present)	He willed
He does	He did (past)	He has done

I'd like to suggest that the inconsistent tenses in this verse actually make a powerful theological point. God does not need to *work* or even *do* anything. *Everything exists as a result of His will*. We see this in the wording of the very first thing ever created.

And God said let there be light; and there was light. (Genesis 1:3)

Notice that the verse does not say, *And God said let there be light; and He created light; and then there was light*. Rather, He just *said* it, and there it was! In other words, He expressed His will that there be light and - voila! - there was light. *God's will alone creates*.

I believe that this is the true meaning of our verse: *all that He wills He has done*. As soon as *He wills* anything, that's it. *It's done*. There is no intermediate step. Once He expresses His will, the intended creation or manipulation in the physical earthly realm is already complete. The change from present to past in our verse speaks directly to the immediacy of this process. Once it is willed by God it is over. It has already happened.

God does not need to *be physical* or engage in the physical world. His reign is by His will alone. This is how a purely spiritual non-physical God – *in heaven* - can be in total control of the material world below.

And our God is in heaven; all that He wills He has done.

Just as in Genesis God created only through His speech, the expression of His will alone, He continues to govern the world by His will. Whatever He wills, it is done.

115:4 *Disappointments of Silver and Gold*

> *Their idols are silver and gold;*
> *the work of human hands.*

The ancient world is famous for its idols. Early pagan religious life was rife with images of stone, wood, gold, and silver believed to house the many deities and powers that were worshipped. Just as in ancient times, humanity today falls prey to the error described in this verse; the worship of silver, gold, and the creations of our own human hands.

To gain a deeper understanding of these lessons, let's draw our attention to two interesting features of our verse:

1. The verse specifically singles out idols of *silver* and *gold* as opposed to other common substances.
2. The verse does not use the usual Biblical Hebrew word for *idol*.

*Two Hebrew Words for _Idol_*

The Hebrew word for *idol* here is ETZeV. The more common word for *idol* in Scripture is PeSeL. PeSeL is from the root PSL meaning *carve*. It refers to the fact that many – if not most – idols were carved of stone or wood. The root of this more unusual word for *idol* - ETZeV - is unclear. Other than the twenty times in Scripture where the word in our verse is used to describe an idol, there are *more than thirty* additional appearances of this root. *In all but one* of them this root means *pain, toil, disappointment,* or *suffering*. (see Genesis 3:16,17, 6:6, Proverbs 14:23)

*This is a good place to point out to readers who are not so familiar with Hebrew that *verb roots* in Hebrew are also usually the basis for related *nouns*.

Why is the Hebrew root whose primary meaning is _toil_, _disappointment_, and _suffering_ also used as a word for _idols_?

The single exception where ETZeV does not mean *pain, toil, disappointment,* or *suffering* is:

Your hands *shaped me* and made me. Will you now turn and destroy me? (Job 10:8)

The word for *shaped me* is a conjugation of the ETZeV root. Perhaps it is this single exception that allows for the word ETZeV to mean *idol*. Just as the more common PeSeL is from the root for *carve*, the word ETZeV would be from the root for *shape*. The problem with this approach is that it is difficult to make the case that the etymology of the word ETZeV for *idol* derives from *a single exceptional instance* of a root that has a different meaning in dozens of other places in Scripture.

To sum up this point:
- The ETZeV root means *pain, toil, disappointment*, or *suffering* in more than thirty places in the Bible.
- The ETZeV root means *shaped* in one place in the Bible.
- It is difficult to suggest that this one exception is the basis for the twenty places where ETZeV means *idol*.

I would like to suggest that the word root ETZeV is used for *idols* based on two points about idolatry:
1. How these false gods were worshipped
2. The Biblical attitude to such worship

Suffering vs. Drawing Near

As I pointed out, the root ETzeV almost universally means *toil, pain, disappointment*, and *suffering*. Put simply, it implies *discomfort*. I'd like to suggest that while there may have been *toil* involved in forming these idols, the reason that they are referred to as ETzeV is that to a pagan mindset it was understood that *to worship* meant *to give something up* or even *to suffer*. This concept took shape through self-affliction in the form of self mutilation, child sacrifice, and a general belief that it is the human responsibility to appease the gods by feeding them from the work of our hands. To serve the gods meant *to suffer and to give something up*.

In contrast, the biblical belief is that the service of God is meant to elevate humanity by drawing us closer to God. We don't have to *give up* anything in order to please God. This point is powerfully illustrated by the Hebrew word for *sacrifice* KoRBaN which is from the root KRB meaning *close* or *near*. *KORBAN* is *that which comes close* or *that which is drawn near*.

The relationship of humans to gods in the pagan Ancient Near East can be summed up as follows: Humans are slaves of the gods and must labor to serve them or suffer their wrath.

The Bible paints a different picture. Man is created in the image of God. *God loves man*. Man's highest goal and yearning is to walk in

God's ways and thereby be close to Him. *You shall be holy for I am holy* (Leviticus 19:2).

Idolatry = Disappointment

I want to suggest that referring to idols as ETZeV is the Bible's way of categorizing the worship of idols as *labor, suffering, pain*, and *disappointment* when these false gods can't deliver. There is no love, no spiritual or moral refinement, and no *closeness to the Divine*.

The psalmist is making this point by using a play on words and choosing the word ETZeV for *idol* rather than the usual PeSeL. It is as though the verse could be read,

Their *disappointments* are silver and gold; the work of human hands.

Still worshiping Silver and Gold

Alternatively, there is a contemporary message in this verse as well. There are all too many people who put their hopes in *silver and gold* and their faith in *the work of human hands*. Silver and gold look great on the outside. Aesthetically beautiful and economically valuable, they provide enjoyment, beauty, and security only in the short term. In the long run, worship of silver and gold leads only to ETZeV – to disappointment and suffering. Gold, silver, and human handiwork are valuable *tools*, but if we put our ultimate trust in them they always disappoint.

Silver and gold are two of the softest metals on earth. In other words, even though they are beautiful, they are not strong. Unlike wood, they are neither alive in any way nor can they nurture life as food. The fact that they are valuable is a creation of man and his desire for superficial aesthetic beauty. Not only what is made by them, but even the fact that silver and gold *have any importance at all* is, as the verse states, *the work of human hands*.

Their idols are silver and gold; the work of human hands.

There is a human tendency to worship silver and gold; to believe that they have power; but they always disappoint. In contrast, our service of the Lord elevates us and brings us closer to His love.

115:5 *Communication Breakdown*

---

*They have a mouth but they do
not speak; they have eyes but
they do not see.*

Paganism = Everything is alive

At first glance it is quite easy to think of idol worship as pure foolishness. After all, why would anyone believe that something made by his own hands is a god that has power over his own life? This is how we tend to think of ancient paganism. But this understanding of idolatry is incorrect. The idol worshippers of the ancient Near East were not irrational stupid people. Once we understand this we can begin to understand both the true meaning of their false beliefs as well the profound beauty and truth of Biblical monotheism that responds to and refutes those beliefs.

In the ancient world it was believed that everything in nature was animate. Everything is conscious. Everything has a will. The rain, the wind, the sky, disease, and every other aspect of the natural world was believed to be alive and willful. The purpose of religious practice was to interact with these forces; to keep them happy and satisfied, and thus to secure safety, health, and prosperity in one's own life.

Idols: Portals not Symbols

Additionally, it was believed that one way to interact directly with all of these living, conscious, independent forces of nature was to create icons and idols that represent their identities and powers. It was believed that by creating a physical object whose form represents a certain power, the object would then become infused with that idea and would consequently contain the power itself. For example, if I create an idol depicting the god of storms – perhaps a wild untamed beast would be appropriate –, by presenting the image of the god of storms it was believed that the object could then house the *idea* of storms and thus the *power* of storms. The god of storms could be served and communicated to through that object.

To sum up this idea, the ancient use of idols and icons was based on the assumption that forms have the ability to house the powers represented by those forms if they are made for that purpose.

"Hey! This thing doesn't work!"

With this in mind we can understand the statement that is made by our verse as well as the two verses that follow it.

> *They have a mouth but they do not speak; they have eyes but they do not see.*

In other words, idols don't actually work. The forces of nature can not be communicated with and do not communicate. Creating a graven or cast image that represents a particular power such as the wind, the sun, or pestilence does not bring the object to life. An icon does not house a certain force or become a portal to communicate with the god in question. There is neither response nor is there any awareness on the part of the idol.

No perception, No communication

Speaking is active communication. *Seeing* is passive perception. The psalm stresses that they have neither. Considering the point of this verse, it is critical to note that both *speaking* and *seeing* are behaviors that are anthropomorphically attributed to God a great many times throughout Scripture. God *sees* human behavior, suffering, and hidden thoughts. God *speaks* His commandments, promises, and rebuke. While these verbs are used metaphorically, in the context of our psalm we can see these activities as indicative not only of physical behavior but of divine interaction with creation as well.

Faced with the fact that his idol does not communicate with him, an adherent of idol worship might argue that while the communication is not perceptible to man, the idol – or god that it houses – is certainly *aware* of the worship being done before it; that the idol serves as a portal to the conscious god even if we humans are not able to see this. To this line of thinking, our verse responds, <u>*Just as*</u> *they have a mouth but they do not speak;* <u>*so too*</u> *they have eyes but they do not see.* They are equally inanimate in *perception* as they are in *expression*.

They have a mouth but they do not speak; = They do not communicate to us.

they have eyes but they do not see. = They do not even have awareness of us.

Only the one God is conscious. Only God makes decisions and communicates His will to the world.

115:6 *Hear no Worship; Smell no Worship*

> *They have ears but do not hear;*
> *they have a nose but do not*
> *smell.*

It seems that at this point the psalm is simply continuing what began in the previous verse with the *mouth* and *eyes* by listing more organs of the senses.

While it is certainly true that these verses poetically refer to all of the sensory abilities that graven idols do not possess, there is a distinct theological point being made in our verse as well.

In my comments to the previous verse I explained that *speech* and *vision* typify *active* and *passive* communication. In other words, the point of the previous verse was that the false gods of idolatry do not communicate at all; neither actively nor passively.

Here in this verse the two senses that are paired have a new and different message.

Hearing, Smelling and Worship

Like *speaking* and *seeing*, both *hearing* and *smelling* are senses that are used in Scripture to describe Godly behavior. As I explained, when Scripture describes God as *speaking* or *seeing* the intent is to express the fact that God is *communicative* and *cognizant*. Now, with the introduction of *hearing* and *smelling* the psalm is making reference specifically to the pagan idols' *failure to respond to worship*.

When Noah leaves the ark after the flood, his first act is to build an altar and bring sacrifices to God.

> Then Noah built an altar to the Lord and, taking some of all the clean animals and clean birds, he sacrificed burnt offerings on it. *The Lord smelled the pleasing aroma...* (Genesis 8:20-21)

Smell continues to be the sense used to describe God's reaction to sacrifices in Leviticus chapters 1 through 3 where the phrase *a pleasing aroma for the Lord* appears numerous times.

Similarly, and even more widespread in its use, the sense of *hearing* is associated with God's acceptance of worship. To bring one example among many,

> Then we cried out to the Lord, the God of our ancestors, and *the Lord heard* our voice and saw our misery, toil, and oppression. (Deuteronomy 26:7)

We see that the two senses mentioned in our verse – *smelling* and *hearing* – are used to indicate not only God's *awareness* of worship, but His affirmative *acceptance* of worship as well.

With this in mind, the message of this verse following the previous verse becomes crystal clear. The previous verse made the statement that the forces of nature believed to be embodied in idols do not communicate. They do not pay attention. They do not *speak*. They do not *see*.

Now, in verse 6, this idea is taken a step further. Lest one think that although they do not pay attention – *see* - or relay clear messages – *speak* -, perhaps, one might argue, if they are worshipped and served in the correct way, these forces are awakened, pleased, and responsive. True, in the absence of worship they pay little attention to us but perhaps that is the very purpose of offerings and gifts of worship. Perhaps this is the way to arouse these forces who are only otherwise uncommunicative.

To this possibility our verse responds. *No! They do not smell. They do not hear*. Neither the smell of offerings nor the sound of prayer yields any reaction at all. There are no buttons of worship to push that awaken or appease these forces. The senses ascribed to God when He *accepts our worship – smell* and *hearing* – do not apply. Worship of the forces of nature is meaningless.

They have ears but do not hear; they have a nose but do not smell.

Only the one Lord, God, responds to worship, accepting our offerings and heeding our prayers.

115:7 *It's Not Alive*

They have hands, but cannot feel. They have feet, but cannot walk. No sounds come from their throats.

This is the final verse of the three verses that describe living functions of which pagan idolatrous gods are incapable. Here we encounter three bodily actions; *feeling, walking,* and *making sounds with the throat*. It is interesting to note that verse 5 already mentioned that false gods do not possess the power of *speech. They have a mouth but they do not speak*. At first glance it seems that the end of our verse is simply repeating this lack of verbal ability in different words. *No sounds come from their throats.*

However, it is precisely the fact that this statement appears to be redundant that calls our attention to it and calls upon us to analyze it more carefully. After all, Scripture does not simply repeat itself without good reason. Furthermore, a close look at the difference between this final clause of verse 7 and the first part of verse 5 gives us the key to understanding the unique message of verse 7 in its entirety.

Not Things that God Does

I mentioned in my commentary to the previous two verses that all of the behaviors mentioned in those verses are used in Scripture to describe God's interactions with creation. I used this fact to explain that the lessons of those verses were specifically alluding to the lack of *divine abilities* that are attributed to God and God alone. I cited verses that describe God doing all of these things. God *speaks*. God *sees*. God *smells*. God *hears*.

The final clause of our verse alerts us to the fact that this verse teaches a fundamentally different lesson from the previous two. *Speech* is associated only with God and human beings. If our verse intended to refer once again to *speech* it would have done so. Instead the psalmist chose the unusual description, *No sounds come from their throats*. In other words, we are no longer referring to *speech* at all. Rather, the point of this verse is to say that these false gods do not even function at the level of *animals!* Animals do not speak but they do make noises with their throats.

With this approach we can understand the choice of the first two clauses in the verse as well. *They have hands, but cannot feel. They have feet, but cannot walk.* As I have pointed out, many times Scripture describes God as *speaking*, *seeing*, *smelling*, and *hearing*. These physical behaviors are anthropomorphically applied to God. Despite the Bible's willingness to use these physical descriptions for God's non-physical behavior, not all bodily functions are attributed to God. Specifically, God is *never described as feeling*; i.e. with touch. He is *never described as walking*.

After two verses listing four bodily functions that are attributed to God, our verse lists three bodily functions that are *never* ascribed to God! More importantly, animals do all three of these. Animals *feel*, *walk*, and *make noise with their throats*.

To put it all together, after detailing the ways in which the idolatrous pagan gods have no ability to behave or respond as God does; our verse takes things one step further. Idols are not even alive at the level of animals! They do not even have physical abilities that are purely animalistic and never attributed to God.

No Manipulation of Nature Through Idols

Theologically speaking, the verse is responding to another common belief of the pagan world. Many ancient people saw the gods as having basic animalistic needs. They believed that they could manipulate the gods by doing this or that behavior precisely because the gods would instinctively respond a particular way to a particular ritual. In other words, a pagan might argue that the gods are powerful forces who are alive and responsive even if they are not fully conscious in a human way. They are forces to be manipulated based on what we know of their instinctive natures much in the same way that animal behavior can be predicted based on hardwired natural tendencies. They saw the gods as powerful living forces much like powerful beasts that can be pleased or irritated by stimuli that arouse their natural reactions.

As the third in this series, our verse declares; *Not only are these false gods unable to respond, communicate, or be conscious of human behavior. They are not even as alive as animals. They are not living forces to be individually manipulated the way one manipulates actual living things.*

Not only do they lack divine or human qualities; they lack even animal qualities as well.

To sum up these three verses:

They do not speak or see	= *No communication in either direction*
They do not hear or smell	= *No response to worship*
They do not feel, or walk, or make sounds	= *No animate response whatsoever*

Only the one true God communicates with us and responds to our prayers. God controls the natural world. It does not exist independent of Him. We can not manipulate it to perform as we wish without God.

115:8 *You are What You Worship*

> *Like them shall be those who make them; all who trust in them.*

After the previous three verses described the inanimate futility of pagan idols, this verse appears to be either nothing more than an insult and epithet of disdain for those who worship idols or a prayer for their downfall and failure.

The Hebrew word – YiHiYU - *they shall be*, the second word in this verse, is used elsewhere in Psalms as a hope or prayer, as in *May it/they be...* (e.g. Psalm 19:14). In fact, there are a number of translations and commentators that see our verse in this same way. They understand it to be prayerfully saying, *May those who make the idols end up just like them.*

Not a Prayer, Not an Insult

I believe that this reading of the verse is incorrect for two reasons.

First, the syntax does not lean this way. Everywhere else that YIHIYU – *they shall be* - is used *as a prayer* or expression of hope it appears as the first word of the sentence. Here, it appears after the word – KEMOHEM - *Like them*. If it were a prayer or hopeful curse upon the idolaters, wishing that they end up as inanimate and impotent as their idols, the verse should have read *May it be that (YIHIYU) those who make them (OSEIHEM) shall be like them (KEMOHEM)*. In other words, if this verse is a prayer, the word order would be an exception to the rules of syntax.

To sum up this point:

The first phrase of our verse is made up of three Hebrew words:

Like them	KeMOHeM
shall be(3rd. pers. pl.)	YiHiYU
those who make them;	OSEIHeM

- The middle word, YiHiYU – *shall be* – is sometimes used in the context of prayer asking God for something to come to pass. When used this way it would be translated *let them be* or *may they be*.
- Whenever YiHiYU is a request or prayer it is the first word of the sentence. Here, of course, it is not.

Secondly, the context makes it unlikely that this verse is meant as a prayer or curse on idolaters. This entire psalm is a praise of God. The focus is on God's greatness and how much better it is to worship Him than to worship inanimate and impotent gods of silver and gold. This is the thrust of the psalm both before and after this verse. The insertion of a prayer for the downfall or failure of the wicked at this point would make little sense contextually.

The alternative common understanding, that it is an insult that pokes fun, so to speak, at idolaters is difficult as well. Is it the way of Scripture to hurl insults and exaggerations about those who have strayed from God? Those who worship and fashion idols are not, in fact, inanimate objects with no ability to speak, smell, or walk. For the psalmist to say, *They will end up just like the idols they worship* seems like a petty *and inaccurate* epithet. What would be the point of such a statement? If it is referring to the fact that the worshippers of idols will die and therefore become as inanimate as those they worship; is that not also true of every one of us?

The common translations of this verse do not make sense. Context and language both indicate that it is neither a curse upon idolaters nor is it a prayer for their downfall.

You are what you worship

I would like to suggest that this verse is making a unique and powerful psychological and theological point.

Any god that any person believes in represents, for the believer, an ideal. In the polytheistic pagan world each god represented a different ideal. The god of beauty, the god of war, the god of pleasure, etc. each represented the perfect ideal of the force that they were believed to represent. To some extent, the same is true of hero worship of *idols* in modern popular culture. For those who idolize entertainers or athletes, these famous people are paradigms of what they strive for or wish to be.

If I believe that there is nothing more powerful than the forces of nature; that there is no way to triumph over nature; then nature becomes the highest ideal. The limitations of nature become my limitations. If I believe that the human being is part of the animal kingdom governed by natural animalistic forces, then my natural animalistic traits become my ideals and my identity. There is no inclination to strive to move beyond them.

On an ethical level, the natural forces – and the pagan gods that were represented by them in ancient times – were understood as a power structure without any morality per se. In this context, it is no wonder that cruelty, slavery, and despotism were commonplace.

Today too, those who reject faith in a caring and giving God; in a God who cares about good and evil reject the ideals implied by an objective God-given morality.

On the other hand, if I believe in a perfectly spiritual God who is above nature, who is not bound and limited by natural physical laws, then those divine traits become my ideals. To emulate my God is to strive to overcome the limitations of nature, for He is not bound by those limitations. I strive to give and do for others regardless of personal benefit because God has given me everything and needs nothing. God does not have base animal instincts, so I strive to transcend my instinctive animal traits. Limitless spirituality – like the God I worship – is the perfection which I seek to imitate.

The Bible teaches us that God created humanity *in the image of God.* (Gen.1:27)

What our verse is powerfully declaring is that *everyone* is created – *or fashions themselves* - in the image of the gods – or God – that they serve. If I serve the one true God, the unlimited and all powerful creator of all, *then this is the image in which I was created.* This is the ideal towards which I strive. My possibilities for spirituality, growth, and perfection are limitless because the God I serve - *the ideal towards which I strive* - is perfect, limitless, and above the restrictions of nature. I can transcend nature because God is above nature and I am in His image.

On the other hand, if I serve gods of silver and gold; limited gods that represent the finite laws of nature then the inevitable result is that I am limited. I am bound by nature.

We all create ourselves in the image of whatever we worship.

Like them shall be those who make them; all who trust in them.

Not a curse. Not an insult. Rather, our verse is stating the inevitable. We are what we worship. It is the image in which we are fashioned.

What we idolize is what we strive to be. What we worship tells us what we are working to become. Our faith in God leads us to try to become like Him.

115:9 *Helper and Shield*

O Israel, trust in the Lord; He is their helper and their shield.

Trust vs. Faith

After the previous verse referred to idolaters *trusting* in their false gods our verse and the next two that follow it contrast the pagan trust in false gods and our trust in the Lord. But what is *trust*? How is it different from *faith*?

The Hebrew word root BTCh – *trust* - refers to *trust* in the sense of *protection* and *security*. Two typical examples of different uses of this root are:

> When you cross the Jordan and live in the land which the Lord your God is giving you to inherit, and He gives you rest from all your surrounding enemies so that you live in *security*, (BeTaCh) (Deuteronomy 12:10)

> They will lay siege to all the cities throughout your land until the high fortified walls in which you *trust* (BoTeaCh) fall down. (Deuteronomy 28:52)

Faith, on the other hand, refers to the *knowledge* and *awareness* that God exists and is in control. For example, upon experiencing the splitting of the Reed Sea and the drowning of the Egyptian army the People of Israel are described as having *faith*:

> And Israel saw the great hand that God enacted upon Egypt; and the people feared the Lord; and they had *faith* in the Lord and in Moses His servant. (Exodus 14:31)

To put it another way, *faith* is the belief that God exists and controls all. *Trust* is the belief and emotional state that says that because God is in control, everything will turn out for the best. *Faith* means that I know that God *is here*. *Trust* means that I know that He *will be there in the future*.

Faith vs. Trust

Faith = God is here now

Trust = God will be there in the future

Helper vs. Shield

This understanding of the meaning of *trust* in God sheds light on the second phrase in our verse. *O Israel, trust in the Lord; <u>He is their helper and their shield</u>.* The word for *helper* – EZeR – does not usually connote *help* in the sense of being saved from danger. Usually it implies *sharing in a task*. The first time this word appears is in the well-known scene describing the creation of the first woman. God says,

> *It is not good for Man to be alone. I will make for him a helper –* EZeR *– matching him* (Genesis 2:18).

There are many other examples in scripture of this connotation of the word EZeR meaning a partner sharing in a joint task.

When the people of Israel are in danger and in need of salvation from harm they need God's *help*, in the sense that they need His protection from harm. That said, in the context of the rest of this psalm I don't believe that this is the type of *help* implied in this verse and the two that follow. This psalm does not describe Israel in danger and being redeemed.

Let's look at the themes in this psalm.

- The *first* eight verses of this psalm are a polemic against the futility and falsehood of pagan idolatry.
- The *last* seven verses of the psalm describe the blessedness of God's people and those who fear Him; and the responsibility that they have to do God's work on earth.

Our verse and the two that follow it are between these two sections. They serve as the transition between those two sections of the psalm.

I would like to suggest that the two words *help* and *shield* are meant to describe two ways that God guarantees that His people's *mission is accomplished* in the long term. There are times when God's people are in a position to do God's work. They are in a position of influence. The task of refuting and defeating the gods of silver and gold, the worship of the forces of nature, is at hand. At those times we trust that God is with us as a *helper*, assisting us in our mission.

At other times, when the forces that oppose us are riding high; when the attacks on God's nation prevent them from being able to do God's work; when all they can do is fight for survival; God is a *shield*. He protects His people from attack.

- *Helper*   in carrying out their mission
- *Shield*   against those attacks that would hold them back

"To" Israel or "About" them

This verse contains a peculiar grammatical change in *person* that requires our attention.

> *O Israel, trust in the Lord; He is <u>their</u> helper and <u>their</u> shield.*

The first half of the verse is in the *second person*, speaking *to* Israel and instructing them to trust in God. The word *trust* here is conjugated in the second person command form. The second half of the verse then speaks *about* Israel in the *third person*. Many translations change either the first phrase or the second in order to make them consistent. I believe that this is a mistake that leads to a misunderstanding of the message of the verse.

Those who change the verse do so because for the verse to be grammatically consistent without changing something, the word *their* in the second clause of the verse cannot refer to the same people who are being addressed in the first clause; Israel.

| *O Israel, trust in the Lord;* | speaking <u>to</u> Israel |
| *He is <u>their</u> helper and <u>their</u> shield.* | speaking <u>about</u> Israel |

This doesn't seem to make sense. So the translators change it. I would like to suggest that *this is precisely the reason for the change.* In other words, the Israel spoken <u>about</u> at the end of the verse is not the same as the Israel spoken <u>to</u> at the beginning!

Let me explain.

As I mentioned, *trust* is about the future. If the second clause of the verse continued addressing Israel in the second person the meaning of the entire verse would simply be, *O Israel, trust in God <u>that</u> He <u>will be</u> your helper and shield*. The change in person means that the people being addressed at the beginning are, in fact, *different than those mentioned in the second half of the verse*. The correct meaning of the verse is as follows; *O Israel, trust in God (in the future) <u>because</u> He has helped <u>those before you</u> and has been <u>their</u> shield.*

To sum up:
1. The change in person – from "you" to "they" - indicates a different group
2. The verse calls on Israel to trust in the future
3. Because He has helped and shielded Israel in the past

In other words, if the verse had not switched from second person to third, the message of the second half would not be understood. Without the change the verse is simply stating that God helps and shields His people. The change in person reveals that the second phrase is *giving a reason why* God's people can feel secure in trusting in Him going forward in to the future. It is giving the support of *past evidence* to embolden God's people – those addressed in the first phrase – to trust in Him because He has already shown Himself to be a helper and a shield in the past to those that came before them.

Our trust in God, that He helps us and protects us, need not be relegated to irrational blind belief. When we look back in history we can see the evidence. He was there as a *shield* in times of trouble. He was there as a *helper* when we went to work for Him. Just as He was there *for them*, He will be there for *us*.

O Israel, trust in the Lord; He is their helper and their shield.

Once again, history is a source of faith and trust in God. When we see how He has preserved and assisted those who have faith in Him we are confident that He will do the same for us.

115:10 *Individual Leaders; Collective Nation*

> *O house of Aaron, trust in the
> Lord; He is their helper and
> their shield.*

After the previous verse called upon Israel to trust in the Lord, there is
an obvious question that demands our attention as to the plain meaning
of this verse that now follows. What is meant by the house of Aaron? Are
the descendants of Aaron, the high priest, not also members of Israel?
If Israel trusts in the Lord, does that not also mean that the house of
Aaron trusts in the Lord? Why are they singled out? What is the difference between the call to Israel to trust in the Lord and the same call to the
house of Aaron?

You(s.) trust vs. You (pl.) trust

Serving as a congregational rabbi in Newport News, Virginia, I was
introduced to the wonderful Southern United States expression of *y'all*, a
contraction of you-all. Without textual context, it is hard to know when
the word *you* is addressing one person or many people since the English
language does not distinguish between second person singular and
second person plural in its verb conjugations. The Southern expression
y'all cuts through it all and lets me know that many people are being
addressed. Y'all provides English with a second person plural!

In the Hebrew language, there is never a doubt if the word *you* is
singular or plural.

With this in mind, we can address a glaring grammatical difference
between these the previous verse and this verse that is not at all evident
in the English translations.

In verse 9, the word *trust* is singular. In verses 10 and 11 it is plural.

When the psalmist is telling Israel to trust in the Lord, it is in the
singular; however, when it comes to the *House of Aaron* and the *Fearers of*

the Lord the call to trust in the Lord is written in the plural. English translations do not pick up this glaring Hebrew grammatical change.

If I could illustrate this with use of the Southern *y'all*, the verses would look like this:

Israel *(you)* trust in the L-rd;	He is their helper and their shield
House of Aaron *(y'all)* trust in L-rd;	He is their helper and their shield
G-d fearers *(y'all)* trust in the L-rd;	He is their helper and their shield

To sum up the question: Why is the collective of *Israel* addressed in the singular while the *house of Aaron* is addressed in the plural?

Helper: Assistant not Savior

Before answering this question, I would like to revisit the word *helper* – EZeR – that appears in these verses. This word or its root appears approximately one hundred times in Scripture. *More than half of the time* it refers to military assistance, often one force helping another. Almost all of the non-military uses of the word are in the context of *assistance with a mission or task*. Sharing in an important project is what is implied by this word more than the kind of *help* that saves someone from danger or alleviates their suffering. To sum this up, the word *helper* used in these verses implies that the Lord provides assistance to Israel, the house of Aaron, and those who fear the Lord in the *success of their missions*.

With this in mind, we can now understand the peculiar change from singular to plural as well as the meaning of this verse in its entirety.

Missions: Collective vs. Personal

Israel has a mission. Their mission is not an individual one. No one member of the chosen people is capable of fulfilling Israel's purpose on this earth. The mission of setting up a Godly society – *a kingdom of priests*

and a holy nation (Exodus 19:6) – in order to bring knowledge of God and
His word to the entire world can only be accomplished by the collective
people of Israel. That is why the psalmist, when telling Israel to trust in
God, that he is their EZeR – their *helper* with their task –, speaks to them
as one singular unit.

No leadership class

The priests, *the house of Aaron,* have a leadership role within Israel.
Despite the fact that the house of Aaron is quite literally *a family* and
therefore more likely than not to view themselves as a single separate
unit, they are spoken to in the plural.

Leaders have to lead. To lead effectively, they must be engaged with
the people. More to the point, the house of Aaron are the priests. Their
mission is to inspire, to teach, and to help others draw closer to God. If
they were to see themselves as a separate distinct unit, they would not be
as effective. To properly fulfill their mission, they dare not see themselves
as a separate *priestly class* that sits above and apart from the rest of Israel.
So long as they see themselves as individuals – as individual priests,
teachers, and spiritual guides – they will identify as members of Israel
who have an integrated leadership role to play within the people. If they
see the house of Aaron as a separate entity, this is the starting point that
leads to an aloof and detached leadership class.

Another way to put is this. Leaders should view themselves *verti-
cally* – as serving the people and their needs – rather than *horizontally* – as
primarily identified with other members of their class or position.

As mentioned above, Israel has a priestly role to play in the world. As
God states just before the covenant of Sinai, they are to become a *kingdom of
priests*...(Exodus 19:6) Like priests to their flocks, their mission as a nation
is to inspire the nations of the world to draw closer to God. This is a collective mission. Nation to nation. It is the mission of the people as a whole.

Within Israel there are internal priests as well, the house of Aaron,
who have a similar mission. They, too, are given the task of inspiration
and leading others towards the divine. However, this task is an individual one – person to person.

The plural language addressing the House of Aaron speaks to each member as an individual as opposed to singular language which would address the House of Aaron as a single collective.

Just as Israel can trust that it will receive Godly assistance in achieving its mission to the world, so too the house of Aaron – charged with the mission to inspire Israel – must trust that God will be their helper in their great task as well.

O house of Aaron, trust in the Lord; He is their helper and their shield.

All who live in covenant with God are charged with the mission to inspire others. But these people of faith also need leaders who in turn inspire them.

115:11 *The Fearers of the Lord*

> *O fearers of the Lord trust in the Lord; He is their helper and their shield.*

Who exactly are the *fearers of the Lord*? What makes them different than, say, *the lovers of the Lord*? (Psalms 97:10, 5:12) What new idea is stated here by calling on them to trust in the Lord?

Special Status for Fearers

The phrase *fearers of the Lord* appears numerous times in Psalms. The *fearers of the Lord* are described as givers of special praise to God;

The fearers of the Lord praise Him. (Psalm 22:24)

They also receive special rewards and divine protection;

How abundant are the good things that You have stored up for *those who fear You*, (Psalm 31:20)

Behold the eye of the Lord is upon *those who fear Him*. (Psalm 33:18; see also Ps. 34:8, 60:6, 103:11, 103:13, 111:5)

God serves the fearers?

Among the many blessings that are bestowed upon the *fearers of the Lord* in the book of Psalms, there are two that stand out as quite extreme.

The secret of the Lord is for those who fear Him; He makes His covenant known to them. (Psalm 25:14)

He fulfills the desires of those who fear Him; He hears their cry and saves them. (Psalm 145:19)

In the first of these verses those who fear the Lord are promised knowledge of *the secret of the Lord* and *His covenant*. This is an astounding gift. Even when God blesses people with health and success in their lives, one thing remains. They still do not know the hidden plan of God. By what merit do those who *fear* Him deserve this amazing revelation?

The second verse that I cited here is even more amazing. *He fulfills the desires of those who fear Him; God* fulfills *their* desires!

So What is a Fearer of the Lord?

To understand this we have to ask an even simpler question. What does it mean to be a *fearer of the Lord*? How does one qualify for this specific title? How is a fearer of the Lord different from a *lover* of the Lord or one who has *faith* in the Lord?

The answer is found in two other verses in Psalms.

Fortunate are all who *fear the Lord, who walk in His ways*. (Psalm 128:1)

Who is the man who *fears the Lord? He will teach him in the way he should choose*. (Psalm 25:12)

In both of these verses *fear of the Lord* is associated with following *God's way*. In other words, *fear of the Lord* means *obedience to His will*. While it is true that those who *love* the Lord may also be obedient, the trait of *absolute obedience* is associated with *fear of the Lord*. The *fearers of the Lord* are those who exemplify obedience.

> *Fearer of the Lord = One who displays absolute obedience*

Abraham: The original fearer

Proof that absolute obedience to God's will and the title *fearer of God* go hand in hand takes us all the way back to the first person who was ever described this way.

When the angel of God prevents Abraham from killing Isaac as a sacrifice for God, the angel says,

> 'Do not lay a hand on the boy', he said. 'Do not do anything to him. Now I know that you are a *fearer of God*, because you have not withheld from me your son, your only son.' (Genesis 22:12)

Bear in mind that the previous eleven chapters in Genesis that lead up to this scene are almost entirely about Abraham and his relationship to God. And yet, it is only now when he showed his willingness to sacrifice his son for God that Abraham earns the title *fearer of God*.

This is because to be a fearer of God is to be obedient. There is no greater example of obedience to the will of God than Abraham's willingness to offer his son Isaac as an offering to God. The reason that this is the greatest act of obedience is that the command made absolutely no sense to Abraham.

God's Irrational Demand

God had already told Abraham that Isaac would be the bearer of the covenant and that a great nation would come from him. How could that happen if Isaac is killed?

Furthermore, Abraham devoted his life to combating the prevailing paganism of his day. One of the most immoral and evil pagan rituals was that of child sacrifice. Abraham preached knowledge of a God of ethics and kindness; a God of life. This commandment from God to sacrifice his son went against the grain of everything Abraham knew to be true about the God he believed in. It made no sense. *And yet he did it.*

Much of the time, our obedience to God involves doing things that we relate to. We know they are the right thing to do. We agree with them. This is certainly admirable and an important part of our service of God. But it is not truly *obedience*. After all, how can we call it complete obedience to *His will* when *our will* agrees with it too?

The true test of obedience is in carrying out the will of God when it makes no sense to us; or even feels like the opposite of what we think is right.

Pure obedience = Serving God even when it makes no sense

The fearers have earned their rewards

Now we can understand why the *fearers of the Lord* are called those who *walk in His ways*. *His* ways. Not *our* ways. Not because they make sense to us, but because *He said so.*

Remember that amazing verse that said that God *fulfills the desire of those who fear Him*? It actually makes a lot of sense. They earned it. If they are willing to do God's will, no questions asked; God repays them in kind. He does their will too.

Fearers of the Lord are able to know the secrets of God – the divine plan that makes no sense to the human mind - because they are willing to disregard their own human calculations and follow the will of God.

Now we can understand the unique message of our verse. In verse 9, Israel was called to trust in the Lord that they would be successful in their collective national mission. In verse 10 the house of Aaron, the priestly spiritual leaders by birth were called upon to trust that God would help them be successful as leaders of the flock. Now in verse 11, all who walk in obedience to God against all human logic, all who set aside their own will and walk only in *His ways*, are called upon to trust in the Lord. It is *trust* that enables us to carry out the will of God; the trust that it is the right way to live even when it makes no sense on a human level.

O fearers of the Lord trust in the Lord; he is their helper and their shield.

When we submit to the will of God in full obedience we truly demonstrate obedience to Him. We become truly His agents in this world and merit special protection.

115:12 *God's Memory*

> *The Lord who remembered us will bless; He will bless the house of Israel; He will bless the house of Aaron.*

God Remembers

What do we mean when we say that God remembers? It's obvious that God is perfect and all powerful and does not forget anything. If He doesn't forget, how can he *remember*?

From the many verses throughout Scripture that refer to God *remembering* it is clear that for God, *remembering* is not merely a state of mind, a mental function of recalling lost information. Wherever God *remembers* there is a result. Here are a few typical examples, including the very first time God remembers.

> And God *remembered* Noah and all the wild animals and the livestock that were with him in the ark, and *He sent a wind over the earth*, and the waters receded. (Genesis 8:1)

> And God *remembered* Rachel; and *He heeded her and enabled her to become pregnant.* (Genesis 30:22. See also Genesis 19:29; Exodus 2:24)

In other words, when God *remembers*, something is going to happen.

When we say that God *remembers* we do not mean that God forgot and that at some later point He remembered. What we mean is that there is something that is part of God's plan for the world – for an individual or for history - that was not being carried out. It did not *seem to be* on the agenda. It appeared as though God forgot about it. And now it is being *remembered* by God. In other words, it is being fulfilled in reality. Whatever was *forgotten* is now at the revealed forefront of God's plan of action. Its time has come. To sum up, God *forgot* means that in God's plan the time had not come yet for whatever it is that we describe as forgotten. God *remembers* means that the time is right.

God Remembers = God Wills

Actually, if God doesn't really forget and all that He needs to do to create anything is to *will it into being*, then His *remembering* isn't even a *prior step to His doing.* It produces the result itself!

I explained this idea back in my commentary to verse 3:

> *"all that He wills He has done."* As soon as He wills anything, that's it. It's done. There is no intermediate step. Once He expresses His will, the intended creation or manipulation in the physical earthly realm is already complete.

In other words, if *remembering* for God means that the time has come for something to be willed into existence, doesn't it follow logically that whatever He remembers is basically already being carried out?

It does. Which is why there is no word *and* between the first two verbs of this verse. Allow me to explain.

The verse states: *The Lord remembered us; He will bless.* It does not state *The Lord remembered us <u>and</u> will bless.* I am pointing this out because twenty out of the fifty English translations that I checked had translated this verse *incorrectly* by including the word *and*. *And* is a word that has meaning. And it is a word that *does not appear in the Hebrew of this verse.*

Adding in the word *and* is a very significant change in the meaning of the verse. If the verse had included the word *and* it would mean that *remembering* and *blessing* are two separate things that God does. First, *The Lord remembered us*. Then *He blessed*. Theoretically, in this reading, He could have *remembered <u>without</u> blessing*. But this is not what it says. The absolutely literal translation of the Hebrew words is, *The Lord remembered us; He will bless*. Because this sounds cumbersome in English, translators need to add something to improve the flow.

On the other hand, if the word *and* was intended by this verse, for the Hebrew to not include it would be quite unusual. More importantly, it changes the meaning of the verse.

The Lord remembered us; He will bless literally implies that the Lord remembered us *whereby* He blessed us. In other words, *the remembering directly causes the blessing.* They are not two separate acts by God. The *blessing* is merely the external and automatic result of the *remembering*.

Our verse is not a prayer asking for blessings that have yet to be bestowed. The verse simply states a fact. *The Lord remembered us; He will bless;* This verse flows directly from the previous three verses. Those verses stated that Israel, the house of Aaron, and the fearers of the Lord all put their trust in the Lord. They trust that He will bring them success and protection. Now in verse 12 the psalmist tells us that God remembers us. As a direct result – as an automatic expression of that remembering by God – He will bless.

This continues the theme of Psalm 115 in its entirety; our confidence that God is the only God and that His will, His promises, and plan are not in doubt. They are a certainty.

A part of God's plan that has yet to come to pass only seems forgot-ten. Actually it's a part of God's will that we can't see. When the time comes God will remember. His will is always done.

115:13 *The Young With the Old*

He will bless the fearers of the Lord; the young with the old.

The Young With the Old

What stands out most in this verse is the second phrase, *the young with the old*. Verses 9 through 11 listed three categories of people who are called upon to trust in God:

- *Israel*
- *the house of Aaron*,
- *the fearers of the Lord*.

Verse 12 then begins to speak of how God will bless each of these groups, with the fearers of the Lord completing the list in the first half of our verse. What exactly is meant by adding on this phrase, *the young with the old*?

One way to understand this phrase is to say that *the young with the old* refers to the *young* of the previous three groups together with the *old* of those same groups. In other words, the verse is saying that the young of Israel will be blessed along with the old of Israel. The young of the house of Aaron will be blessed along with the old of the house of Aaron. The young fearers of the Lord will be blessed along with the older fearers of the Lord.

The problem with this explanation is that it raises an obvious ques-tion. When the previous verse stated that God will bless the house of Israel did it not mean that the young of Israel would be blessed as a part of that group? Is there any reason to believe that the young were not included in that blessing? A similar question could be asked regarding the house of Aaron. The term *house of* always refers to a family or tribe. Why would the *house of Aaron* not include the young?

Furthermore, verses 9 through 11 allotted a separate verse for each of the three groups – Israel (v.9), house of Aaron (v.10), and fearers of the Lord (v.11). Each group has its own verse stating that it trusts in the Lord. Then, in verses 12 and 13, when stating that God blesses these same groups, Israel and the house of Aaron are mentioned in verse 12 together. The fearers of the Lord are mentioned separately in verse 13 along with this new phrase *the young with the old*. If the phrase *the young with the old* refers to all three groups, why is it separated from the first two and placed in a separate verse together with *the fearers of the Lord*?

With not And

It is also worth noting that the verse does not say *the young and the old*, but *the young with the old*. The verse is not merely pointing out that the young are included and blessed in addition to the old. For this, the word *and* would have been sufficient. The word *with* implies that the young are blessed by the very same blessing that the old receive. The old are blessed. The young are blessed *with* them.

To sum up our questions:
1. What does *the young with the old* refer to?
2. Didn't *Israel* and the *House of Aaron* include their young and old?
3. Why are *Israel* and the *House of Aaron* together in one verse while *the fearers of the Lord* are in a separate verse with the addition of *the young with the old*?

In light of all of this, I would like to suggest that the phrase *the young with the old* is directly connected to the blessing bestowed upon *the fearers of the Lord*. *The fearers of the Lord* are in a separate verse in order to make this connection in and to make a powerful point.

Notice that *the young* are not called upon to trust in the Lord in verses 9 through 11. The Lord is not said to be their *helper* and *shield*. They are not yet full participants in God's mission. They are not yet influencing the world as *Israel* does. They are not inspiring Israel as the *house of Aaron* does. They are certainly not in a position to fully embrace the lofty obedience to God of *the fearers of the Lord*.

In the Shadow of the Fearers

While they are not expected to reach the level of trust that we see in verses 9 through 11, they are included in the blessing, but in a different way. They are blessed along with *the fearers of the Lord*. More precisely, when *the fearers of the Lord* are blessed, the result is that the young are blessed.

As I explained in verse 11, *the fearers of the Lord* are those who profess and practice outstanding obedience to the will of God. They are paragons of humility, self-sacrifice, and piety. These great people are not necessarily in positions of leadership. But everyone knows who they are. *The fearers of the Lord* among us are those people in society whom we look to as examples of how to live. *We hope and pray that our children will too.*

Unfortunately, their effectiveness as examples is often undermined by their position in society. If the pious and humble God-fearers among us are also in positions of struggle and difficulty, it is that much harder to convince our children to emulate them. No young person easily takes on a path in life that leads to hardship, no matter how admirable that path may be.

This is why the bestowing of blessings on *the fearers of the Lord* brings a special and unique result. The young are blessed *along with them*. When the righteous paradigms of fear of the Lord are blessed – when they rise to prominence and success – the result is that the young are blessed as well.

I should point out that there are many different kinds of blessing. Prominence and success are not the only blessings that God bestows. I will discuss the concept of blessing more extensively in the verses that follow. That said, we should not underestimate the resulting impact that wealth and prominence have on one's ability to positively influence others, especially the young.

God will bless *the fearers of the Lord. Along with* that blessing, He *thereby* blesses the young who are now more inclined to look to those shining examples of obedience to the Lord as examples for their own lives and become *fearers of the Lord themselves.*

He will bless the fearers of the Lord; the young with the old.

We must promote those around us who serve as examples of fear of the Lord and obedience to His will. With the success of such people, our children will be more easily inspired by them.

115:14 *Add Upon vs. Add To*

May the Lord add upon you; upon you and your children.

More blessings! The previous two verses stated that God will bless *Israel, the house of Aaron,* and *the fearers of the Lord.* This verse appears to be continuing that theme by saying that the blessing will be increased more and more.

A closer look at the Hebrew word here for *add* uncovers a more precise – and slightly different – understanding.

Add To vs. Add Upon

The Hebrew word for *add* used here is YOSeF. It may look familiar as the name of the famous Joseph from the book of Genesis. This is because he was named after this word. As his mother Rachel declared at the time of his naming:

> She named him Joseph, and said, "May the Lord *add to* me another son" (Genesis 30:24)

When Rachel used this word, notice that she said *add to.* When this word YOSeF is used in Scripture it is sometimes followed by the Hebrew for *to* and sometimes followed by the word AL - *upon*. Simply put, sometimes YOSeF is *add to* and sometimes it is *add upon*.

The difference between them is actually quite straightforward. Rachel has just given birth to her first child. She would like *another* one. So, she asks the Lord to *add to* me *another son*. She is the recipient of the gift. The additional son would be the gift itself.

When the word AL – *upon* is used with YOSeF the meaning is quite different. There are seven such instances in Scripture. Four of them are in an identical context.

It is forbidden to misuse sacred objects designated for use in the temple. If someone damages or consumes something sacred to the temple, that person must pay. When making such a payment, the law states that they must add a fifth to the value. When this rule is stated, the verse uses the word YOSeF – *add*.

> And he shall make restitution for what he has done amiss in the holy thing, and shall *add* a fifth *upon* it, and give it to the priest; (Leviticus 5:16)

The identical rule applies to the redemption of an object that was sanctified for the temple. For example, if someone dedicated a certain object or animal to the temple and then changed their mind and wanted to give something else to the temple instead they would need to redeem the object. Money equaling the value of the original object would then be given to the temple in its place. In this situation as well, a penalty of a fifth would be added on to the value of the object being redeemed. This penalty prevented people from dedicating objects to the temple only to renege on the pledge at their convenience if the item later went up in value.

As I mentioned, there are four almost identical verses referring to these twenty percent penalties. All of them use the words YOSeF AL – *add upon*.

The other three instances of YOSeF AL are our verse here in Psalm 115 and these two:

> May the Lord, the God of your ancestors, increase (*add upon*) you a thousand times and bless you as he has promised! (Deuteronomy 1:11)

> But Joab replied, "May the Lord multiply (*add upon*) his troops a hundred times over." (1 Chronicles 21:3)

As we can clearly see, in all of these verses the addition is that there will be more of the thing being added to. As opposed to *add to*, like in Rachel's case, there is no mention of a recipient of the increase. YOSeF AL – *add upon* – clearly means that what is being referred to will *multiply* in number; *that there will be more of it.* Money is being paid to the temple. An additional fifth – also money – is added on. In the verse from Deuteronomy, Moses is telling Israel that God will *multiply them* in number– not that they will receive some other blessing.

This is why when Rachel prays for another son the word is *add to.* She doesn't want another Rachel. She wants another son given *to her.*

YOSeF Le	YOSeF AL
Add *to* X	Add *upon* X
X receives more	X is multiplied

Add Upon You = More of You

Now we can understand our verse.

> May the Lord <u>add upon you</u>; <u>upon</u> you and your children.

The verse is not saying that the blessings of the previous two verses – whatever they may be - will increase upon you and your children. This verse is telling us exactly what the blessing of the previous verses is!

The previous verses told us that the Lord *will bless*. In our verse we are told *how* He will bless. The blessing is that you will increase in number. You will multiply and survive to future generations.

Let's recall that this psalm began with the words *Not to us, O Lord, not to us, but to Your name give glory*. The psalm went on in the first few verses to praise God in contrast to the false pagan idols. It may seem strange, then, that a psalm that started by saying *Not to us* has turned into a celebration of blessings bestowed upon *us* by God! What is the theme of this psalm? Is it *Not to us*, or is it *God will bless us*?

For this we need to turn our attention to the next verse.

The greatest blessing that we can ask for as servants of the Lord is for Him to grant us children who continue in our mission to serve Him.

115:15 *Being For God*

Blessed are you of the Lord,
maker of heaven and earth.

Not To Us… Bless Us??

At the end of my comments to the previous verse I asked a question. I will explain it here once again.

This psalm began with the powerful statement, *Not to us!* With this opening line, the psalm emphatically declared that the salvation of God's people and their protection is not for the people themselves. Rather, all the miracles of redemption are for one purpose and one purpose only; the glory of God Almighty. Following this theme, the psalm went on to describe how God is the only true God in contrast to the impotent and inanimate pagan idols of silver and gold. The theme of the psalm was clear; that all kindnesses done to His people are *in reality* meant only to facilitate the glory of the one true God.

If this is the theme of the psalm then why have the past six verses – 9 through 14 – been all about how God will protect, help, and bestow His blessings upon His people? *What happened to "Not to us"*? It seems like the psalm has suddenly become *all about "us"*!

Blessed of the Lord

The key to understanding the answer to this question can be found in the third Hebrew word of this verse. *Blessed are you of the Lord...*

Of the Lord is made up of one Hebrew word. The word is the name of God with the prefix L' or La. This prefix has numerous related meanings. It can mean *to, of,* or *for*. Most translations ignore these options and translate the verse *Blessed are you by the Lord*. However, as I just said, *by* is not one of the meanings of the prefix La.

Hebrew prefix L' or La	**LADONAI (our verse)**
Option #1: *to*	**to the Lord**
Option #2: *for*	**for the Lord**
Option #3: *of*	**of the Lord**

In all other translations the verse appears as *Blessed are you of the Lord*. While this is an accurate translation, it is also vague. What does it mean to be blessed *of* the Lord? The word *of* in English can mean *from*, as in Pesach Wolicki *of* Jerusalem. The problem is that this is not what is meant by the prefix La when translated as *of*. To say *from*, Hebrew would use the prefix *Me* not La.

Alternatively, *of* in English can mean *about*. As in, "I was thinking *of* you." Here the Hebrew would use the word AL, not La.

There is only one English use of the word *of* that would work for the Hebrew prefix La.

> *Of* every kind of bird, *of* every kind of animal, and *of* every kind of thing that crawls on the ground, two of each will come to you; that you may keep them alive. (Genesis 6:20)

Where I have italicized the word *of* the prefix La appears in the Hebrew.

In this usage, the word *of* indicates a specific identity or detail within a category. If we try to use this meaning in our verse we are still left unsure of the meaning. Does our verse mean that we are blessed as members of a larger category called *the Lord*; i.e. *of the Lord*?

To keep this simple: in our verse translating LADONAI as *of the Lord* is problematic and unclear.

As I mentioned above, the prefix La most commonly means *for* or *to*. More to the point of our verse, the word in our verse LADONAI – *for/to/of the Lord* – appears no less than five hundred times in Scripture! Other than two exceptions where the meaning is unclear, in all five hundred of them the meaning is quite simply, *for the Lord*. Our verse is one of the two exceptions. The other exception is equally vague.

Of the Lord = For the Lord

I would like to suggest that the translation and meaning of our verse is actually quite straightforward.

As I explained in the previous verse, God's blessing in our psalm is very specific. It is the blessing of increase in number of those who are blessed. *Israel, the house of Aaron, the fearers of God, the young and old* of these blessed groups. All of those who are in relationship with God and devoted to His mission will be multiplied and made abundant.

After telling us that the Lord will assist, protect, and multiply us, our verse returns to the theme that started the psalm.

Blessed are you *for the Lord* - LADONAI, maker of heaven and earth.

It is not about us! It is true that God protects and blesses His people. It is true that He helps them and makes them abundant. But it's not about them. It's *for the Lord*!

Now the sequence of ideas in our psalm makes perfect sense.

1. It's not for us but for God's glory.
2. He is the one true God.
3. He assists and protects those who trust in Him
4. He blesses them and makes them abundant...
5. ... *so that* they can continue to spread His glory.

Quite simply, those who are devoted to and trust in God are blessed *for God's sake*, not for their own. When they are assisted in their work, when they are protected, when they are made more abundant in number, God's glory is increased.

Our verse tells us *why* God blesses us. *For Him, not for us.*

Blessed are you FOR the Lord, maker of heaven and earth.

Those who serve the Lord are increased and blessed in order to have the means to succeed even further in the mission of creating His kingdom. This is the purpose of the creation of heaven and earth.

115:16 *Heaven on Earth*

*The heavens are the heavens for
the Lord; and the earth He gave
to humanity.*

He's up there. We're down here...??

What exactly is this verse saying? It seems to state that God is up there in heaven and we are down here on earth and these are two separate realms. This, of course, cannot be the case. Is it implying that God has no influence here on earth? Of course not.

Furthermore, looking at context, our psalm and the preceding two psalms have emphasized over and over again that God is sole master of all that happens *on earth*. As verse 3 of this psalm stated so clearly, *Our God is in Heaven; all that He wills is done.* Obviously, this means that all that

He wills on heaven or *on earth* is done. Why do we now seem to be saying that the heavens are the Lord's and the earth is ours?

It is useful to point out that the word *heaven* has two different meanings throughout scripture. There are many instances where *heaven* simply refers to the sky; i.e. the physical place which produces rain and houses the celestial bodies. (e.g. Deuteronomy 11:17) A second meaning of *heaven* which appears elsewhere refers to the spiritual realm.

> And you shall know today and place well upon your heart that the Lord is God in the *heavens* above and upon the earth below; there is no other. (Deuteronomy 4:39)

> Gaze down from Your abode of holiness, from the *heavens*, and bless Your people Israel and the land that You gave us just as You swore to our forefathers; a land flowing with milk and honey. (Deuteronomy 26:15)

Obviously, these verses do not mean to say that the Lord is God up in the atmosphere where the clouds are located; that His abode of holiness is to be found somewhere in the night sky. *Heavens* here refers to the spiritual world in contrast to the physical one.

Heavens = Spiritual Realm

Which brings us back to our verse.

Heavens are Heavens?

The heavens are the heavens for the Lord. Why not state more simply *The heavens are the Lord's*? Why the repetition of the word *heavens*? It seems that the point is not that the heavens are the Lord's. Rather, the verse is stating that the *heavens* are *heavens for the Lord*. What does this mean?

The verse says:	Why didn't it say?:
The heavens are the heavens for the Lord	*The heavens are the Lord's*

A close look at the second half of the verse will help us solve this question.

And the earth He gave to humanity. If this statement stood alone as its own verse in Psalms or any other book of the bible we could easily understand it to mean that God granted human beings mastery over this earth. However, when we consider our context we see that this verse means something very different.

Our psalm began with the words *Not to us.* The theme of the psalm is that God rather than humanity is deserving of the glory for what goes on here on earth. To be more exact, the point of this entire psalm is that even where it appears that humans – or other forces – deserve some credit for the happenings on earth we must not be mistaken. It is only to God that all glory must be given. Not to man. Not to the forces of nature. Only God.

The psalm then went on to describe how God assists and increases the numbers of those who are actively involved in the mission to bring glory to His name; *Israel, the house of Aaron,* and *the fearers of the Lord.* As the previous verse stated so clearly, *You are blessed (i.e. increased) for the Lord.*

Now we can understand the riddle of our verse.

After stating repeatedly that God is in sole control of everything one might ask, why does He need to increase and assist those who praise Him? If God is in control of everything, let Him perform supernatural acts and bring the entire world to know and praise Him. Why does He need us?

Our verse answers this question.

Making Earth into Heaven

The heavens are the heavens for the Lord; In other words, in a context of pure spirituality God is clearly seen. *The heavens* – the spiritual realm – *are the heavens for the Lord* – is a context in which God is easily seen. *And the earth He gave to humanity;* however, the task of building awareness and glory of God here on earth in the material world was given to humanity. It is our job to reveal Godliness in the physical arena. Of course, God could reveal Himself and perform great miracles. He could force humanity to see Him. But that does not give humanity the opportunity or responsibility of finding God; of choosing Him. If God would force His presence upon us He would prevent us from giving Him His true glory.

The earth is under the influence of man not because God has no control. It is under the influence of man because God wants it that way; because we benefit from our faith and awareness of God when we choose Him. That is why the verse states *and the earth <u>He gave</u> to humanity*. God wants it this way.

With this in mind I'd like to suggest that the double mention of the word *heavens* implies our mission. In other words, the verse could be understood as follows:

The heavens are the heavens for the Lord; – In the context of pure spirituality, there is always full awareness of God. *Heaven is already heaven.*

The earth He gave to humanity. – But in the material world, it is man's job to reveal Godliness. To create a second heaven here on earth.

Our task on this earth is to reveal God's presence in every aspect of creation. In this way we transform the physical realm into a spiritual place. This is the kingdom of God.

115:17 *The Dead and the Dying*

It is not the dead who will praise the Lord; nor all who descend into silence

---

The dead do not praise the Lord. Isn't this obvious? They are dead. The same can be said for those mentioned in the second phrase in our verse, *those who descend in silence*. They are silent. They do not praise anybody. What is this verse saying?

To fully understand this we have to look at our verse in the context of the entire psalm.

A summary of the key points of Psalm 115 up to this point:

- God's kindness and salvation is for His sake; not ours. (v.1)
- Heathens and pagans do not believe in a God that they cannot see. (v. 2-3)
- Pagan idol worship is futile and pointless. (v. 4-8)
- Those who trust in God are assisted by Him (v. 9-11)
- They are blessed by God in order to complete their mission. (v. 12-15)
- God gave the responsibility to glorify His name on earth to humanity. (v.16)

Our verse, the second to last in the psalm comes next.

Nature Dies

The pagan world of the Ancient Near East was obsessed with death. Egyptian religion was so concerned with death that their book of mythology describing the godly world is called The Book of the Dead. The greatest monuments that remain from Egypt are tombs. Sir James Frazer, in the preface to his classic encyclopedic work on ancient religion, The Golden Bough, refers to death as *the most powerful force in the making of primitive religion.*

This makes a lot of sense. Focus on death is the natural extension of a faith system that believes that the forces of nature are all powerful.

All natural living things follow the same path of life. They begin by sprouting or are born. They grow to their fullest size, beauty, and strength during the first quarter to third of life. Then they begin a gradual decline until they wither away and die. This is true of plants, animals, and human beings alike. To put it another way, all living things are involved – for most of their existence – in the gradual process of *dying*.

The Soul is not Natural

There is one living thing that is an exception. The soul. The human spirit, consciousness, and intellect do not fit this pattern. Human beings do not reach the height of their intellectual powers, spiritual development, or emotional maturity at the same time as their bodies reach their peak. Long after the body has embarked on its long steady journey of decline towards death, the human spirit is still growing, expanding, and developing to greater and greater heights.

In fact, if not for physical infirmity and illness which hampers further development, the human soul would continue to develop forever.

This is because the soul is not *natural*. It is *supernatural*. It is above nature. It does not quickly rise to its peak and then gradually deteriorate and die. More to the point, it is not in the process of *dying*.

The Dying do Not Praise

The Hebrew word for the dead in our verse is HaMeTIM. It is the plural present tense of the verb *to die*. It is equally accurate to translate this word as *the dead* or as *the dying*. In fact, the end of our verse suggests that the translation here should be *the dying*. If the meaning of HaMeTIM here was the dead, the second phrase should have been *nor all those who* <u>descended</u> *into silence*; in the past tense or *nor all those who* <u>are silent</u>, as a present tense parallel to *the dead*. The way it is written, *All those who* <u>descend</u> *into silence* indicates that the people in question are *in the process of descending*. To be consistent, the first half of the verse should be read as a present tense process as well. Confused? Let me sum up:

- HaMeTIM at the beginning of the verse can translate either as *the dead* or as *the dying*.
- Since, the second phrase of the verse is stated in the present continuous form *all who descend*,
- Therefore contextual consistency dictates that HaMeTIM should be in the continuous form *the dying* as well.

I would like to suggest that the most accurate translation is:

> *It is not* <u>the dying</u> *who will praise the Lord; nor all* <u>who descend</u> *into silence*

In other words, those who put their faith in nature; who identify as part of the natural cannot praise the Lord. They do not believe in the supernatural immortal soul. They do not believe that our natural inclinations are not all that we are meant to be. They do not believe that nature can be overcome. *And natural things are always dying.*

Therefore, they are incapable of praising God. They do not have the ability to see that nature is not all that there is.

This verse refers to people who are doing nothing but dying and descending into silence, who regard their existence as nothing more than physical. For them, death is final. Without a belief in the immortality of the human soul there can be no blessed connection to the eternal God.

Although nature is in a constant state of deterioration towards death, our souls are forever growing and alive. It is through this eternal spark of God within each of us that we are able to praise the Eternal God.

115:18 *Hallelu-YAH!*

And we will bless the Lord
from now and until eternity;
Halleluyah.

In my comments on verse 113:2 I explained the meaning of *blessing* God. To review, *blessing* means *increase*. Since there is nothing that God needs and He cannot be added to or subtracted from, to *bless* God means to *increase awareness* of Him; to multiply His glory in the world.

In almost every single English translation the name of God used here in this verse is *the Lord*. This is, of course, the standard translation whenever the tetragrammaton YHVH appears. A few translations that I saw had Jehovah for God's name in our verse. The problem with all of these translations is that *this is not the name of God used here.*

YaH as a Distinct Name of God

The name of God in this verse as well as the one before it is YaH, often written as Jah in English. This is the name that makes up the last syllable of the word Halleluyah, or *praise the Lord.*

Most translators write *the Lord* for YaH because this name is, in fact, the first two letters of YHVH which, as I mentioned, is always translated as *the Lord*. While this is an understandable choice, the result is that reader of Scripture in English is unaware that YHVH is not the name in this verse. *In addition, the unique meaning of the divine name YaH is lost in translation.*

What YHVH means

To understand the true meaning of YaH we must first understand the meaning of YHVH. A longer and more detailed explanation can be found in the section of this book titled, *A Note on the Names of God*. You can read there for the full explanation. For now, I will sum up the key points.

The name YHVH, like every name of God, is a Hebrew word. It is a very holy and lofty Hebrew word, but it is a word, nonetheless. Like every Hebrew word, YHVH has a root. The root of YHVH is the verb *to be* or *to exist*. The form or conjugation of this root that is YHVH is an impossible mix of past, present, and future tenses.

YHVH, as a Hebrew word, essentially means *the cause of all existence past, present, and future.* Pretty good name for God, right?

Different parts of the four letters of YHVH contain grammatical elements of these three different tenses. The Y at the beginning indicates future tense. The V in the middle indicates present. The aH sound at the end is for the past tense. Future, present, past. Does this seem out of order?

Actually, the order is correct. Think about it. Everything in existence first exists in the *future*. Then it becomes part of the *present*. It then slips into the *past*. Before I sat down to write this, my writing was a part of the future. Right now, as I am writing it is in the present. After I am done it will be part of the past. The same is true for every created being and every moment in time. So in actuality, *future, present, past* is the order of existence.

What YaH means

The name YaH or YH – the beginning of YHVH - is the *future* part of God's name. In other words, it represents *God's will*; His plan *before* we see it. That's where all of existence and all of history *is* before it happens. It is part of the *future*; still part of God's will and plan waiting to be revealed.

When we see events unfolding and believe and declare that we see *God's plan*, what we mean is that we believe that God thought of this and willed it before it happened. That from the beginning of time, all the events that we experience *already existed in the future tense.*

The pagans who believed in the gods of nature certainly believed in higher forces. They were not atheists. However, they did not believe that there was any kind of long term program for the world. Their faith had no room for a god or gods who have a goal for humanity or the world and a plan to get there. When events unfolded around them, like the atheists of modern times, they did not see evidence of a prior will. They did believe that the godly powers had acted. *But they could not recognize YaH – the divine planner of the future!*

With this understanding we can now understand the full meaning of the closing phrase of our verse and of Psalm 115.

> And we bless YaH <u>*from now until eternity*</u>, Halleluyah!

We bless YaH – we increase awareness of God who has a plan and program for the future – for all that will unfold *from now until eternity!*

Hallelu-YaH! – Praise the One who plans and wills and carries out His will into the future.

A final thought for Psalm 115

For many years I have been interested in ancient pagan beliefs. It's one of the pet topics that I like to read about. It struck me years ago that if I understood the way people thought about things prior to Abraham and to Sinai I would better understand what the Bible is trying to accomplish; what it's responding to.

I like to think about ancient pre-Biblical religion as the attempts by humans to understand the powers that govern the world without God ever speaking to them and introducing Himself.

As I mentioned in my comments to verse 5, ancient pagans were not fools. They did their best to make sense of the world in which God was not yet revealed through prophecy.

I highly recommend to anyone who loves God and loves Scripture to read books about Ancient Near Eastern beliefs and practices. The more I learn about these societies the more I appreciate the beauty and wisdom of the Bible. There are so many details within Scripture that I never noticed or never understood until I learned about the erroneous beliefs of ancient Mesopotamians or Egyptians.

The way I see it, if the Bible is out to eradicate idolatry maybe I should get to know idolatry so I know what I am working towards.

The simplest and most profound example may be right there in Genesis chapter 1. Humanity is created in the image of God. What a departure from the dominant creation stories of the Ancient Near East in which the human species is pathetic and hopeless; created to labor as a slave for the greedy hungry gods and to suffer!

The Ancient Near East was a world without right and wrong. Only crass pragmatism motivated even religious practices. Academic scholars identify the introduction of morality as a basis for choice as fairly late in the history of these societies.

The more I learn about these long forgotten beliefs, the more beautiful is the word of God.

But there's a second effect that these studies have had on me that I didn't expect.

Fundamentally, the faith of ancient people focused on the forces of nature. These forces do not care for us. They do not have a plan. Most importantly, they are all that there is. Nothing is beyond them.

The more I learned about this ancient mindset the more I realized that the Biblical battle against this world view has never ended. In fact, this battle is being fought more fiercely now than ever before.

Today, just as then, there is a prominent world view that sees nature as all that there is; that sees the processes of nature and history as impersonal; that denies that there is a Divine Plan or that there is any objective right and wrong.

Concurrently, there are all too many people who put their ultimate trust in gods and ideals *of silver and gold; the work of human hands.*

The message of Psalm 115 is not a message of the past. It is a message of the present. Now more than ever before.

Those who trust in the Lord need the protection, assistance, and increase in their numbers in order to be victorious in the ongoing battle against the new pagan culture.

Today, just as it was almost 4000 years ago when Abraham walked this earth, our mission is to bring knowledge of God to all humanity; to replace the belief in a finite, natural, and ever-dying world with faith in the infinite, supernatural, and eternal One God.

Psalm 116

From the Personal
to the Universal

My experience writing the commentary to Psalm 116 was markedly different than what I went through with the other five psalms in this book. Although I have known the words of Psalm 116 by heart for most of my life, I must confess that until I worked on the commentary that you see before you I had no idea what messages this psalm contained.

Most people familiar with the Bible know of two well known books that deal with the topic of suffering. One is Job and the other is the Scroll of Lamentations. Job is the story of a person who suffers for no reason known to him or to any other mortal. Lamentations describes the suffering of Israel as a result of their sins. Job examines the question of the unjust suffering of the righteous. Lamentations is about suffering that is deserved and must be corrected through repentance and atonement.

Psalm 116 is a completely unique *third Biblical approach to suffering*. It neither asks nor seeks to answer the question of why people suffer. Instead, this psalm explores a more existential theological question. How ought we to react to suffering? How do we derive meaning from suffering? What is the content of the meaning that we can derive? In what ways do we grow and change as a result of suffering and the emergence from it?

The most striking textual feature of Psalm 116 is prominently displayed immediately by the opening word. *I love.* The previous three psalms in our series had the psalmist speaking in the first person plural. Psalm 116 switches to first person singular.

This change sets up the remarkably intimate journey that unfolds in this psalm. The psalmist is suffering, fearing death, and feels alone. He cries out to the Lord. He then begins a theological contemplation of the righteousness and mercy of God to find meaning in His suffering.

The meaning that he discovers is twofold.

First, he realizes the redemptive effect of the experience of suffering itself. He appreciates the unique power of crisis to stimulate focused thinking about one's values and beliefs coupled with the ability of suffering to steer us clear of carelessness and frivolous behavior.

Then, after emerging redeemed, he discovers a second way to infuse his suffering with meaning. Beyond being grateful to God for salvation, he asks himself what the entire experience of the hand of God in his life demands of him. He uses the clarity and focus that he has acquired to see God's gifts for their higher purpose. By asking the question, "What can I give back to the Lord?" he infuses his entire journey of suffering and redemption with sanctity.

He declares his new found mission to call out the name of the Lord to all the world. First, in celebration; then in worship. He thus uses his own personal experience of the hand of God as a springboard for the universal vision of God's Kingdom on earth.

Psalm 116

א אָהַבְתִּי כִּי יִשְׁמַע יְהוָה אֶת קוֹלִי, תַּחֲנוּנָי.

1. *I love; because the Lord will hear my voice, my supplication.*

ב כִּי הִטָּה אָזְנוֹ לִי; וּבְיָמַי אֶקְרָא.

2. *For He has inclined His ear to me; and in my days I call out.*

אֲפָפוּנִי חֶבְלֵי מָוֶת וּמְצָרֵי שְׁאוֹל מְצָאוּנִי; צָרָה וְיָגוֹן אֶמְצָא.	ג 3.	*The cords of death have encompassed me and the constrictions of the grave found me; suffering and anguish have I found.*
וּבְשֵׁם יְהוָה אֶקְרָא: אָנָּה יְהוָה, מַלְּטָה נַפְשִׁי.	ד 4.	*And I call out in the Name of the Lord; "Please, Lord, deliver my soul."*
חַנּוּן יְהוָה וְצַדִּיק; וֵאלֹהֵינוּ מְרַחֵם.	ה 5.	*Gracious is the Lord and righteous; and our God bestows mercy.*
שֹׁמֵר פְּתָאיִם יְהוָה; דַּלֹּתִי, וְלִי יְהוֹשִׁיעַ.	ו 6.	*The Lord protects the unwary; I was brought low; but for me it brings salvation.*
שׁוּבִי נַפְשִׁי לִמְנוּחָיְכִי: כִּי יְהוָה גָּמַל עָלָיְכִי.	ז 7.	*Return, my soul, to your restfulness for the Lord has bestowed this upon you.*
כִּי חִלַּצְתָּ נַפְשִׁי מִמָּוֶת: אֶת עֵינִי מִן דִּמְעָה; אֶת רַגְלִי מִדֶּחִי.	ח 8.	*For You have rescued my soul from death, my eyes from tears, my feet from stumbling;*
אֶתְהַלֵּךְ לִפְנֵי יְהוָה בְּאַרְצוֹת הַחַיִּים.	ט 9.	*I will walk before the Lord in the lands of the living.*
הֶאֱמַנְתִּי כִּי אֲדַבֵּר; אֲנִי עָנִיתִי מְאֹד.	י 10.	*I had faith when I spoke; I was greatly afflicted.*
אֲנִי אָמַרְתִּי בְחָפְזִי: כָּל הָאָדָם כֹּזֵב.	יא 11.	*And I said in my haste, "All humanity is deceiving."*

מָה אָשִׁיב לַיהוָה כָּל־תַּגְמוּלוֹהִי עָלָי. | יב | 12. | *What can I give back to the Lord?; all that He has bestowed is upon me.*

כּוֹס יְשׁוּעוֹת אֶשָּׂא; וּבְשֵׁם יְהוָה אֶקְרָא. | יג | 13. | *I will raise the cup of salvations; and I will call out in the name of the Lord.*

נְדָרַי לַיהוָה אֲשַׁלֵּם; נֶגְדָה נָּא לְכָל עַמּוֹ. | יד | 14. | *I will fulfill my vows to the Lord; now in the presence of all His people.*

יָקָר בְּעֵינֵי יְהוָה הַמָּוְתָה לַחֲסִידָיו. טז אָנָּה יְהוָה, כִּי אֲנִי עַבְדֶּךָ:
אֲנִי עַבְדְּךָ, בֶּן אֲמָתֶךָ; פִּתַּחְתָּ לְמוֹסֵרָי. | טו | 15. | *It is costly in the eyes of the Lord; the death of his pious ones.*

אָנָּה יְהוָה, כִּי אֲנִי עַבְדֶּךָ:
נִי עַבְדְּךָ, בֶּן אֲמָתֶךָ; פִּתַּחְתָּ לְמוֹסֵרָי. | טז | 16. | *Please, O Lord, for I am Your servant; I am Your servant, the son of your maidservant. You have released my bonds.*

לְךָ אֶזְבַּח זֶבַח תּוֹדָה; וּבְשֵׁם יְהוָה אֶקְרָא. | יז | 17. | *To You I shall offer a sacrifice of thanksgiving; and I will call out in the name of the Lord.*

נְדָרַי לַיהוָה אֲשַׁלֵּם; נֶגְדָה נָּא לְכָל עַמּוֹ. | יח | 18. | *I will fulfill my vows to the Lord; now in the presence of all His people.*

בְּחַצְרוֹת בֵּית יְהוָה בְּתוֹכֵכִי יְרוּשָׁלָ͏ִם: הַלְלוּיָהּ. | יט | 19. | *In the courtyards of the house of the Lord— in your midst, Jerusalem. Praise the Lord.*

116:1 *What Do I Love?*

I love; because the Lord
will hear my voice, my
supplications.

The opening verse of Psalm 116 poses a number of translation problems.

Too many translations
    I checked fifty-three different translations of this verse. Forty-eight of them translated the opening clause of the verse the same way:

> *I love <u>the Lord because</u>* He hears my voice, my supplication

Two translations had this:

> *I love, <u>because</u> the Lord* will hear the voice of my supplication.

One translation had this:

> *I love <u>that</u> the Lord* will hear my voice, my supplication.

And one translation had this:

> *I love <u>when</u> the Lord* hears my voice, my supplication.

Yet another had this:

> *I love – because the Lord hears –* my voice of supplication.

    In other words, I love my voice of praying and supplicating because of the fact that the Lord hears.

How can one simple verse be translated so many different ways?
There are two reasons for all of these differences.

But first, let's get familiar with the literal word by word translation
of the Hebrew.

AHaVTI	*I loved*
KI	*but / because / when / that*
YiSHMA	*He hears / He will hear*
ADONAI	*the Lord*
ET	(signifies the direct object)
KOLI	*my voice*
TAHANUNAI	*my supplications*

Problem #1: What is being loved?

The first word of the verse – AHAVTI - means *I loved* or *I love*. What
is difficult to determine is what exactly is being loved. The verb *to love*
requires a direct object that is being loved. In Hebrew the object of love
is always* indicated with the word ET – the fifth word in our verse. It
is an untranslatable word which tells us what a particular verb is acting
upon. For example, if I wanted to say "I read the Torah" the Hebrew
would be:

ANI	I
KORE	read
ET	
HaTORAH	the Torah

The reading is being done *to* the Torah. ET tells us what the verb is
acting upon.

Here's a well known verse from Scripture as a second example.

---

* There are two exceptions in all of scripture where a different conjunctive word indicating
the direct object is used. Nevertheless, the direct object must be indicated.

*You shall love the **Lord** your God with all your heart and with all your soul and with all your might. (Deuteronomy 6:5)*

In between the Hebrew word for *You shall love* and the word for *the Lord* the word ET appears. Like this:

VeAHaVTa	*You shall love*
ET	
ADONAI	*the Lord*
ELOHECHA	*your God*

The word ET is necessary in Hebrew grammar to connect the verb to its object.

And this is the problem with our verse. There is no ET that tells us *what is being loved*. The ET in our verse tells us what *the Lord hears*, not what *I loved*.

So the first problem in our verse is that we are not told what is being loved. In fact, in our verse here at the start of Psalm 116, all of the ancient Hebrew commentaries discuss the lack of the word ET and the ambiguity that it causes.

Confused? Let's make it simple.

Problem #1
The verse does not tell us what is being loved.

Problem #2: Because, When, or That
The second translation problem relates to the second word of the verse. After the word AHAVTI – *I love* - is the word KI. This word is one of the most common words in all of Scripture, appearing well over 4000 times. KI has four different meanings; *but, because, when,* and *that.* Generally, we know from context which meaning is the correct one. In our verse *but* is clearly not an option. Other than that, our verse is one example where it is hard to know what KI means.

Problem #2

The second word in our verse – KI - could mean
because, when, *or* **that**

Now we can understand the wide range of differences in translation of our verse. If KI means *because,* then the object of the love is not stated clearly. The verse would actually read like this:

I love (AHAVTI) because (KI) the Lord hears my voice; my supplication.

This is the approach taken by the majority of translators. In this translation, the object of love is left unstated. The implication is that *the Lord* is being loved. These translations avoid the awkwardness of the wording by moving words around. They then render the verse:

I love *the Lord because* He hears my voice; my supplication

If, on the other hand, the word KI means *that,* then the verse would mean something quite different:

I love *that* the Lord will hear my voice; my supplication.

Why this matters

This is not merely a matter of words. The theological difference in meaning between these is significant.

*   First translation: *the Lord* is the object of the love *because He hears.*
*   Second translation: the very *fact that the Lord listens* is the object that is loved.

Think about this. According to the first option, the love of the Lord is based on the fact that He heeds prayers. *I love the Lord because...* In contrast, according to the second translation love *of the Lord* is not the subject. The psalmist is saying that he loves *the fact that the Lord heeds his prayers.*

And neither of these translations is completely satisfying based on the precise wording of the verse.

The first option – *I love the Lord* - is too far from the precise reading of the words. Neither *I love that* nor *I love because* – the two most direct translations of AHAVTI KI - accommodate this meaning.

The second option - *I love that* - is a better fit with the wording. However, it is not as satisfying theologically. According to this translation the psalmist is not declaring his love for God but for *the fact that God heeds his prayers*. This seems a bit self serving. It sounds almost as if he is saying, "I love that I get what I ask for."

A careful look at the other translations mentioned earlier shows that these two issues – what is being loved and what is the meaning of the word KI – cause all of the differences.

Layers of meaning in the Bible

I would like to suggest that *all of these translations are correct*.

Let's start with the obvious point. *The prophetic author of these words deliberately chose wording that would leave the object of love vague.* Think about that.

The fact that there is no clear definite object of love is not because the author of the psalm is a poor writer or doesn't know grammar. The fact that the meaning of KI is unclear in this context is not because the psalmist did not know how to express his ideas properly.

When a verse in scripture is written in a grammatically awkward manner it is not a mistake! When a verse in scripture can be legitimately interpreted in multiple ways there is a simple reason for it. *We are supposed to interpret it in multiple ways!*

This is true of many hundreds of verses throughout the Bible. Unusual or grammatically strange wording opens us up to the layers of meaning that are all embedded in the words.

I love the Lord when He hears my prayers.
I love the Lord because He hears my prayers.

I love the fact that the Lord hears my prayers.
I love praying because I know that the Lord is listening.

How wonderful and amazing it is that the poetry of a single verse in Psalms is able to convey so many different messages at the same time!

Scripture was written to inspire us; to connect us with God. Each and every one of us. The *words* are the same for everyone. But we are all different people. We read these words at different times in our lives, with different experiences in our backgrounds. We are each in our own unique place in our own developing relationship with God. This verse, like many others in Scripture, allows us to relate to the many different layers of meaning hidden within the sacred word.

The different interpretations that the language of Scripture allows for show the depth and beauty of the sacred word. Like the different seasons of our lives, the words of the Bible are multi-layered and multi-faceted.

116:2 *The Right Time to Call to the Lord*

> *For He has inclined His ear to*
> *me; and in my days I call out.*

The previous verse stated that God *hears my voice*. Now the psalmist refers to God *inclining His ear*.

Inclining vs Hearing

The symbolism of this imagery is simple and powerful. *Hearing* is a mostly passive behavior. While it is true that quite often in order to hear one must pay attention, nevertheless, the point remains that hearing generally neither requires nor displays any particular effort.

Inclining the ear is an action. A person who inclines his ear to hear is taking active steps to hear that person. He is not merely listening to what is audible. He is making a concerted effort to put himself in a position to hear what may otherwise not be heard.

When the psalmist says that *God has inclined His ear to me*, he is stating that fact that *God wants to hear me*. He anticipates my voice. He desires my prayer.

Hearing   =   passive, does not indicate intent
Inclining the Ear =   active, indicates intent and concern

This is a good place to point out a significant transition that took place at the start of Psalm 116. The three psalms that began the Hallel, 113 through 115, were entirely written in the first person plural. "Not to *us*", "*We* will bless the Lord." etc.

Psalm 116 is written in the *singular*. In other words, while the previous psalms described a collective relationship to God – with Israel, with the nations, with the fearers of the Lord, etc. – this psalm describes a *personal relationship* with God.

With this in mind, the phrase *For He has inclined His ear to me* is even more striking. Whereas the previous two psalms dealt with the redemption of Israel and the declaration and praise of God to the world, this psalm is about the *individual*. God listens to each an every one of us. Not only does He listen, *He has inclined his ear*; He *comes towards* us as individuals and wants to hear each of us speak to Him.

What are "my days"?

The second half of this verse is unclear. What is the meaning of *in my days I call out*? Many translations render it as *all of my days, as long as I live*, or *my entire life*. The problem is that this is not what the Hebrew says. In Psalms, when the intent is to refer to *all* of a person's life, the verse states that clearly. For example:

One thing have I desired of the Lord; that will I seek after: that I may dwell in the house of the Lord *all the days of my life*, (Psalm 27:4)

Or

> Only goodness and loving kindness will pursue me *all the days
> of my life*, and I will dwell in the house of the Lord *for the length
> of my days*. (Psalm 23:7)

In these verses, the words *all* – KOL - and *for the length of* – LeORECH -
are stated. In our verse, there is no such word. Our verse simply states,
and in my days I call out. I do not believe that the meaning of this phrase
is that the psalmist will call out to God <u>all</u> *the days of His life*. Rather, I
believe that the verse is simply stating that *I call out to the Lord <u>when it is
day for me</u>*.

But what is *day*? Throughout Psalms, *day* and *night* are repeatedly
used to symbolize happy and difficult times respectively. The examples
are too numerous to list here.

The rest of this psalm describes first how the psalmist calls out to
and praises God first during difficult times of suffering (verses 3 -11)
followed by a description of praise and thanks to God when times are
happy and all is good (12-19).

Calling out to God in Psalm 116

In times of difficulty and struggle	verses 3 through 11
In happy seasons of life	verses 12 through 19

Good or Bad: I call on His name

I would like to suggest that our verse – right at the beginning of this
psalm – introduces these two themes.

For He has inclined His ear to me; - In other words, when He knows
that I am suffering and expects me to seek Him and pray to Him, He is
already there waiting and listening.

<u>*and*</u> *in my days I call out*. – and when times are good I don't forget
about the need for prayer and praise even when I don't have worldly
needs. I call out to Him in *my days*.

This understanding of our verse is suggested by the two times later in the psalm when the identical phrase *Then I call on the name of the Lord* appears.

> I was overcome by distress and sorrow. *Then I call on the name of the Lord*: (v.3-4)

> What shall I return to the Lord for all his goodness to me? I will lift up the cup of salvation and *I will call on the name of the Lord* (v. 12-13)

In other words, whether I am experiencing difficulties or happy times the response is the same. *I call out the name of the Lord.*

We must not reserve our prayers for times of struggle and difficulty. Whether I am experiencing difficulties or happy times the response is the same. I call on the name of the Lord.

116:3 *Three Kinds of Suffering*

> *The cords of death have encompassed me and the constrictions of the grave found me; suffering and anguish have I found.*

This verse introduces the images that follow to set up how the merciful God rescues the psalmist and heeds his cries for help.

It is important to note that unlike most verses in Psalms, this verse is made up of three phrases. Most verses in Psalms are written as couplets; composed of two phrases. A quick glance at the other verses in this book will show that quite clearly. One other exception that we saw was back in Psalm 115:7 which had three phrases, similar to our verse.

Let's take a look at the first two phrases in this verse. At first glance they seem repetitive. *Cords of death. Constrictions of the grave.*

There are a few of plays on words here in the Hebrew that are worthy of our attention.

The <u>cords</u> of death. The word for *cords* – HEVLEI – has two meanings depending on context.

1. *Cords* or *ropes.* The Hebrew word HEVEL means *rope.*
2. Alternatively, this word appears in eight separate verses in Scripture where it means *pangs.* For example:

   What will you say when the Lord sets over you those you cultivated as your special allies? Will not *pain* grip you like that of a woman in labor? (Jeremiah 13:21)

The etymological connection may be the fact that one who is in severe *pain* feels as though they are *bound* and *ensnared*; unable to escape.

HEVLEI – two meanings

1. *Cords, ropes*
2. *Pangs, sharp pains*

<u>Constrictions</u> *of the grave.* A second word in our verse that has a double meaning is the word *constrictions.* The Hebrew word METZAREI is the plural of METZAR – *constriction* or *tight place.* This is a word that we will encounter again in Psalm 118 verse 5. For now, a quick look at variant translations both here and in 118:5 will show that many translate this word as *distress* or *suffering. Constriction* and *distress* are both accurate meanings of this word. Once again, the two meanings have a clear link. One who is *suffering* or in pain feels figuratively that they are *constrained* and *limited.* There is a feeling of being in a *tight place.*

Nothing could be quite as limiting and hopeless as death; the grave.

METZAREI – two meanings

1. *Constriction, tight place*
2. *Suffering, distress*

While these two phrases are somewhat repetitive, there is a subtle difference in the imagery.

Cords ensnare me indicates that a trap was laid for me or that someone *intentionally* captured me and tied me up. Seen this way, the *cords of death* would indicate a mortal danger of being killed by a deliberate and willful enemy.

Constrictions of the grave has a different connotation. Everyone dies. Feeling death closing in does not necessarily imply that one is being attacked or pursued.

With this in mind, we may sum up these first two seemingly redundant phrases as follows: When all is lost and hopeless whether because I am being actively pursued and ensnared by adversaries or simply heading toward my own inevitable and unavoidable demise…

Suffering and anguish I have found

This third phrase of our verse presents a fascinating grammatical contrast with the first two. The verb in this phrase is in the first person. This is of critical importance.

In the first two phrases, - The cords of death *have encompassed me* and the constrictions of the grave *found me* – the psalmist is passive. His peril and suffering is something that is being done *to him*. It's not his fault. In the third phrase, *suffering and anguish <u>I have found</u>*, he is active. Suffering and anguish have not found him. *He has found them*. The implication is that somehow his own behavior has led him to his current state of despair.

Rather than being repetitive, our verse actually describes a *progression* leading to the prayer and salvation of the Lord in the following verses.

- *The cords of death <u>have encompassed me</u>* – whether my suffering is the result of active premeditated attack by enemies,
- *The constrictions of the grave <u>found me</u>* – or it is the result of natural decay and suffering of old age,
- *suffering and anguish <u>I have found</u>* – or even if my hardship is of my own doing.

In all of these situations I cry out to the Lord for help. (see the next verse)

The progression makes a lot of sense.

When people experience suffering they often are hesitant to pray because they are not sure that they deserve to be helped. Many people, even very religious ones, feel unworthy of Divine assistance in times of trouble. Our verse responds:

Whether I am actually ensnared by enemies through no fault of my own or I am even undergoing the natural sufferings that one cannot rightfully complain about; or even if I am at fault for causing my own suffering, I still call out to God for His help. There is no such thing as being undeserving of God's help.

Regardless of the source of our pain and anguish. Regardless of how hopeless things look. Calling out to God for help is always the correct course of action.

116:4 *Please. vs. PLEASE!!*

> *And I call out in the Name of the Lord; "Please, Lord, deliver my soul."*

When all reasonable hope seems lost and despair, death, and suffering are closing in, the response is always to call out to the Lord for deliverance.

Please vs. PLEASE!!

The Hebrew word for *please* used here is ANA. ANA as *please* appears only 13 times in Scripture. The more common word for *please* is a shorter version of the same word – NA - which appears almost 400 times.

The difference between ANA and NA is clear from context. ANA is always in the context of a subordinate speaking to a master. In 12 out of the 13 instances of ANA it is God who is being addressed. The one exception is when Joseph's brothers beg him for forgiveness after their father Jacob's death. Joseph is a sovereign ruler in Egypt and the brothers are terrified of his vengeance for their treatment of him.

A good way to think about this distinction between the more casual NA and the more formal ANA in English is to compare it to the difference between *please* spoken in a normal conversation and the more formal *I beseech you*. In fact, many translations render ANA this way.

Certainly ANA is the appropriate form of *please* here. Feeling death and suffering closing in, the psalmist cries out to God to help. ANA – *Please!*

ANaH or ANA

But there is a more striking yet subtle nuance in the Hebrew that is impossible to see in any English translation of this verse.

As I mentioned, ANA appears 13 times in Scripture. What's fascinating is that it is spelled two different ways. In seven instances the spelling is ANA: A- Aleph, N – Nun, A - Aleph. The other six times it is spelled ANaH: A – Aleph, N – Nun, H – Heh. It is important to understand that the pronunciation is identical. It's similar to the difference in English between the names Sara and Sarah. No change in pronunciation. The only way to tell would be to see how it is written. The spelling in our verse is the second one; Aleph, Nun, Heh – ANaH.

So to sum up, in six out of thirteen times ANaH with the H is used for *please*. The other seven uses of ANA are spelled without the H.

The ancient Hebrew commentaries do not suggest any distinction in meaning between ANA and ANaH. However, a careful look at context reveals a very powerful idea about prayer.

So what's the difference?

ANA and ANaH both mean *please*. Despite there being no difference in *translation* between ANA and ANaH context reveals an important distinction that lies beneath the surface.

In the seven places where ANA *please* is spelled *without the letter Heh* the context is almost always a plea either for forgiveness (see Genesis 50:17, Exodus 32:31) or for God to keep His covenantal promises to Israel (see Daniel 9:4, Nehemiah 1:5) When ANaH is spelled *with the Heh* – identical to *where to* and *until when* – the context is almost always *salvation from the threat of death.* (see II Kings 20:3, Isaiah 38:3, Jonah 1:14) In short:

ANA = plea for forgiveness or covenantal fulfillment
ANaH = plea for salvation from mortal danger

I would like to suggest that when *please* is spelled ANaH, as it is in our verse, there is a tone of despair and fear that is implied *by the spelling*. God's covenantal promises are guaranteed as is His forgiveness for our sins. There is no *despair* or *fear* in the verses asking God for forgiveness or fulfillment of the covenant. On the other hand, fear of death, like in our verse here, is another matter.

God hears the "spelling"
The psalmist feels that all hope is lost. Death and the grave are closing in. There is no way out. He cries out to God *Please!*

This is a powerful lesson about our prayers. A human being listening to this cry hears the word *please*. But the fear and despair implied by the *spelling* are not perceptible in the pronunciation, but they are there. *God hears the spelling too.*

The Lord hears the unspoken and hidden layers of fears and feelings that lie beneath the word that come out of mouths. He hears what we mean and not only what we say.

116:5 *Gracious, Righteous, & Bestows Mercy*

Gracious is the Lord and righteous; and our God bestows mercy.

After stating that he calls out to God in times of suffering and despair, the psalmist now expresses the reasons that he is confident that God hears his prayers.

Three characteristics of God are mentioned here.

Gracious is the Lord and *righteous*; and our God *bestows mercy*.

Gracious:	He gives us blessings that we don't deserve.
Righteous:	He deals justly; any suffering that we experience is deserved.
Bestows mercy:	He feels our pain and alleviates our hardship.

Almost every translation that I saw rendered the last phrase of the verse as *our God is merciful (or compassionate)*. This translation is simply incorrect. Let me explain.

Traits vs. Actions

Gracious and *righteous* are both adjectives. These translations are accurate as the words that appear in the Hebrew are adjectives as well. *The third description is not written as an adjective but as a verb.* For the sake of comparison;

He has caused His wondrous works to be remembered; the Lord is *gracious and merciful*. (Psalm 111:4)

Or

> So rend your heart, and not your garments; Return to the Lord
> your God, For He is *gracious and merciful*, Slow to anger, and
> of great kindness; And He relents from doing harm. (Joel 2:13)

In both of these examples – as well as in nine more verses in Scripture –
God is described as *merciful*. *Merciful* is an adjective. It describes one of
God's characteristics. The Hebrew for merciful is RaHUM.

Here in our verse a different word is used. The word here is not the
adjective *merciful* – RaHUM. It is the active verb *acts mercifully* or, as I
translated it, *bestows mercy* – in Hebrew, MeRaHeM.

To sum up, the first two descriptions are of traits of God, i.e. what He
is. The third description is of what God *does*.

Gracious	=	adjective
Righteous	=	adjective
Bestows Mercy	=	action / verb

This distinction is made even more striking by the fact that God's characteristics of *graciousness* and *mercy* appear together 12 times in Scripture.
Eleven out of twelve times the word to describe God's *graciousness* is the
adjective – RaHUM. Look back at the two verses I just quoted; *gracious
and merciful*. Two adjectives. The same pair appears in Exodus 34:6, Jonah
4:2, Psalms 86:15, 103:8, 112:4, and 145:8, Nehemiah 9:17 and 31, and II
Chronicles 30:9.

Our verse is the only exception. This is the *only verse* in all of Scripture
where the trait of *mercy* appears not as the adjective - *merciful* but as a
verb - *bestows mercy*.

We can understand the importance of this exception by looking at
one other exception.

God vs. the Lord

Our verse is the *only verse in Scripture* which pairs the trait of *mercy*
with the name ELOHEINU – *God*, rather than the four letter name of God

YHVH; usually translated as *the Lord*. In other words, with the exception of our verse *every single time* that God is described as *merciful* He is named as *the Lord, YHVH*.

What's more, Psalm 116 mentions God by name sixteen times. This is an extremely high number for a psalm of nineteen verses. Fifteen out of sixteen times the name for God used is *YHVH – the Lord*. The only exception is this phrase; *and our God bestows mercy*. Fifteen *the Lords*. One *our God*. From a literary perspective, this should force us to sit up and take note.

The Names of God in Psalm 116

YHVH – *the Lord*   15 times
ELOHEINU – *God*   1 time

To sum up these two exceptional features of this phrase:
* Only place in the Bible that pairs God's *mercy* with a name other than *YHVH – the Lord*
* Only use of a divine name other than *YHVH* in Psalm 116

What do God's names really mean?

The name ELOHEINU – *our God* – is the possessive form of the name ELOHIM – *God*. This is the only name of God that appears in Genesis 1, the six days of the creation of the world. The name YHVH – *the Lord* does not appear there. Furthermore, the name YHVH is never pronounced as it is written. As I explained in the <u>Note on the names of God</u> at the beginning of this book, *the Lord* is not a translation of YHVH at all, as YHVH has no meaning in Hebrew outside of being God's name. The popular translation of YHVH, *The Lord,* is a translation of the Hebrew *euphemism* used as a *replacement* for YHVH, ADONAI – which means *Lord*.

To sum up:
* ELOHEINU (our God) and ELOHIM (God) are pronounced as written.
* YHVH (the Lord) is not.

Why is this so? The answer is both simple and profound. YHVH is a name that refers to God's *timelessness* and *total omniscience*. These are concepts that, while we *believe* them to be traits of God, we can not really *understand* or relate to them. As limited human beings, we can not imagine what timelessness or omniscience are in our reality. ELOHIM, on the other hand, refers to the God that I can see. The God of creation. God revealed in nature.

"God" vs. "Our God"

ELOHIM is *God*. ELOHEINU is *Our God*. ELOHIM is the God of creation, God who governs the world around me. ELOHEINU is personal. He cares about us. His control of the natural world takes our specific needs into account. He is not just God. He is *Our* God.

Traits vs. Actions

To say that someone is *merciful* or *gracious* refers to a character trait that they possess. But a trait is not always outwardly expressed in action. It is often hidden from view even though it is there in potential. You can't see the fact that someone *is merciful*. Only when a person *performs an act of mercy* do we see that trait.

Now we can understand the power and meaning of our verse.

Gracious is the Lord and righteous; - Even though I don't always see it, I know that YHVH, the all knowing, all powerful God possesses the traits of grace and righteousness.

and our God bestows mercy; - ELOHEINU - the *personal God of my experience* is not just *merciful* as a trait that I may not see; He *bestows mercy* that I experience and perceive with my senses.

To sum up these last three verses: No matter how desperate or hopeless my situation; whether I see my suffering as my own doing or the result of the attacks of others; I call out to God. Not only is He gracious and just; He shows me that He is personally and emotionally involved in my life and the lives of those around me; *our God bestows mercy.*

Even when we are struggling and feel like God is distant, He is not. He is here and involved. He bestows mercy on us.

116:6 *Hidden Benefit of Hard Times*

> *The Lord protects the unwary;*
> *I was brought low; but for me*
> *it brings salvation.*

Why are we discussing the unwary?

The previous verses described the psalmist despairing, suffering, in danger. He calls out to the Lord in plaintive prayer and is confident that the Lord hears him. What, then, is the point of this verse? *The Lord protects the unwary?* What is the relevance to the context of this psalm? *I was brought low* could just as easily fit in with the earlier statements in verse 3; *The cords of death have encompassed me and the constrictions of the grave found me; suffering and anguish have I found.* What is the new idea here and what does it have to do with the Lord protecting *the unwary?*

Furthermore, what is the relevance of the first phrase - *The Lord protects the unwary;* - to the rest of the verse - *when I was brought low, he saved me.* Are we to assume that all of the suffering and despair in the earlier verses is now being defined solely as the result of foolish carelessness?

Understanding the accurate meaning of this verse will reveal a powerful lesson in faith and will allow us to properly understand the verses that follow.

Alert! Translation issue

If you take a quick look at almost any translation of this verse you will find something different than my translation above.

A typical rendering of this verse would be:

> The Lord protects the unwary; I was brought low; and He saved me.

The differences are in the translation of the last phrase.

1. Almost every translation available has either *and He saved me* or *He saved me* without the word *and*. Out of approximately 50 translations, I found only four that included the word *but,* as I did.

2. Every single translation had God as the subject of the final verb; as the one doing the saving. *He saved me.*

I find these translations problematic primarily because of the unique choice of words in this phrase.

He saved to me (??)

Anyone reading this verse in Hebrew immediately notices the cumbersome and unusual syntax. The end of the verse, usually translated as *I was brought low; and He saved me* is actually quite difficult to translate word for word. This entire quote is comprised of three Hebrew words. I will translate and show both the literal and the common translation.

	common translation	literal translation
DaLoTI	I was brought low	I was brought low
Ve-LI	and me	and to me / and for me
YeHOShIA	He saved	He / it causes salvation

This may look like no big deal, but it is. Allow me to explain. Simply put, in Hebrew *He saved me* can not be written this way.

The word Ve-LI – *and me* is the most difficult word to translate here. Li means *to me* or *for me*. Ve is the prefix *and*. A literal translation of our verse is *I was brought low and He saved for me*. As I said before, anyone reading the Hebrew is struck by the awkwardness of the verse. But awkward or not, there is just no way to justify the common translation of VeLi as *me*.

The real meaning of VeLi

Surprisingly, the word Ve-Li appears only seven times in Scripture. Li – *to me* or *for me* - is an extremely common word and appears over 700 times. However, once the prefix Ve –*and* – is added; only seven.

In at least three of these seven instances, the meaning of the prefix Ve – which usually means *and* – is *but*.

> Then Samson's wife harassed him with tears, and she said, "You really hate me, you don't love me. You posed a riddle to my countrymen, *but to me* (VeLi) you did not tell the answer;" (Judges 14:16)

> Saul was very angry; this statement displeased him greatly. 'They have credited David with tens of thousands,' he thought, '*but to me* (VeLi) only thousands. What more can he get but the kingdom?' (I Samuel 18:8)

> Right now they are eating and drinking with him and saying, 'Long live King Adonijah!' *But to me* (VeLi) your servant, and Zadok the priest, and Benaiah son of Jehoiada, and your servant Solomon he did not call to join. (I Kings 1:25-26)

I'd like to suggest that this is the meaning in our verse as well.

Suffering and Sin

In the previous verse the psalmist refers to God not only as gracious and as one who acts mercifully, he also referred to the Lord as *righteous*. This word, when referring to God, always implies that His judgments, rewards, and punishments are always justified. He is a just God.

Our verse continues that thought. The psalmist is marveling at God's latent kindness inherent in the suffering that he is experiencing. Someone who is in a weakened, limited, perilous state is usually incapable of sin. Even if physically capable, someone in a state of acute suffering is usually not interested or inclined to sin.

I was brought low – I am in a weakened state, restricted, suffering.

But for me it brought salvation – my limited state of weakness actually saved my soul!

Now we can understand the peculiar opening words of the verse. *The unwary* in Hebrew are called PeTAIM. This word is from the same root as the word for *seduction*. (e.g. Deuteronomy 11:16, Exodus 22:15) In other words, this is a particular type of carelessness; that of being blind to the moral dangers inherent in a tantalizing and inviting, yet sinful, experience.

The psalmist is suffering. He is weak, fearing death. He knows that God is just. He knows that God cares for him and wants only the best for him. He has a revelation! Even when God causes me to be weak and in a lowered state; He does this out of love to save me from my carelessness and protect my soul!

The Lord protects the unwary; I was brought low; but for me it brings salvation.

Although we do not invite suffering upon ourselves, we can recognize that such experiences often save us from the more frivolous and careless behaviors into which we slip.

116:7 *Me, My Soul, and I*

Return, my soul, to your restfulness, for the Lord has bestowed this upon you.

Talking to yourself?

In a dramatic turn, the psalmist poetically speaks directly to his soul. A less poetic version of the same verse would be:

I will return to my restfulness, for the Lord has bestowed this upon me.

This second person address directly *to his soul* is particularly interesting as this is one of three consecutive times in this psalm where the psalmist refers to his *soul* rather than to himself as *me*. Allow me to elaborate.

Verses 1-3: Me

In the opening three verses of the psalm, the author directly refers to himself numerous times. For example, verse 3.

> The cords of death have encompassed *me* and the constrictions of the grave found *me*; suffering and anguish have *I* found.

This verse could just as easily have been written like this:

> The cords of death have encompassed *my soul* and the constrictions of the grave found *my soul*; suffering and anguish has *my soul* found.

Any or all of these self references could have been changed in this way and the meaning would be seemingly identical. The same is true for the self references in verses 1 and 2.

Three mentions of "my soul"

And then in verse 4 the psalmist calls out *Please, Lord, deliver my soul;* rather than calling out *deliver me.*

Now again, here in verse 7 the psalmist refers to *his soul* rather than himself in the first person. The third and final example immediately follows this in verse 8.

> For you have delivered *my soul* from death, my eyes from tears, my feet from stumbling;

From verse 8 until the conclusion of the psalm there are no more mentions of the psalmist's soul. He returns completely to referring to himself in the first person.

Alert! Translation issue

Before we explain these references to *my soul*, there is a translation issue that must be addressed.

I translated the second half of the verse *for the Lord has bestowed this upon you.*

But this is not what you will find in most – dare I say, *any* – other translations.

22 of the translations available on the internet had exactly the same wording:

For the Lord has dealt bountifully with you

Another 16 translations had some version of this:

For the Lord has been good to you

And then there were a few that were so far from the original Hebrew that they are not even worth mentioning here.

Here's the problem. There is no indication that God has dealt *bountifully* or bestowed anything *good* here. *Bountifully* implies abundance; that *a lot* of something was given. There is no indication whatsoever that what was given was a lot, a little, or even quantifiable at all! Even the translation *has been good* is problematic. The Hebrew words simply state:

KI	for
YHVH	the Lord
GaMaL	bestowed / meted out
ALAICHI	to you / upon you

GaMaL – The Good, the Bad, and the Vague

The key word here, of course, is GaMaL. This verb in various conjugations appears more than 20 times in Scripture. Approximately half of those refer to the *meting out of punishment* or simply to someone doing *something bad* to someone else. In many other instances it refers to the granting of positive gifts, blessings, or rewards. One example of a negative use should suffice to make the point.

O Daughter of Babylon, doomed to destruction, happy is the
one who pays you *what you deserve* for what *you have done* to us.
(Psalm 137:8)

Both italicized phrases are uses of the word GaMaL. The evil perpetrated
by Babylon upon Israel is GaMaL in noun form and the punishment that
they deserve for it is GaMaL as well, this time as a verb. As I said, this
is only one of approximately ten examples. I say *approximately*, because
there are even a few instances where it is *ambiguous as to whether what is
being bestowed is bad or good.*

And that is precisely the point of our verse!
　　In the opening verses the psalmist describes how he cries out to the
Lord in times of great suffering and danger (v. 1-4). He knows God is just.
He knows God is merciful and gracious (v.5). And yet he is suffering.
Besides the physical suffering, *his soul* is in turmoil as well. Why is this
happening to me? What is the purpose of this hardship?
　　As I explained, in the previous verse the psalmist realizes that sometimes hardship is sent by God to keep him from careless sinful thoughts
and behavior. It is not uncommon for people who feel weak and fear
death to find the experience reminding them of higher values that they
may have been neglecting in their lives. This happens precisely because
suffering is a context that facilitates this kind of focus. Earthly temporal
desires fade into the background. Our psalmist understands that his suffering is itself a form of salvation. That was verse 6.
　　Now in verse 7, with this realization in hand, he turns to his confused and beleaguered soul and says.
　　Return, my soul, to your restfulness - You can relax. You need not be in
turmoil haunted by questions of why this suffering has befallen us. Yes,
our body is still in pain; but, you - my soul - need not be tormented.
　　for the Lord has bestowed this upon you. – Is it good? Is it bad? Nobody
welcomes suffering. It is certainly to be avoided. But there is good in it as
well; for it is from the Lord.

No matter how painful or confusing, what the Lord bestows is good because it comes from Him. The pain and the benefit go hand in hand.

116:8 *My Soul, My Eyes, My Feet*

For You have rescued my soul from death, my eyes from tears, my feet from stumbling;

The most striking feature of this verse is that it is spoken *to* God and not <u>about</u> Him. The entire psalm up to this point has referred to the Lord or God in the third person. Even in verse 4 when the psalmist prays to the Lord this prayer appears in a narrative form as a quote: *And I call out in the Name of the Lord; "Please, Lord, deliver my soul."*

Our verse, on the other hand, is addressed *to God*. It's worth pointing out that this kind of transition between talking *about* God to talking *to* God and vice versa is quite common throughout the book of Psalms. *And it is always worth studying.*

Here we see three rescues; *soul from death, eyes from tears*, and *feet from stumbling*. Together they encompass all of the experiences that have been referred to in the psalm up until this point. Each one on its own represents a unique form of peril from which God saves us.

My soul from Death

These words refer back to the imagery of verse 3:

The cords of death have encompassed me and the constrictions of the grave found me;

With the words *you have rescued my soul from death* the psalmist is praising God for saving him from mortal danger. Yet at the same time, he alludes to the spiritual danger from which he was rescued as well. Notice that the verse does not say *you have rescued ME from death*; which would have adequately referred to the mortal danger of verse 3 on its own. The psalmist recognizes that when God saved him from mortal danger and fear, in addition to steering him away from sin, He has rescued *his soul* from death – the combined spiritual deaths of fear and sin.

> The Lord is my light and my salvation; whom shall I fear? The Lord is the stronghold of my life; of whom shall I be afraid? (Psalm 27:1)

My eyes from tears

Tears, of course, refer to sadness. Specifically, when we feel helpless to improve the situation and have given up hope, tears begin to flow. While in his original state of peril the psalmist felt complete despair. He saw no upside to his suffering. It caused only sadness. Then, upon realizing that even his hardship is a tool that God uses to help him, that his suffering is a sign of God's love, he no longer had reason to cry. Where there is hope there are no tears.

My feet from stumbling

Here God is neither saving him from imminent danger nor is he giving him reason to be happy. *Stumbling feet* are not a form of suffering. They are, quite literally, *missteps*. In this statement the psalmist is praising God for steering him on the right path and lighting his way towards God and away from sin.

These three salvations encompass all that we yearn for when we encounter difficult times. Fear, sadness, and making mistakes that only dig us deeper into the hole in which we find ourselves. To put it another way, fear focuses on dangers from without. Sadness prevents us from thinking positively and hopefully. Stumbling is the danger within us when we feel distant from God and make wrongful choices. God loves us and saves us from all of these.

My soul from death	=	You gave me life, both physical and spiritual
My eyes from tears	=	You saved me from anguish and despair
My feet from stumbling	=	You steered my away from careless sinfulness

From "Him" to" You"

When we are suffering, lose hope, or are carelessly following our baser instincts there is a tendency to feel distant from God. As we contemplate our situation and remind ourselves of God's love for us we feel our faith being restored. We begin to feel His presence. We feel close to Him again. The third person implies that the person we are speaking about is not present. Even if they are present, we are not facing them and engaging them. We are speaking to somebody else. The poetic transition from third person to second person reflects an *increase in intimacy.* The psalmist, realizing the greatness of God's salvation and love, now realizes that God is right there with him. Figuratively, he turns to God because he realizes that He is there.

When we speak to God we are more conscious of His closeness to us; of our direct relationship with Him.

116:9 *Walking Before God*

I will walk before the Lord in the lands of the living.

A particularly baffling translation

Throughout this book I have pointed out translations that I felt were imprecise. I have made the point that the efforts by translators to clean up awkward syntax causes the English reader of Scripture to lose the poetic nuance of the original Hebrew. At other times the translators are faced with an impossible grammatical structure such as a sudden switch of person or tense in mid sentence. I have shown over and over that if an unexpected word or cumbersome grammatical form is used *that is because it is deliberate.* It is specifically in these situations that we are called upon to notice the layers of deeper meaning embedded in this sacred poetry.

There are other times when the translators are forced to make a legitimate choice between two possible translations of a word that has multiple meanings. Inevitably, they must sacrifice the nuanced double meaning of the word. While these instances are regrettable, the choices are understandable. After all, translators need their texts to read smoothly and not appear poorly written.

However, even by these standards, the translation issue that we find in this verse is difficult to understand.

Out of fifty published English translations that I looked at, only four translated the word *lands* in the plural as I did here. The other forty-six translated the verse as:

I will walk before the Lord in the *land* of the living.

The Hebrew word here is unmistakably plural; *the lands of the living.* It is not singular. Rather than *correcting* this plural word as the translators chose to do, we ought to ask ourselves, *what lesson is the psalmist trying to teach us? What lands are being referred to?*

Walk before vs Walk with

The verse opens with the words *I will walk before the Lord.* Notice that it doesn't say *I will walk with the Lord.* What does it mean to walk *before* the Lord?

What's fascinating about this question is that in the book of Genesis there are two people who are described as walking *with God* and two who are described as walking *before God.*

And Enoch *walked with God…* (Genesis 5:22, 24)

These are the generations of Noah. Noah was a just man and perfect in his generations, and Noah *walked <u>with</u>* God. (Genesis 6:9)

When Abram was ninety-nine years old, the Lord appeared to him and said, "I am God Almighty; *walk <u>before</u> me* and be without fault." (Genesis 17:1; see also Gen. 24:40)

Then he [Jacob] blessed Joseph and said, "May *the God <u>before</u> whom* my fathers Abraham and Isaac *walked*, the God who has been my shepherd all my life to this day," (Genesis 48:15)

Enoch and Noah walked *with* God. Abraham and Isaac walked *before* God. I believe that if we just think about the difference between Enoch and Noah on one hand and Abraham and Isaac on the other we will see that the meaning of these verses is simple. Enoch and Noah were certainly both righteous men of faith. However, neither of them had any significant influence on the world. Neither Enoch nor Noah had followers who spread their faith in God to the society around them. Neither of them became the founder of a nation charged with the mission to bring knowledge of God to all the peoples of the earth. They were pious men, but not influential.

The Covenant of Walking before God

It is important to note the context in which God appears to Abram and commands him to *walk before me*. If we look carefully at the verses that immediately follow this command we will understand what it means to *walk before God*.

When Abram was ninety-nine years old, the Lord appeared to him and said, "I am God Almighty; *walk before me* and be without fault. Then I will make my covenant between me and you and will greatly increase your numbers." Abram fell facedown, and God said to him, "As for me, this is my covenant with you: *You will be the father of many nations. No longer will you be called Abram; your name will be Abraham, for I have made you a father of many nations."* (Genesis 17:1-5)

Abraham's name change from Abram to Abraham indicates a change in mission. Abraham is to be a father of *many nations*. This is a new covenantal mission. He is now charged with the task of bringing knowledge of the One God to *all the families of the earth.*

Enoch and Noah were personally righteous men who did not follow the evil pagan ways of their time and place. They walked *with* God. Abraham took things to a different level. Abraham was not merely faithful and pious as an individual. Abraham did not merely walk *with God.* He walked *before God.* Like a herald before the king, Abraham was out in the world calling out the name of the Lord for all to hear. (see Genesis 12:8; 13:4; 21:33)

Abraham passes this covenantal mission on to Isaac and to all his offspring after him; to *walk before God* – to broadcast knowledge of Him to the world.

Lands, not Land

Now we can answer our original question. The psalmist is declaring his readiness to continue Abraham's mission. He is saying, in effect, I am dedicated to telling everyone – wherever they may be – *in every place, in every land, in every society* about You. I will not stay in my place and keep God to myself. I will invite others into the relationship with Him.

I will walk <u>before</u> the Lord in the <u>lands</u> of the living.

As devoted servants of God we are charged not only to have faith in Him but to promote knowledge and faith of Him to all peoples in all lands.

116:10 *Speaking the Faith*

*I had faith when I spoke; I was
greatly afflicted.*

The first half of this verse is composed of three Hebrew words.

HEEMANTI	*I had faith*
KI	*but / because / that / when*
ADABER	*I speak*

In my comments to verse 1 of this psalm I explained that KI can *mean because, when, that,* or *but.* Despite these options, most translations translate KI in this verse as *therefore.* The most common translation of the verse being something along the lines of:

I believed, therefore I spoke, "I am greatly afflicted."

I would like to suggest that KI in this verse retains a conventional meaning. The two most common meanings of KI are *because* and *when.* I believe that either of these translations fits the plain meaning of this verse and teaches us a profound lesson about faith.

Context Matters!

The first nine verses in this psalm describe the experience of one who is in a state of mortal danger and suffering; he feels that all hope is lost. (v.3) He calls out to the Lord (v.4) and then begins to contemplate the fact that God knows what's best for him (v.5). He reminds himself that not only does God save and protect, but even when He causes him to suffer, He has his best interests in mind (v.6). After reminding himself of the core principles of his faith in God; after finding meaning in his suffering He declares his intention to devote his life to declaring the glory of God in the world (v.7-9).

Now, the psalmist reflects on this experience. He shares a powerful lesson about faith that he learned along the way.

I had faith when/because I spoke

Back in verse 3 the psalmist was terrified and felt helpless in the face of dire circumstances. How, then, did he get himself out of that state? First, he called out to the Lord. But then after calling out to the Lord he began to express his faith. He reminded himself of the benevolent and merciful traits of God (v.5). He spoke soothingly to his troubled soul (v.7). He reaffirmed his beliefs and values and gained strength to cope with his situation and even to grow from it (v.9).

One of the most powerful tools that we have to help us in time of suffering is our own expression. When we express our faith; when we articulate it and remind ourselves of that which we know in our hearts and minds to be true; that God loves us, that He is with us in our suffering, that when He saves us from peril He saves us so that we can live more meaningful lives; we deepen that faith. The faith that had previously escaped us when we had given up hope returns to us and gives us optimism and strength.

I had faith when I spoke. Because I expressed my *beliefs*; as a result of expressing what I *know to be true* about God and His love for me; my faith returned.

And why was this necessary? - *I was greatly afflicted*. Extreme situations test our faith. It is a natural reaction to suffering to wonder if God has abandoned us and to lose the feeling of faith in Him. It takes work to bring it back. Speaking about God, articulating His great kindness and love for us even as we suffer brings faith back.

I had faith when I spoke; I was greatly afflicted.

When we feel it slipping, verbalizing our belief in God reconnects us to Him. Speaking about faith leads to a strengthening of faith.

116:11 *Rethinking the Meaning of Life*

---

*And I said in my haste, "All
humanity is deceiving."*

Who's deceiving whom?

This verse appears out of place. The psalmist seems to be referring to human enemies who deceive him. This is strange because the danger and suffering that was mentioned in this psalm has heretofore made no mention of any human antagonists. "Pangs of death" (v.3), "the grave" (v.3), "I was weakened" (v.6).

Said in haste = mistaken

Furthermore, the phrase *I said in my haste* implies that whatever was said *in haste* was later refuted or realized to be incorrect. Put simply, "I *hastily* thought X. Now I know I was wrong." To illustrate, let's look at the one other appearance of this phrase in Scripture, right here in the book of Psalms.

I said in my haste, "I am cut off from before Your eyes." But You heard the voice of my petitions when I cried to You. (Psalm 31:23)

In other words, I *hastily thought* that I was cut off from God's protection but I was wrong.

This makes sense. To say that something was *said in haste* means that it was carelessly stated and was later seen to be incorrect. Seen this way, our verse seems to be saying, *I hastily thought that all humanity is deceptive, but I was wrong.* Again, what is the message of this verse in a psalm that has been all about praising God for salvation in time of trouble?

In my haste I said "X" = "X" turned out to be incorrect

False vs. Deceptive

Hebrew has a number of words for *falsehood*. Falsehood comes in different forms. The most common Hebrew word for *falsehood* is SHeKeR. The word in our verse is KoZeV, which is the verb form of the root, KaZaV. This word often refers not to falsehood generally, but specifically to *deception*. What's the difference between *falsehood* and *deception*? Falsehood is simply, *false*. There is zero evidence or reality to support it. It is false.

Deception, on the other hand, means that there is an *appearance* of truth. It seems true. In other words, there is reason to believe it at the time, but down the road the truth comes out. To put it another way, *deception* refers to something that seemed solid and verifiable in the short term but really was not true at all.

The Entirety of Man

I'd like to suggest that the words *All humanity* – KOL HaADAM in Hebrew - should be understood as they are used at the end of Ecclesiastes.

> The end of the whole matter let us hear: - Fear God, and keep His commands, for this [is] *the entirety of man* – KOL HaADAM. (Ecclesiastes 12:13)

In this verse in Ecclesiastes KOL HaADAM does not mean *all people*. Rather, it refers to the entirety of the human endeavor, *the ultimate purpose of humanity*.

To put this together with the word KoZeV – *deception* – I believe that our verse is saying the following:

When I was suffering and felt helpless and hopeless *I hastily* came to the conclusion that KOL HaADAM - *the entirety of humanity*; i.e. the purpose of human existence - KoZeV – *is deceiving*. It seems solid, meaningful, and full of eternal purpose - but it's not. *It's all a big deception. Human life is pointless.*

In that state of despair, I had not yet gained perspective and did not understand the meaning that God brought to my life through this experience. So...

I said in my haste,	=	I wrongly concluded that
all humanity	=	the entire human enterprise on this earth
is deceiving.	=	is meaningless and devoid of purpose.

But that was before God *rescued my soul from death, my eyes from tears, my feet from stumbling* (v.8). It was before I rediscovered *faith when I spoke* (v.10). Now, *I will walk before the Lord* declaring His greatness *in the lands of the living* (v.9).

I should point out that the psalmist is reflecting back on his thoughts and feelings at the time that he was suffering. He realizes just how far gone he was; how he felt distant from God, questioned his faith, and even doubted the point of human existence. In the context of this point in the psalm he is contrasting how he felt in retrospect with how he feels now that he appreciated how God has redeemed him from the brink of despair.

When we experience hardship we may slip into a sense that life has no meaning. When God pulls us through we can reflect and see more clearly.

116:12 *Beyond Gratitude*

What can I give back to the Lord? All that He has bestowed is upon me.

Each and every one of us has been through experiences that cause us to feel grateful to God. We face difficulties. We pray. We look to the Lord for help. Later, after we make it through we are overwhelmed by feelings of gratitude. We thank the Lord for hearing our prayers and helping us in our time of need.

But this verse is not about *thanking* the Lord. It goes far beyond that. The psalmist wishes to *give back to the Lord*. He feels that he must *repay* the kindness that God bestowed upon him.

The key to understanding this important message is in the final Hebrew word in the verse. *Upon me* is one word in Hebrew. The simple reading of the verse seems to be saying *What can I give back to the Lord for all that He has bestowed upon me.* But there is no word or prefix which means *for* in this verse. In terms of pure and precise grammar, the two phrases in the verse read as two separate complete sentences.

The first half as a question: *What can I give back to the Lord?*
The second half as a sentence: *All that He has bestowed is upon me.*

Upon me = I am responsible

The last word of the verse, the Hebrew word ALAI – *upon me* – often means *incumbent upon me*. I am responsible for that. The word *incumbent* or *responsible* is implied. This is similar to the English slang, "It's on me." Here are two examples among many:

Example #1

One of the soldiers in King David's army tells the general Joab that he saw Absalom, who was rebelling against the king, hanging by his hair from a tree.

Joab said to the man who had told him this, "What! You saw him? Why didn't you strike him to the ground right there? Then *I would have had to* –ALAI - give you ten shekels of silver and a warrior's belt." (II Samuel 18:11)

Example #2:

A traveler passing through the town of Gibeah is invited by a local resident to spend the night:

> And the old man said, "Peace be with you! However, all your needs *are my responsibility* - ALAI; only do not spend the night in the open square." (Judges 19:20)

I would like to suggest that this is the meaning of ALAI – *upon me* in our verse as well. Beyond being thankful for God's salvation, he is overwhelmed by a *sense of obligation* to *repay* God for the kindness done to him. The kindness done for him by the Lord gives him responsibility.

Beyond Thanks

This is an important and relevant lesson for all people of faith. When we experience God's gifts in our lives we are certainly required to thank Him. And we do. We are overcome by thankfulness and we express it. I believe that the vast majority of God fearing people do not neglect to thank God after feeling the divine hand assisting them in times of trouble. But do we take it to next level? Do we ask ourselves the question in this verse? *What can I give back to the Lord?* What responsibility do I have to God?

Why don't we go beyond thanks?

I believe that there are two reasons that we are lax in this regard. First, we know, as does our psalmist, that God needs nothing. We know that there is nothing lacking in Him, so we believe that there is nothing we can give Him. But does this fact exempt us from the sense of obligation expressed in this verse? Even if God does not lack anything, isn't there still a great value in *feeling that we ought to be repaying Him*; that we owe Him something and we want to give Him something if only there was something He needed?

Second, there is so much talk about how much God loves us and gives to us selflessly as a parent gives a child; how he asks for nothing in return; that we forget that *He does want something from us.*

God made it very clear what He wants from us. God wants us to live sanctified lives. He wants us to declare His name to the world. He wants us to serve Him and build His kingdom here on earth. He gave us clear instructions. God has told us these things in no uncertain terms. Our psalmist knows this *and we know it too*. The verses that follow show us exactly how to repay Him.

The message of this verse is simple and powerful. Yes we must feel grateful for God's kindness to us. We must thank Him. But there is something beyond thanks. God's blessings and salvation are meant to instill in us a feeling of indebtedness; to remind us of our obligations to Him. To serve Him by building His kingdom here on earth.

What can I give back to the Lord?; all that He has bestowed is upon me.

Beyond thanking God for the gifts in our lives we ought to see ourselves as indebted to God. We must continually ask ourselves, "What can I give back to the Lord?"

116:13 *Calling In God's Name*

*I will raise the cup of
salvations; and I will call out
in the name of the Lord.*

A toast is always public

To *raise a cup* is a sign of celebration. It is a symbol that is familiar to us as a practice that we still engage in today. We raise a cup. We make a toast. Drinking wine has always been a primary way that people celebrate. When we drink to celebrate, the drinking is about something. This is not merely a cup of wine. It is a *cup of salvations!*

Implicit in this image is that it is public. There is no reason to *raise a cup* if one is alone. This is what is meant by the second half of the verse *and I will call out the name of the Lord*. I will publicize Him. I will declare the greatness of His kindness to me; I will tell the story of my salvation.

Call out to God even after He helps

Beyond simply saying, "Let's celebrate!", in the context of this psalm there is a deeper meaning to this verse. Let's return to verses 3 and 4.

> The cords of death have encompassed me and the constrictions of the grave found me; suffering and anguish have I found. *And I call out the Name of the Lord*; "Please, Lord, deliver my soul."

And then a few verses after ours, in verse 17 we read:

> I will offer to You the sacrifice of thanksgiving, *And I will call out the name of the Lord.*

Exactly the same phrase appears three times in this psalm. The message is unmistakable. When I am scared and facing mortal danger *I call out the name of the Lord.* When I am saved, too, *I call out the name of the Lord.* I called on Him when I needed Him. I did not forget to call on Him after He helped me as well.

Calling IN God's name vs. Calling TO God

It is interesting to note that in the Hebrew the word *name* in these verses includes a prefix. The full word is BeSHEM.

SHEM	=	name
BeSHEM	=	in the name

The Be prefix in Hebrew means *in* or *with*. In fact, there are many instances in Scripture that refer to people calling out – BeSHEM – *in the name of the Lord*. The most notable person who calls out - BeSHEM – *in the name of the Lord* is Abraham. In Genesis 12:8, 13:4, and 21:33 *Abraham calls out in the name of the Lord.* He was not in trouble or danger of any kind in any of those situations. From context it is clear that all three instances refer to Abraham publicizing and spreading the name of God to those around him.

In fact, when calling out to God *in time of need* the Hebrew usually uses a different form. A few examples:

As for me, I call *to God*, and the Lord saves me (Psalm 55:17)

I cry out *to God* Most High, *to God*, who vindicates me (Psalm 57:3)

These verses as well as many others describe a plea to God in times of suffering and use the word EL meaning *to* rather than the prefix Be – *in*.

I'd like to suggest that, like Abraham, to call out *Be* – *in the name of God* describes the proclaiming of the greatness and glory of God. It does not refer to actually asking God to do anything. To call out *in* the name of the Lord is to advertise God's greatness to others. In contrast, calling out EL – *to God* is, simply put, a cry for help.

So what about verse 4 in our psalm? Why does it use the form BeSHEM – *in the name of the Lord*? Wasn't that a cry for help in time of trouble? Yes and no. Yes, the psalmist felt helpless and called out to God, *"Please, Lord, deliver my soul."* But look what followed that plea. There is no evidence that the perceived danger was removed or that his situation actually changed in any way. The verses that follow that plea are a theological contemplation by the psalmist of the condition of his suffering. He thinks about why a gracious and merciful God would allow this to happen. He comes to the conclusion that his difficult situation is itself a gift from God. In other words, his calling out the name of the Lord was really a calling out *in the name of the Lord*. In other words it was a declaration of faith more than a cry for help. It was a statement that he understood the great love that God has shown him, even when making him weak and helpless.

With this repetition of this exact phrase, *And I will call out the name of the Lord,* we see a direct link between verse 4, our verse, and verse 17.

4   And <u>I call out in the Name of the Lord</u>; "Please, Lord, deliver my
      soul."

13   I will raise the cup of salvations; and <u>I will call out in the name of the
      Lord</u>.

17   To You I shall offer a sacrifice of thanksgiving; and <u>I will call out in the
      name of the Lord</u>.

As a thread that links the beginning of the psalm to its end, this repetition poetically announces the theme of the entire Psalm 116. As I wrote at the end of my comments to verse 2:

> *In my days I call out* (v.2), whether I am experiencing difficulties or happy times the response is the same. *I call on the name of the Lord*.

All too often, devout believers in God who worship Him regularly and live life in relationship with Him think that a God centered life is supposed to be trouble free. True devotion to God does not mean automatic protection from all earthly suffering and an abundance of worldly blessings. True faith means that my life is not about me. *It is about Him.* God wants us to live lives of sanctification. He shows His love for us by helping us get there. Sometimes the best way for us to live more Godly lives is through God's tough love found in a painful dose of trials and tribulations.

Whatever God throws our way, in good times or in difficulty, *we call out in the name of the Lord.*

In both good times and difficult ones, we are called upon to continue what Abraham started in a world that did not know God. To call out in the name of the Lord.

116:14 *Keeping Our Vows*

---

*I will fulfill my vows to the
Lord; now in the presence
of all His people.*

One very common reaction that many people have when experiencing hardship is the taking of vows. We all do it. When we plead with the Lord to help us through a difficult test our prayers often include some commitment to God on our part. "Lord, if you help me through this I will…" Now, some people may be cynical about this kind of vow. I disagree with this cynicism for two reasons. First, vows of this nature are usually extremely personal expressions of our relationship to God; of what we feel we need to be doing. Second, as I will explain, they are critical to the process of transforming our suffering into a meaningful and productive spiritual experience.

Sanctifying moments of suffering

In my comments to the previous verse I wrote that we are called upon to live *sanctified lives*. What does this mean? Well, in the simplest terms, something is *sanctified* when it is elevated from a mundane neutral state to a state of holiness; i.e. it is dedicated for Godly purposes. The most common examples are found in the myriad rules and regulations regarding the Holy Tabernacle that we find in Exodus and Leviticus. Mundane objects such as gold, wood, and livestock became *sanctified* when dedicated for use in the temple service. Similarly, when we recognize that a moment is *sacred* or *sanctified*, what we mean is that we can perceive that the particular event or moment is about more than the mundane act or event. It is about something Godly; *something holy*.

To say that we are called upon to live sanctified lives means that it is our duty as people of faith to take every opportunity possible to realize the potential in each particular moment and experience in our lives for glorifying and publicizing God's name on earth. This is, of course, a very personal and individualized process. Each and every one of us has unique abilities and unique experiences in the unique context of our own life.

In my comments to verse 7 I wrote that it is not uncommon for people who are suffering to find that hardship reminds them of higher values that they may have been neglecting. The unfortunate reality is that in the regular course of our lives we sometimes need suffering to wake us out of the slumber that often results from comfort and stability. We allow our weaknesses and personal flaws to linger. When things are good we don't find ourselves turning to God with the same urgency and sincerity as when we feel helpless.

Vows = the value of our suffering

Nobody knows our failings better than we do. When we go through difficult times it is natural to contemplate the ways in which we have fallen short of our best; the unfinished business of making our lives as good and holy as they ought to be.

So, in times of trial and hardship, we make vows. We make vows not only as a way of bargaining with God, "If you save me, I'll do X for you." It is true that there is definitely something to be said for using our sense of indebtedness to God as incentive to live holier and greater lives. The first person to do this was Jacob. After securing the blessings from his father Isaac, Jacob left home to escape the wrath of his brother Esau. On the road for the first time and headed to a distant land alone, Jacob had his famous dream of the ladder with angels ascending and descending. In his dream God promised to protect him. Nevertheless, when Jacob awoke he made a vow.

> Then Jacob made a vow, saying, "If God will be with me and will watch over me on this journey I am taking and will give me food to eat and clothes to wear so that I return safely to my father's household, then the Lord will be my God; and this stone that I have set up as a pillar will be God's house, and of all that You give me I will give You a tenth." (Genesis 28:20-22)

The "If You get me through this I will do X for You" type of vow certainly has value and, as we see it has a Biblical precedent. At the same time, I believe that there is a deeper motivation in the vows we make at difficult points in our lives. In part we make vows because suffering brings our higher values into focus and we know that we owe it to God and to ourselves to be better.

This is how we sanctify our suffering. When we use the experience of suffering as a stimulus to live holier and more Godly lives, we have sanctified the experience; i.e. we have used it in the service of God.

Which brings us to our verse. The fulfillment of vows made during difficult times is not merely making good on a commitment so that we are true to our word. Following through on those introspective resolutions that we made when we needed God most is the way that we give *lasting meaning and value* to what we went through. This way we elevate even our worst moments in life to a higher sanctified purpose.

I will fulfill my vows to the Lord; now in the presence of all His people.

Note: for discussion of the second half of the verse *now in the presence of all His people* see my comments to verse 18 below.

The commitments that we make during times of crisis often serve to remind us of that which we were supposed to be doing all along. Fulfillment of these vows brings purpose to the difficult experiences that we endure.

116:15 *Being a Good Investment*

It is costly in the eyes of the Lord; the death of his pious ones.

Precious or Expensive

The Hebrew word YAKAR which I have translated as *costly* is usually translated as *precious*. Both are correct. YAKAR literally means *of great value. Precious, expensive, costly,* and *rare* are all legitimate translations of YAKAR and it appears in all of these uses throughout Scripture. In fact, the English word *precious* contains within it all of these meanings as well. The problem is that these connotations are very different. To say that something is *costly* can very different than to describe the same thing as *precious. Precious,* besides referring to actual price, brings with it a definitely positive association. To illustrate, nobody would describe a very expensive and badly needed repair to their car as *precious. Costly,* yes; *precious,* certainly not. Yet, in Hebrew YAKAR would be the word used for both.

Based on this, there are those who make the mistake of interpreting this verse as a statement that the Lord finds great positive value in the death of the pious. In other words, they take the word YAKAR to mean precious with all of its positive implications. The problem with this interpretation is twofold.

Context: Salvation from death

First, the context of the rest of this psalm does not support a positive understanding of the word YAKAR. The psalmist began by describing how he felt death and mortal danger closing in on him (v.3). He then cried out to the Lord (v.4). He realizes the great meaning inherent in his suffering and commits himself to celebrating God's salvation and promoting greater knowledge of God on earth (v. 5-11). He sees this reaction as incumbent upon him as a result of the divine rescue from death that he has experienced (v. 12-14). In the midst of the verses in which he is praising God and declaring his indebtedness to Him for saving his life, it would make no sense to state that God sees *preciousness;* i.e. *positive value,* in the deaths of pious people.

While there may be passages in Scripture which give appropriate context for a statement that God sees positive value in the deaths of the pious, *this is not one of them.* There are certainly numerous examples of righteous people who die the death of martyrs in the Bible. There are even mentions of such deaths in Psalms. However, this is neither the subject nor the thematic thrust of this psalm.

Broader Context: Psalm 72

The second reason that a positive interpretation of YAKAR as *precious* is problematic is based on another verse with very similar language right here in the Book of Psalms.

> He will take pity on the weak and the needy and save the needy from death. He will rescue them from oppression and violence, for *precious is their blood in His eyes.* (Psalm 72:13-14)

We see that the phrase *precious in the eyes of the Lord* in the context of rescue from death – precisely the context of our psalm as well – refers to God *guarding* those He wishes to save *from danger*. It does not refer to God looking favorably upon their deaths.

YAKAR = Expensive

Over two thirds of the thirty six times that the adjective YAKAR appears in the Bible it refers to either precious stones or actual wealth. In other words, *expensive*, rather than the emotionally positive *precious*, is actually the most commonly accurate translation of the word.

With the meaning of YAKAR more fully explained we can better understand the intent of our verse.

Being a good investment for God

As previously explained, the psalmist does not stop at being grateful that God has saved him from peril. He sees the fact that God saved him as a responsibility. He asks himself, "Why did God save me? What must I do to justify this kindness?" He realized that his debt to God must be repaid by becoming a vehicle for the increase in awareness and glory of God in the world.

Now in our verse, he deepens our understanding of why God saved him. In effect he is saying that so long as he is committed to living a Godly life he is a *good investment for God*. God has an incentive, so to speak, to keep him alive. To let him die would mean one less person publicizing God's name in the world; one less person promoting divine morality and faith. It would be *costly* for God's plan for the world for such a person to die.

The lesson for us is powerful and challenging. Each of us should ask ourselves, "Am I a good investment for God? Would it be *costly* for God to let me go?" We dare not forget that we are here to serve Him. By serving Him, doing His good works, and by spreading knowledge of Him we literally make ourselves *more valuable in the eyes of the Lord.*

It is costly in the eyes of the Lord; the death of his pious ones.

Ask yourself, "Am I a good investment for God?" As His servant, do I produce? Am I contributing to His kingdom?

116:16 *What is Freedom?*

> *Please, O Lord, for I am Your servant; I am Your servant, the son of Your maidservant. You have released my bonds.*

Is the psalmist a servant or is he free? The verse appears contradictory. First, *I am your servant.* Then immediately, *You have released my bonds.*

Tagore's Violin String

Rabindranath Tagore (1861-1941) was a Nobel Prize winning Bengali poet, artist, author. In one of his most profound poetic statements he gives us the answer to the riddle of our verse.

> I have on my table a violin string. It is free to move in any direction I like. If I twist one end, it responds; it is free.
> But it is not free to sing. So I take it and fix it into my violin. I bind it and when it is bound, it is free for the first time to sing.

What is *freedom*? Does *freedom* mean that I have no rules or responsibilities? Are wild animals free? Tagore's short poem responds to this common misconception. The formula is quite simple. That which limits me is servitude. That which allows me to fulfill my full potential; to soar to my highest heights is freedom. To do as I please and give in to any and every desire of the moment my look like freedom. It is the freedom of untamed nature. It is actually not freedom at all. It is submission and slavery to my basest urges; it shrinks my potential greatness. True freedom – higher freedom – is the freedom that comes specifically from submitting to a greater power; from being bound to a force that allows us to sing.

> *That which limits me is slavery.*
> *That which allows me to fulfill my full potential is freedom.*

The Freedom of Sinai

The greatest example of this is the Exodus from Egypt. The People of Israel were freed from slavery to Pharaoh; a slavery that suppressed them and did not allow them to fulfill their covenantal mission. A few weeks later they stood at Sinai and became servants of God, bound by a comprehensive set of rules and regulations about which they had no choice. They were slaves again. Only this time, their slavery meant freedom. *Freedom to sing*; freedom to fulfill their covenantal potential as *a kingdom of priests and a holy nation.*

Limitation = Slavery

In verse 3 the psalmist described the sense of hopelessness and fear that paralyzed him. Then, in verse 6 he referred to himself as *unwary*, which I explained as referring to carelessly giving in to the desires of the moment. Both the despair of verse 3 and the base impulsiveness of verse 6 are forms of *slavery*. Both are limitations on my best self. Both hold me back from fulfilling my potential as a being created in the image of God.

Our verse teaches us what freedom really means. In effect, what our verse is saying is:

Please, O Lord, for I am Your servant; - as a result of the fact that I am *your servant*; I am neither controlled by the fear and despair of worldly dangers nor am I a slave to my every momentary urge,

You have released my bonds. – I am truly free. In freeing myself of the earthly restrictions and limitations on my potential; *in choosing to serve You, I am now truly free.* I am now free to soar to the highest heights; by serving You I am free to be greater than I ever imagined.

The son of a maidservant

The son of a maidservant is a servant by birth. Referring to himself in this way, the psalmist takes the message even deeper. There is a fundamental psychological difference between someone born into slavery and one who was born free and made into a slave. One who was born free and became a slave is a slave against his will. His natural identity is not that of a servant. By contrast, for one born into slavery it is the only identity he has ever known.

By adding in the phrase *I am Your servant, the son of Your maidservant*, the psalmist is saying, "Lord, I realize not only the liberating transcendent value of servitude to You; I realize, too, that this is *my natural state of being*; that this was my purpose and my identity *from birth*. I embrace this servitude not as one forced into this against his will. Rather, I am as comfortable as Your servant as I am with my most natural identity; with my mother."

Can we say the same? Are we comfortable as God's servants? Do we embrace our servitude to Him as our natural state of being? Do we fully appreciate the *freedom to sing* that the Lord gives us when we serve only Him?

Perhaps this is the meaning of the strange use of the word *please* at the beginning of this verse. Every English translation ignores or changes this word. With our understanding of the verse it is a beautiful and heartfelt prayer. In effect, it is saying, "Please, Lord. I want to reach this point. I want to feel such comfort and ease in serving You that it feels as natural as my mother's embrace. I want to serve You. I want to be free."

Please, O Lord, for I am Your servant; I am Your servant, the son of Your maidservant. You have released my bonds.

Let us embrace the higher freedom that we achieve as we submit to the higher will of the Almighty. In this submission we feel the freedom that comes with doing what we were created to do.

116:17 *Sacrifice of Thanksgiving*

To You I shall offer a sacrifice of thanksgiving; and I will call out in the name of the Lord.

At this point in the psalm the reader is immediately struck by the phrase *and I will call out in the name of the Lord*. This is the third time in this Psalm that these exact words have appeared. The first was in verse 4 when the psalmist was describing his call to God in a state of suffering and hopelessness. More recently, these words were used in verse 13 when celebrating and praising God for his personal salvation. Then again here in verse 17 the phrase is repeated.

Here are the two verses side by side.

I will raise the cup of salvations; and I will call out in the name of the Lord. (v.13)

To You I shall offer a sacrifice of thanksgiving; and I will call out in the name of the Lord. (v.17)

What is the difference between these two types of worshipful celebration; *raise the cup of salvations* and *offer a sacrifice of thanksgiving*?

Context is Key

The key to understanding the messages of these two verses can be found in the context.

Here is a paraphrase of the five verses leading up to ours; verses 12 through 16:

- *How can I repay the Lord? I am so indebted to Him (12).*
- *I will publicly celebrate, call out His name (13),*
- *and fulfill my vows to Him (14).*
- *Wait a minute! If God saved me, I must be very valuable to Him. He must want something more from me (15).*
- *I must be completely subservient to Him. I must serve Him as a servant serves a master. Through serving Him I will fulfill my greatest potential (16).*

This is the immediate context of our verse.

I'd like to suggest that the difference between *raising a cup of salvations* and *offering a sacrifice of thanksgiving* is the difference between *praising God* and *serving God*. Of course, *praise* is a form of *worship*. But there is a difference.

The Cup vs. The Offering

Raising a cup is a celebration. It is a sign of joy. The sentiment that is expressed is one of thanks and praise to God for His great kindness and blessing. I believe that the fact that this verse is stated first indicates that it is a more instinctive and spontaneous form of thanks to the Lord. It should be noted that while libations of wine were poured in the temple as a component of sacrifices, no wine was ever consumed by anyone as any part of any temple service. In other words, this *raising of the cup* is decidedly *not* a form of *worship*.

A *thanksgiving sacrifice* is not a spontaneous act at all. In Leviticus 7 the thanksgiving sacrifice is described as follows:

> If one offers [a sacrifice] as an expression of thankfulness, then along with this thank offering they are to offer unleavened loaves made without yeast and with oil mixed in, unleavened

> loaves made without yeast and brushed with oil, and cakes
> of the finest flour well-kneaded and with oil mixed in. This
> offering, along with cakes of leavened bread he shall offer
> along with his thanksgiving ... The meat of their fellowship
> offering of thanksgiving must be eaten on the day it is offered;
> they must leave none of it till morning. (Leviticus 7:12-13,15)

A thanksgiving sacrifice in the temple was an animal, usually an ox or a sheep, and it included many loaves of bread and cakes. As the verses above state, the entirety of the offering had to be eaten in one day. Considering the amount of meat and bread involved in this offering, it would be very nearly impossible for any one person to consume this quantity of food in a single day. Clearly, this offering was meant to be shared. In fact, thanksgiving offerings in temple times were an occasion for the person bringing the offering to invite friends, relatives, and probably even perfect strangers to partake of the celebration. After all, it was forbidden to leave any meat left over until the next day. Anything that wasn't eaten would go to waste. As opposed to the more spontaneous *raising of a cup*, the thanksgiving offering was an event that required planning and involved a significant financial commitment.

Think about it. The thanksgiving sacrifice was designed to give a person who has experience God's benevolence the opportunity – and responsibility - to include others in the celebration. At the same time, it is not just a party. It is an offering to God slaughtered in the temple in Jerusalem. It is *worship*.

Spontaneity and Commitment

I believe that both types of thanks and praise are necessary when we have experienced God's hand in our lives. Each one is a different but equally profound and authentic expression of gratitude towards the Lord. The spontaneous impulse to cry out in thankfulness at the moment of salvation is powerful. We have all felt this at moments when we have been redeemed from our own personal suffering. We feel a surge of gratitude for God. We want to *raise our cup* and tell all who will listen about the great things God has done. The fact that this is our instinct is a beautiful sign of our faith and we would be remiss if we did not react this way.

Later, when the emotional surge subsides, we begin to reflect. We think about what we have been through. We take stock of our lives. We ask ourselves important questions. *Why did God save me? What does He want from me? Am I fulfilling my potential as His faithful servant?* With the benefit of perspective and some distance from the euphoria that we originally felt we now feel a new and different kind of gratitude. It is a gratitude that is intermingled with a broader sense of mission for our lives. The statement made by bringing a sacrifice of thanksgiving is powerful. It is a commitment, an investment, and an act of worship.

First *I will raise the cup of salvations; and I will call out in the name of the Lord.* I will channel the natural sudden surge of emotion at the moment of salvation towards God.

And then later I will not forget to take this gratitude with me; to bring it into my life. I will not only thank Him; *I will serve Him. And I will invite others into this commitment that I have made.*

I shall offer a sacrifice of thanksgiving; and I will call out in the name of the Lord.

After we experienced those sudden high moments when we are aware of the gifts of the Lord in our lives we must also express our gratitude through longer term commitment to serving Him. We must continue to thank Him by worshipping Him.

116:18 *All of God's People*

> *I will fulfill my vows to the*
> *Lord; now in the presence*
> *of all His people.*

This verse is an exact repetition of verse 14. Both verses appear right after the words *and I will call out in the name of the Lord.* Why the repetition? Is there a difference in meaning between them?

"Vows" not "Vow"

It is interesting to note that the word *vows* is plural. What particular *vows* did our psalmist make? Let's look carefully at the different verses that led up to verse 14 and our verse respectively.

What can I give back to the Lord? All that He has bestowed is upon me. (v.12)

I will raise the cup of salvations; and I will call out in the name of the Lord. (v.13)

In verse 12 he contemplates the fact that he must make a commitment to God. In verse 13 he makes that commitment. Notice that there are two vows in this verse.

- First vow: *I will raise the cup of salvations*
- Second vow: *I will call out in the name of the Lord.*

The first vow is a commitment to celebrate and publicly declare praise and thanksgiving to the Lord. The second vow, *and I will call out in the name of the Lord*, takes this further. As I explained in my comments to verse 13, to *call out in the name of the Lord* means to emulate Abraham in spreading knowledge of God to others who do not know of Him.

Two vows. First, to celebrate and praise God publicly for His kindness and salvation; then to spread more knowledge of Him to the world.

Verse 18, like verse 14, is preceded by a two vows.

To You I shall offer a sacrifice of thanksgiving; and I will call out in the name of the Lord.

- First vow: *To You I shall offer a sacrifice of thanksgiving*
- Second vow: *I will call out in the name of the Lord.*

In my comments to verse 17, I explained the profound difference between *raising a cup of salvations* and *offering a sacrifice of thanksgiving*. Briefly, the former describes a spontaneous outpouring of thanks and praise, the latter refers to an investment of both time and finances for worshipful service of God.

Two "Callings in the name of the Lord"

With this in mind, I would like to suggest that the *calling out in the name of the Lord* in verses 13 and 17 are not the same. While *calling out in the name of the Lord* certainly describes the spreading and publicizing of God's name in the world as Abraham did, there are different ways for this to be done.

In verse 13 the psalmist is excitedly and spontaneously spreading the word about the great kindness that God performed in his life. His *calling out in the name of the Lord* directly follows and is directly related to *raising the cup of salvations*. He is euphoric, elated, and thankful; and he is sharing this with others. He is telling the world about God's miracles in his life.

In verse 17 *calling out in the name of the Lord* is right after he brings a *sacrifice of thanksgiving*. Here, he is sharing the message of our obligation to serve God and worship Him. He is sharing the story of his salvation from suffering as a wake up call. He is spreading the message that God wants His servants to serve Him.

So, while verses 14 and 18 may appear identical, they are not. The vows to be fulfilled are actually quite different.

Who are "all of His people"?

These vows are to be fulfilled *in the presence of all His people*. The use of the word *all* is peculiar. Why doesn't the verse say *in the presence of His people*. What does the word *all* add?

If the verse refers to God's chosen people, the People of Israel, why use the word *all*? Now, you might think that I am nitpicking. But consider this: Israel is referred to as *God's people* – AMO in Hebrew - literally hundreds of times in Scripture. *This is the only time in the entire Bible* that the expression KOL AMO – *all of His people* is stated reference to God.

Out of the hundreds of references to *God's people*, this one is different. What does *all* add?

Zechariah chapter 2 describes the acceptance of God by all humanity at the End of Times.

> *Many nations* will be joined with the Lord in that day *and will become my people.* I will live among you and you will know that the Lord Almighty has sent me to you. The Lord will inherit Judah as His portion in the holy land and will again choose Jerusalem. Be still before the Lord, *all mankind*, because He has roused Himself from His holy dwelling. (Zechariah 2:15-17)

It should be noted that this passage in Zechariah is the only place in Scripture where nations other than Israel are called God's people. Everywhere else, *God's people* refers only to Israel.

I believe that the words *in the presence of all of His people* refer, quite simply, to *all* of God's people, not just Israel. After all, the Biblical vision is a universal one. The Nation of Israel is charged by God to spread knowledge of Him to all peoples. The end goal is shared faith in and worship of the One God, God of Abraham, Isaac, and Jacob; creator of heaven and earth.

The two verses of Psalm 117 that follow soon after this would support this assertion. There, all peoples and all nations are invited to join the praise and exaltation of God for all that He has done for Israel.

The psalmist thanks God and declares his vow to spread God's name to others as Abraham did before him. Abraham's mission was not about the People of Israel; it was about the entire world. The task of every person of faith has always been this, to fulfill our commitments to the Lord and to call out His name to all who are listening; *in the presence of all of His people.*

I will fulfill my vows to the Lord; now in the presence of all His people.

When we call out the name of the Lord in thanksgiving we must invite others to join us in our renewed commitments in response to what He has done for us.

116:19   *The House of Prayer for All*

In the courtyards of the house
of the Lord— in your midst,
Jerusalem. Praise the Lord.

The concluding verse of Psalm 116 is an incomplete sentence. Grammatically speaking, it is a continuation of the previous verse. Nevertheless, they are separated into two verses because they convey two distinct ideas. First, let's look at them together.

> (18) I will fulfill my vows to the Lord; now in the presence of all His people (19) in the courtyards of the house of the Lord— in your midst, Jerusalem. Praise the Lord.

As we can see, the two verses combine to form one complete sentence. The first verse says that the *thanksgiving offering* along with *calling out in the name of the Lord* of the previous verse is to be a public demonstration of praise and worship. Our verse tells us where this will take place. The holy temple in Jerusalem.

Why the courtyards?

Notice that the verse specifically states that the location of this thanksgiving offering and publicizing of the God's name is *in the courtyards of the house of the Lord*. This is because the courtyards were the only place in the temple area where non-priests could assemble. In other words, our verse does not primarily refer to the actual *sacrifice* of the thanksgiving offering. The sacrifice itself would happen inside the sanctuary where nobody but the priests would see it. Rather, our phrase refers to the large gathering of friends, family, and others assembled to eat the offering and hear the stories of praise and thanks to God for His kindness.

Why only Jerusalem?

Our verse is very specific in mentioning Jerusalem. At this point I'd like to raise a simple question for any Bible believing person. Why is it so important that this thanksgiving offering be offered in the temple in Jerusalem? Why can't it be offered on an altar anywhere one chooses? Why is there only one place for sacrificial offerings?

The answer to this question will teach us not only a general Biblical lesson, it will open our eyes to the specific spiritual journey described in the entire nineteen verses of Psalm 116.

Unified Temple = Unified People

In Exodus 25 God commanded Israel to build a Tabernacle.

> They shall build for me a sanctuary; and I will dwell among them.

The choice of words is precise. It does not say *I will dwell in it*. Rather, God declares that He will *dwell among them* – among the people – if they build a sanctuary for Him.

For God to dwell among His people there must be only one temple. Multiple places of worship inevitably lead a fracturing of the people into different sects. People are not all the same. They have different spiritual tastes, strengths, and weaknesses. It is only natural for people to seek a range of points of emphasis in their spiritual lives. The division of a religion into numerous denominations is the result of this natural tendency. Unfortunately, this division can very quickly create multiple identities and ultimately, the dissolution of the unity of the people. This point is emphasized over and over in Deuteronomy chapter 12.

But you are to seek *the place the Lord your God will choose* from among all your tribes to put His Name there for His dwelling. *To that place* you must go; there bring your burnt offerings and sacrifices, your tithes and special gifts, what you have vowed to give and your freewill offerings, and the firstborn of your herds and flocks. *There*, in the presence of the Lord your God, you and your families shall eat and shall rejoice in everything you have put your hand to, because the Lord your God has blessed you. (Deuteronomy 12:5-7)

And then a few verses later:

To the place the Lord your God will choose as a dwelling for His Name—*there* you are to bring everything I command you: your burnt offerings and sacrifices, your tithes and special gifts, and all the choice possessions you have vowed to the Lord. And *there* rejoice before the Lord your God—you, your sons and daughters, your male and female servants, and the Levites from your towns who have no allotment or inheritance of their own. *Be careful not to sacrifice your burnt offerings anywhere you please. Offer them only at the place the Lord will choose* in one of your tribes, and there observe everything I command you. (Deuteronomy 12:11-14)

One temple. One place to offer sacrifices.

It's not about me

But prevention of the breakup of the nation into different religious sects is not the only benefit of a single temple. There is an important message for the individual as well. You are not allowed to bring your thanksgiving offering to God in your own backyard. You must go to the one place that He has chosen for everyone. Simply put, your relationship to God, His blessings and salvation in your personal life, and your praise and worship of Him *are not about you.*

Now we can understand our psalm in its entirety.

Look back at the psalms of praise that came before ours. Psalms 113 through 115 are written entirely in the plural.

Who is like the Lord, *our* God... (113:5)

When *Israel* came out of Egypt... (114:1)

Not to *us*, O Lord, not to *us*... (115:1)

Then, in a sudden change, Psalm 116 is written *entirely in the singular*.

I love; because the Lord will hear *my* voice; *my* supplication (v.1);
for He has inclined His ear to *me*; and in *my* days *I* call out. (v.2)

In the early verses our psalmist reflects on the danger that he personally experienced and his thankfulness that the Lord heard his cries and saved him. Then, after verse 12 - *What can I give back to the Lord* – he begins to transform his feeling of gratitude into a sense of responsibility. He commits himself to involve others; to celebrate with others; to spread God's Name to the world. He realizes that when the Lord answered his cries and saved him from trouble *it wasn't about him at all*. God saved him so that he could serve the Lord by sharing and spreading the story of His glory. Ultimately, this transformation from individual prayer to collective concern is completed in the closing two verses.

I will fulfill my vows to the Lord; now in the presence of all His people in the courts of the house of the Lord— in your midst, Jerusalem. Praise the Lord. (v.18-19)

This is the message of Psalm 116 to each and every one of us. *It's not about me.* It's not about those in my immediate vicinity. It's not even about the here and now. God answers my personal prayers so that I can make my contribution to His kingdom over all humanity on this earth; to building His temple in Jerusalem.

> *Their burnt offerings and sacrifices will be accepted on my altar; for my house will be called a house of prayer for all nations. (Isaiah 56:7)*

Although there are many different spiritual tastes and inclinations, God wants his children to be unified in service of Him. He wants us to be together in the one House of Prayer for All Nations.

A final thought for Psalm 116

As I spend more and more time with Christians, as they tell me their personal stories they often describe what they call "A personal relationship with God." They tell stories of very personal, private encounters with the Lord.

When I noticed the recurrence of this phrase, it sounded strange to me. It's not that Judaism does not believe in a personal relationship with God. We certainly do. The countless lessons from my schooling about the importance of prayer inevitably described God as taking a personal interest in each and every individual. Similarly, I was taught that my sins are a personal private affront to Him. And yet, while the idea of a *personal relationship with God* was certainly discussed, it was never the center of religious identity.

For Jews and Judaism the emphasis is always on the collective; the People of Israel. All of our prayers are stated in the plural. "*We* sinned." "*We* love you." "Thank you for giving *us* your Torah." "Redeem *us* from the exile." "Heal *us*." The lines in our liturgy that are stated in the singular are so few and far between that they stand out as exceptions. This, together with the fact that the text has remained almost identical for almost 2000 years adds to this collective identity. I am praying in the plural *and* I am saying the same words that are said by Jews everywhere in all places and in all times going back centuries.

For Jews, it's always about *us*. Rarely is it about *me*.

And in my conversations with Christians I saw something different. Hearing stories and testimonies from my Christian friends I sensed an intimacy and immediacy in their feelings for God. The more I listened, the more I realized that the intensity of this personal connection was new to me. My relationship to God is much more about history, the covenantal prophecies, obedience to Torah law, and fixing the world to create God's kingdom on earth.

And while I have no doubt in my own faith that this is what God wants from me, I am continually inspired by the beauty and depth of the personal relationship to God that I see in my Christian friends. I have tried to learn from it. I have worked to incorporate more spontaneous words of prayer into my daily worship. I have worked to cultivate a greater awareness of God's hand in my own private affairs.

This is what I have learned most from the Christians that I have met; and my life as a Jew – as a servant of God – has been enriched more than I can measure.

But even though so much of Jewish faith and practice is based on and fosters a collective identity, that doesn't mean that it's easy to think outside myself as an individual.

While we are called upon to think beyond ourselves, - to think collectively - life is not lived and experienced by collectives; but by individuals. And individuals are concerned with, first and foremost, their own private needs.

How does one grow from the natural focus on private concerns to a broader feeling of shared mission for all of humanity? What is the road map for this process?

This is the journey of Psalm 116. Danger, fear, and gratitude are very private feelings. Times of personal hardship help us cultivate intense personal feelings of faith. Without that sense of intimacy; the knowledge that God cares for each and every one of us individually; we will never really have faith nor will we acknowledge God's hand in our lives. But here we are taught that when we do experience that intimacy with God in our personal lives we must ask ourselves, as the psalmist did, *what can I give back to the Lord?* (116:12) How can I transform my personal sense of gratitude into a public display of praise and worship for the glory of God?

After personally experiencing God's kindness, (116:1-11) the psalmist commits himself to repay the Lord by offering a *sacrifice of thanksgiving*, thereby publicly sharing his gratitude and declaring the praises of God to all. (116:12-19)

Then in the two verses of Psalm 117, he expands the scope of his public praise by inviting all the nations of the earth to join him.

The journey of Psalm 116 speaks to the very definition of our identities as people of faith.

This journey begins with personal private concerns and ends with a commitment to use the private experience – ones own gratitude for God's salvation - as a springboard for the broadest possible public display of collective praise of God. *Praise the Lord all nations; exalt Him all peoples!*

It is not about us. It is about God. Even the blessings and salvation of the Lord that we experience in our own private lives are not about us; they are not an end in and of themselves. Rather, they are intended to force us to ask, as the psalmist did, *What can I give back to the Lord?* (116:12) And the answer is always the same.

We repay the Lord for His blessings by sharing stories of His glory with others; by including them. We channel our personal relationship to God into the collective responsibility to build the Kingdom. All are invited; those near us and those farther away; with all peoples and all nations.

PSALM 117

WHERE EVERYTHING LEADS

As Psalm 116 came to a close, the psalmist declared his commitment to share his gratitude and praise of the Lord *in the courtyards of the house of the Lord* in Jerusalem. This was the culmination of his journey from personal private redemption to the broader vision and mission to build God's kingdom over all the earth.

With this newfound sense of purpose, the psalmist repeated his promise to fulfill his vows to the Lord *in the presence of all of His people* (verses 14 & 18). As I explained in my comments to verse 18, the word *all* is unique in Scripture when referring to God's people, calling upon us to depart from our standard understanding of *God's people*. *God's people* throughout the Bible refers to Israel alone. *All of His people* – a term used *only here* – must include something more.

The opening words of Psalm 117 provide the context for us to see who exactly was intended by this once-in-Scripture term. *Praise the Lord all nations. Exalt Him all peoples!*

With this call, the message of Psalm 116 reaches its peak. What began as a cry to the Lord in times of personal distress and despair culminates in the actualization of the most universal realization of God's kingdom. *All nations* and *all peoples* praising the Lord for the same reason *in the courtyards of the house of the Lord* in Jerusalem; in what Isaiah referred to as *the house of prayer for all nations.*

The second verse of Psalm 117 completes the idea – and the sentence – begun in verse 1. What is the context of this praise and exaltation? What are the *nations* and *peoples* of the earth reacting to?

As I mentioned in the introduction to this book, what is described in Psalm 117 is, historically speaking, as miraculous as any of the wonders of the Exodus from Egypt. Considering the historical relationship of the nations of the world to Israel, the idea that all the peoples of the earth would praise God for His abundant kindness to Israel was a literal impossibility up until very recent history.

Today, this vision is becoming a reality. Those among the nations who praise the Lord for His kindnesses to Israel grow in number by the day. Words that seemed so impossible are increasingly part of our current reality. As verse 2 of our psalm states so succinctly, *His kindness has overwhelmed us.*

Psalm 117

הַלְלוּ אֶת יְהוָה כָּל גּוֹיִם;
שַׁבְּחוּהוּ, כָּל הָאֻמִּים.

א

1. *Praise the Lord all nations;*
   exalt Him all peoples

כִּי גָבַר עָלֵינוּ חַסְדּוֹ וֶאֱמֶת יְהוָה לְעוֹלָם:
הַלְלוּיָהּ

ב

2. *For His kindness has been*
   great upon us; and the truth of
   the Lord is forever, Hallelujah.

117:1 *Nations and Peoples*

Praise the Lord all nations;
exalt Him all peoples

What is the difference between a *nation* and a *people*? Why is *praise* associated with one and *exalt* with the other?

GOYIM vs. UMIM

The two Hebrew words used here are GOYIM – *nations* – and UMIM – *peoples*. They are almost exact synonyms. However, based on careful attention to precise usages and context of each word throughout the Bible, the ancient Hebrew linguists explain the difference between them as follows.

GOYIM refers to nations as they are identified either in terms of race and lineage or in terms of land. To illustrate this nuance, the word GOYIM is used in the phrase "nations of *the land*" – eleven times in Scripture.

The second word, UMIM – sometimes appearing as LE'UMIM – implies a people bound together not by lineage or geography, but rather by ideology or leadership. This word never appears as connected to land or tribe.

GOYIM - *nations*	**UMIM - *peoples***
United by race, ethnicity, lineage, land	United by values, ideas, faith, leadership

This psalm, the shortest in the book of Psalms, calls upon all the nations of the world to praise and exalt God for the kindnesses that He has bestowed upon His people. This context and the exact wording – GOYIM and UMIM – remind us of another verse in Psalms that presents what appears to be the mirror image of our verse.

Psalm 2 – the opposite of 117

> Why are the *nations* – GOYIM - agitated; and the *peoples* – LE'UMIM - utter vain things? The kings of the earth rise up and the rulers band together against the Lord and against His anointed. (Psalm 2:1-2)

Psalm 2, like Psalm 117 describes a reaction of the nations to God's plan for history. In Psalm 2 the nations and peoples are opposed to God's plan. In Psalm 117 they exalt and praise Him for it.

The two reactions of the nations to God's plan
Psalm 2 – Against God
Why are the nations – GOYIM - agitated;
and the peoples – LE'UMIM - utter vain things?

Psalm 117 – With God

Praise the Lord all nations – GOYIM.
Exalt Him all peoples – UMIM.

With our better knowledge of the precise meanings of GOYIM and UMIM we can understand what these verses are trying to teach us.

As I mentioned, GOYIM are *nations,* as in *nationalities.* The word does not imply anything about what they believe. They are simply peoples of various nationalities and ethnicities who are witnessing what is happening in history. In Psalm 2 they do not like what they see; they are *agitated.* They work to fight against the direction that God has chosen. They are not motivated by faith or ideology. They are GOYIM – *nations; races.* In this context, they are motivated by their own nationalistic identities. Their own sense of nationalism can not tolerate seeing God's blessings upon someone else. They reject the idea that God has chosen any one nation as His people.

LE'UMIM / UMIM are bound together not by race but by values or faith. Their opposition to God's plan in Psalm 2 stems from the fact that it contradicts *their belief system. They utter vain things.* In other words, they profess faith in a plan for the world and a set of values that are false. When God moves events on this earth in a direction that doesn't fit their beliefs their response is to *utter vain things.* The events that contradict their ideology or theology are explained away so as not to disrupt their preconceived notions of how things are supposed to turn out. They do battle with God differently than the nationalistic GOYIM who are agitated and take action against God's plan. The UMIM don't take action, per se. They *utter vain things;* they stubbornly twist the meaning of what God is doing to fit their own ideas of what ought to happen.

Now look again at Psalm 2 verses 1 and 2.

Why are the nations – GOYIM - agitated; and the peoples – LE'UMIM - utter vain things? The kings of the earth rise up and the rulers band together *against the Lord* and *against His anointed*. (Psalm 2:1-2)

The verses are written as couplets. Let's line them up to see the parallel structure of the phrases.

	A	B
Psalm 2 verse 1:	*Nations agitated.*	*Peoples utter vain things.*
Psalm 2 verse 2:	*Against the Lord*	*against His anointed.*

Motivated not by faith but by self-centered nationalism the *nations* don't accept that there is a Divine plan. They deny the concept of God's control of history altogether. They are *agitated against the Lord*.

The *peoples*, on the other hand, think of themselves as people of faith. They claim to believe in God. The problem with their faith is that they have their own ideas about how God is supposed to act. They refuse to accept that they may not know God's plan; that they may not have it right. In the face of God's salvation of His chosen people they do not deny that God has a plan; but they deny that the plan is happening when it doesn't fit their own vain erroneous ideas. They do not *utter vain things against the Lord*. They profess faith in the Lord. Rather, they *utter vain things against His anointed*.

Praise vs. Exalt

Now that we have seen the reaction of those who are opposed to or in denial of God's plan, let's return to Psalm 117.

Praise the Lord all nations; *exalt* Him all peoples

Psalm 117 describes the reactions of both groups to the abundant kindness that He has bestowed upon His people.

Praise implies acceptance and awareness of greatness. This is obvious. If someone is praising God, it must mean that he believes in Him.

The Hebrew word root for *exalt* in our verse is ShaBeCh. This word also means *to raise in value*. To say that something has value means that it matters; that it has an effect. Simply put, *it is worth something*. In other words, *to praise* is to acknowledge greatness that I have witnessed, *to exalt* implies that this greatness has meaning for me; *that I value it beyond the experience of seeing it*.

Praise = expresses awareness of greatness
Exalt = expresses that one values greatness

My point is that while *praise* and *exalt* are synonyms, the connotations are different. This difference is in terms of the extent of the integration of the experience. I am arguing that *Exalt* is more integrated and more personal than *praise*.

Psalm 117 describes the universal reaction when witnessing that God has done great things for His chosen people.

Praise the Lord all GOYIM

First, they will set aside their nationalistic self interest and in exchange they will embrace and rejoice in the fulfillment of God's promises to His people. The natural reaction to the witnessing of greatness is to open one's mouth and *praise* what one has seen. Praise can be done by one who is impressed by what he sees even if it has no other effect on him.

Exalt Him all UMIM

For those who have faith in God the experience is more integrated and more personal. For those who never doubted that God has a plan, the actualization of the plan does not cause them to believe. They already believed. They certainly join in *praising* Him; but they praised Him as well even before He revealed His miraculous plan. For people of faith when God's plan is revealed it has a deeper effect. They already believed. They already praised. But now He is something more.

As Job declared after God spoke to him,

My ears had heard of you; but now my eyes have seen you. (Job 42:5)

Even for those of us who have faith in God, no matter how certain we are in His promises, we long to see more of Him. We yearn for the actualization of His Divine plan so that we can see it with our own eyes. We should not feel ashamed to say that even though we have perfect faith in Him, it will mean so much more when we actually see it. It is not a flaw in our faith that we know that seeing is more powerful than believing. The fact is that when we see the fulfillment of God's promises our faith is transformed. When we open our eyes and see with our eyes that which we had only heard or read about, we move beyond *praise; we exalt*. God becomes *even more* to us because of what He has done.

We must be humble as we witness God's plan unfolding. We must embrace it even if it is not what we expected it to be. We must internalize the greatness of what we are living through. We must exalt Him and value the effect that God's plan has on our lives.

117:2 *His Kindness and His Truth*

For His kindness has overwhelmed us; and the truth of the Lord is forever, Hallelujah.

After calling upon all *nations* and *peoples* to *praise* and *exalt* the Lord, our verse tells us *why*. Two distinct reasons are given:

1. *For His kindness has overwhelmed us;*
2. *and the truth of the Lord is forever*

The Hebrew words HeSeD - *kindness* and EMeT - *truth* used here are the same as appeared in Psalm 115 verse 1. As I explained in my comments there,

> HeSeD – kindness is not merely kindness in the sense of politeness. The word always implies something that is *given*. Specifically, something that is not even earned or deserved. If I work and get paid my agreed upon wage we would not call that *kindness*. If I receive a nice tip over and above my salary, - something not necessarily earned or deserved – it would be an expression of *kindness*.

This is a very significant point when the topic is God's redemption of Israel, His chosen people. For centuries there have been nay-sayers who have claimed that God's covenant with Israel was broken due to their sins. In other words, God would not fulfill the many prophecies of redemption of Israel in the future because Israel was no longer deserving of this redemption. Although the covenant is referred to as an everlasting covenant many times in Scripture, their response to this was that even so, it is conditional. It must be deserved.

But it is not only the word HeSeD – *kindness* – in our verse that makes this important point. There is a peculiar word choice that points in this direction as well.

First, I should point out that my translation differs from what you will generally find for this verse. A more common translation is *His kindness has been abundant upon us* or *His kindness has been great upon us*. My choice, *His kindness has overwhelmed us*, is based on the following.

For this analysis let's begin with the more conventional translation of GAVAR.

This phrase in Hebrew is made up of three words:

GaVaR ALEINU HaSDo – *His kindness was great upon us.*

GaVaR	=	*was great*
ALEINU	=	*upon us*
HaSDo	=	*His kindness*

The verb root GaVaR appears twenty-five times in Scripture. It variously means *to grow, to become powerful*, and *to become abundant*. Of the twenty-five, there are only five instances where this verb appears together with the word AL – *upon*, as it does in our verse - GaVaR <u>AL</u>EINU. Two of these five, our verse and Psalm 103 verse 11 are identical in meaning, referring to the bestowing of God's kindness on His people. Here are the other three. The English for GaVaR AL is italicized.

> Your father's blessings *are greater than* the blessings of the ancient mountains; than the bounty of the age-old hills. Let all these rest on the head of Joseph, on the brow of the prince among his brothers. (Genesis 49:26)

> The messenger said to David, "The men *overpowered us* and came out against us in the open, but we drove them back to the entrance of the city gate." (II Samuel 11:23)

> The Lord shall go forth like a mighty man; He shall stir up zeal like a man of war. He shall cry out, yes, shout aloud; *over His enemies He shall prevail*. (Isaiah 42:13)

In all of these verses the meaning of GaVaR AL – is not merely *to be great*. Rather, it means *to be greater than*, or, more precisely, *to overcome* or *to overwhelm*.

In the context of God's everlasting promise to redeem Israel, specifically with reference to the nations of the world recognizing the fulfillment of these promises, this precise wording carries a powerful message.

Israel may have sinned. For their sins the Temple in Jerusalem was destroyed and they were sent into exile. If their redemption was, in fact, dependent upon their merit it is quite possible that they would not be worthy of God's miracles. *But the redemption of Israel is not dependent on merit*. It does not have to be earned. It is HeSeD – *kindness*. And lest anyone dare to think that the transgressions or imperfections of Israel stand in the way of God's kindness, our psalm responds. No! God's everlasting promises to redeem Israel and to restore them to their land *are more powerful* than any misdeeds that Israel may have committed.

GaVaR ALEINU HaSDo – *His kindness is greater than us!* His unconditional love for Israel is *more powerful* than anything they may have done.

Having made the point that God's promises of kindness to His people are more powerful than anything they may have done, the psalmist takes it a step further.

And the truth of the Lord is forever

God's plan does not change. He does not change course. He does not break His promises. As the prophet Samuel said,

> The Eternal One of Israel does not lie or change His mind; for
> He is not a human who changes His will. (I Samuel 15:29)

In other words, the idea that God changed His mind suggests an imperfection in Him. Such a belief is actually a grave theological error. To believe that God's will is open to change questions the eternal nature of God's truth.

There is an inclination by many people of faith to attempt to figure out God's plan for history. It is understandable. People who believe in God yearn to see Him working in the world. They seek evidence of His hand in world events. But there is a dangerous downside to this. Often, when theologians and other people of faith think that they have figured out how things are supposed to play out, they hold stubbornly to their assumptions even when actual events call them into question. This is a grave mistake that can blind us to what God is actually doing. It behooves us to remind ourselves that God's plan is not known to us. Yes, we have hints from Scripture, but what those hints actually mean is known only to Him. And so our verse ends appropriately with the word Hallelujah – *Praise YaH*. As I explained in my comments on verse 115:18:

The name YaH or YH is the *future* part of God's name. In other words, it represents God's will; *His plan before we see it*. That's what all of existence and all of history is before it happens. It is part of God's will and plan.

God's will is unknown to us. It is not for us to figure it out or to arrogantly decide in advance how He is supposed to carry out His plan. It is for us to marvel as it unfolds and to praise Him when we see it.
  Hallelu – Yah!

A final thought for Psalm 117

In the introduction to this book as well as in the introduction to this psalm I made reference to the present day phenomenon of Christian support for Israel. I truly believe that Christian Zionism is as obvious a sign of the beginning of the redemption of Israel as are the ingathering of millions of Jews to the land of Israel and the existence of the State of Israel itself. And if you have read this far into this book, chances are that you see things more or less the way that I do. But there are many people who don't share this perspective.

In the Jewish community there are still many who are wary of Christian friendship and support. Many Jews are suspicious of an ulterior motivation to convert Jews to Christianity that they fear underlies this political partnership. Others who may not share this fear are still ambivalent about the growth of Christian Zionism as they just don't see it as relevant to the Jewish story of exile and redemption.

When I speak to Jewish audiences about my work in Jewish-Christian bridge building, I always point them to the many chapters in the Bible that speak of members of the nations of the world who will join us in the era of the ingathering of the exiles. Zephaniah 3, Zechariah 8, and Isaiah 2 are a few examples. I ask them a simple question: If you believe that the step by step process of God's redemption of Israel is underway; if you believe that we are living in the times foretold in Deuteronomy 30 when we will be ingathered after a long exile; then how about this other critical piece of the story? How about the repeated prophecies of the nations and peoples of the earth joining us? Doesn't that process happen step by step as well? Do we embrace and celebrate the beginning steps of our own ingathering? Shouldn't we equally celebrate the beginning of the redemption of the nations?

And what about the purpose of Israel? From Abraham being called to bring blessings to all the families of the earth to the call at Sinai to be a kingdom of priests, isn't the entire purpose of Israel to bring the whole world into relationship with God?

Israel's mission is a universal one. The Jewish people were told at Sinai that their job is to teach the entire world about God. This statement of purpose was reiterated by Moses over and over again throughout the book of Deuteronomy. It was restated by many of the prophets who followed. But the task must have seemed impossible. At the time that Israel was told this, almost nobody knew anything other than ancient pagan beliefs. To be a kingdom of priests would mean living a life of separateness and ridicule. And how would the idea of the Lord, our God be spread to all the families of the earth?

In the course of our history this universal mission was pushed to the background and largely forgotten. The Jewish people were not in a position to teach anyone about anything. Persecuted and reviled, we spent most of the last few thousand years just trying to survive and pass the baton to the next generation. The task of teaching the rest of the world about God – of being a light unto the nations – was not on the agenda. So Jews forgot who we are and what we are on this earth to do. How do you influence the world if nobody cares what you have to say?

But times have changed. The long awaited return to our home-land brought about a return to center stage for the people of Israel. But more importantly, there are millions among the nations who are paying close attention to what we have to say. While Jews were in exile and trying to survive, another development was underway. Christianity was spreading across the globe. Stories of Abraham, Isaac, and Jacob. The words of Isaiah, Jeremiah, and Ezekiel. The Psalms of David. All of the core values and ideas of Israel were being spread to the most distant corners of the earth. Neither Jews nor Christians realized that they were partners in God's plan all along.

The ironies of history can be stunning. For most of this history Christianity held firmly to anti Jewish theological positions. The results were often horrific. But without the spread of this very same Christianity throughout the millennia, the mission of Israel to bring revelation of God to all nations would be a much more distant possibility today. Simply put, without widespread faith in the words of Deuteronomy, Isaiah, and Zechariah, there would be no recognition by millions of non-Jews that the modern State of Israel is the beginning of the fulfillment of God's long awaited plan for the world.

Without Christianity, the fulfillment of Psalm 117 would be as impossible today as it was when it was written. It is the shared faith in the living word of God in the Bible that allows Jew and Christian alike to see the hand of God in modern Jewish history.

Among Christians there are many as well who still deny the abundant kindness that God has bestowed upon Israel. They cling to outdated Augustinian ideas about Israel having been replaced and rejected. For centuries, the primary evidence for this position was the seemingly perpetual exile of the Jews. The idea was simple. The promises of return would never be fulfilled and the covenant was no longer in force. To this claim, Jews – and a minority in Christianity that rejected this replacement theology – claimed that the promises of Deuteronomy 30 were still in force and destined to be carried out.

But what is the argument now, in our times, when millions of Jews have been ingathered to our land and been made *more prosperous and more numerous than our ancestors* (Deut. 30:5)? In the face of historical developments that contradict their theology, they opt for a *denial of reality* rather then question a point of theology that has no direct basis in Scripture – even in their own Christian books. After all, how can any Bible believing person claim that

God's covenant with Israel is no longer in force in light of the modern State of Israel? It is as though they believe that God is bound by their theology!

Think about it this way. Originally, the claim that God's covenant with the Jews was no longer binding was *proven* by the reality on the ground that the Jews were in a seemingly endless exile. Now that the exile is ending, the proponents of this theology reject the reality on the ground because it contradicts the theology. But the basis for the theology was the fact of the exile! Now the theology must be upheld despite the end of the exile!? This is circular logic in the extreme.

In my opinion, the rejection by Christian Zionists of long standing mainstream doctrines of Christianity displays both courage and humility. Courage; because they expose themselves to criticism from other Christians who see them as compromising their Christian faith. Humility; because they enthusiastically embrace a theology that places a people other than themselves at the center of the Biblical narrative of redemption. As a rabbi who has had the privilege of getting to know these Christian communities, my gratitude to them is boundless.

Psalm 115 had the nations mocking and rhetorically asking, "Where now is their god?" This taunt echoes the centuries of people who short-sightedly looked at the condition of the people of Israel and were certain that God was not with them. Such people are still out there. But more and more, it is not the nations of Psalm 115 but the nations of Psalm 117 who are growing in number and joining with God and His people.

Yes, it's true. It's happening. What seemed impossible a few generations ago is increasingly the world in which we live. As our psalm concludes, *the truth of the Lord is <u>forever</u>* – the short term view of Jewish history will always deceive. *The truth of the Lord* is to be found in the long term course of God's plan. *Hallelu-Yah!*

PSALM 118

GATHERED AT THE FEAST

Psalm 118 begins and ends with the same verse. These "bookends" explicitly state the theme of the psalm. *Give thanks to the Lord*. This is a shift in theme. From the opening words of Psalm 113 at the very beginning of our series– *Praise the Lord* – all the way through to the closing words of Psalm 117, *Halleluyah*, the theme has been praise. Now, in Psalm 118, the word *praise* does not appear even once. In its place, the word *thanks* has taken over as the thread linking all the verses together.

Despite this departure, Psalm 118 does not stand alone in the Hallel series. On the contrary, this psalm serves to connect all of the previous themes together. From God's total mastery of human affairs (113), to the miraculous providence over Israel (114), to the mission to defeat false beliefs (115), to the journey from private faith to universal mission (116 and 117), Psalm 118 brings the entire series into focus as a single discourse.

The imagery is similar to that of Psalm 116. An individual is telling his story of suffering and redemption. However, unlike Psalm 116, this psalm uses the individual language to describe the experience of the entire collective of Israel. It is as though God's people are all one single person.

Figuratively, we are present at the feast of thanksgiving that was promised in 116:17. We have been invited to hear the tale of redemption, to give glory to the Lord, and to renew our own commitments to do our part in the building of His kingdom.

Gratitude to the Lord is the theme and message of Psalm 118. It is through this gate that all who enter into a right relationship with Him must enter. On the foundation of this personal gratitude and sense of debt to the Lord, a sense of collective responsibility for God's kingdom is built.

Although the psalmist, Israel personified, has graduated to a broader mission beyond the personal, the psalm closes with a reminder to hold dear to and nurture the intimacy of that private relationship with the Lord even as one works towards a universal mission.

Psalm 118

א	הוֹדוּ לַיהוָה כִּי טוֹב: כִּי לְעוֹלָם חַסְדּוֹ.	1. *Give thanks to the Lord for He is good; for His kindness is eternal.*
ב	יֹאמַר נָא יִשְׂרָאֵל: כִּי לְעוֹלָם חַסְדּוֹ.	2. *Say, now, O Israel; for His kindness is eternal.*
ג	יֹאמְרוּ נָא בֵית-אַהֲרֹן: כִּי לְעוֹלָם חַסְדּוֹ.	3. *Say, now, O house of Aaron; for His kindness is eternal.*
ד	יֹאמְרוּ נָא יִרְאֵי יְהוָה: כִּי לְעוֹלָם חַסְדּוֹ.	4. *Say, now, O fearers of the Lord; for His kindness is eternal.*
ה	מִן הַמֵּצַר, קָרָאתִי יָּהּ; עָנָנִי בַמֶּרְחָב יָהּ.	5. *From the narrow place I called out "Lord" [Yah]; He answered me with the wide open space; Lord [Yah].*
ו	יְהוָה לִי, לֹא אִירָא; מַה יַּעֲשֶׂה לִי אָדָם.	6. *The Lord is for me, I will not fear; what can man do to me?*
ז	יְהוָה לִי בְּעֹזְרָי; וַאֲנִי אֶרְאֶה בְשֹׂנְאָי.	7. *The Lord is for me in those who help me; and I will perceive my enemies.*
ח	טוֹב לַחֲסוֹת בַּיהוָה מִבְּטֹחַ בָּאָדָם.	8. *It is better to take refuge in the Lord than to trust in humanity.*
ט	טוֹב לַחֲסוֹת בַּיהוָה מִבְּטֹחַ בִּנְדִיבִים.	9. *It is better to take refuge in the Lord than to trust in nobles.*
י	כָּל גּוֹיִם סְבָבוּנִי; בְּשֵׁם יְהוָה כִּי אֲמִילַם.	10. *All nations surrounded me; it was in the name of the Lord that I cut them down.*

סַבּוּנִי גַם סְבָבוּנִי; בְּשֵׁם יְהוָה כִּי אֲמִילַם.	יא	11. *They encircled me - indeed they surrounded me; it was in the name of the Lord that I cut them down.*
סַבּוּנִי כִדְבוֹרִים דֹּעֲכוּ כְּאֵשׁ קוֹצִים; בְּשֵׁם יְהוָה כִּי אֲמִילַם.	יב	12. *They encircled me like bees; they were extinguished like the fire of thorns; it was in the name of the Lord that I cut them down.*
דַּחֹה דְחִיתַנִי לִנְפֹּל; וַיהוָה עֲזָרָנִי.	יג	13. *You have surely pushed me to the point of falling; but the Lord has assisted me.*
עָזִּי וְזִמְרָת יָהּ; וַיְהִי לִי לִישׁוּעָה.	יד	14. *My bold strength and the song of praise of the Lord; for me was a salvation.*
קוֹל רִנָּה וִישׁוּעָה בְּאָהֳלֵי צַדִּיקִים; יְמִין יְהוָה עֹשָׂה חָיִל.	טו	15. *There is a voice of joyful sing-ing and salvation in the tents of the righteous; the right hand of the Lord acts valiantly.*
יְמִין יְהוָה רוֹמֵמָה; יְמִין יְהוָה עֹשָׂה חָיִל.	טז	16. *The right hand of the Lord is most high; the right hand of the Lord acts valiantly.*
לֹא אָמוּת כִּי אֶחְיֶה; וַאֲסַפֵּר מַעֲשֵׂי יָהּ.	יז	17. *I will not die for I shall live and I will recount the acts of the Lord.*
יַסֹּר יִסְּרַנִּי יָּהּ; וְלַמָּוֶת, לֹא נְתָנָנִי.	יח	18. *The Lord has surely chastised me; and to death He has not delivered me.*
פִּתְחוּ לִי שַׁעֲרֵי צֶדֶק; אָבֹא בָם אוֹדֶה יָהּ.	יט	19. *Open for me the gates of righ-teousness. I will enter them; I will thank the Lord.*
זֶה הַשַּׁעַר לַיהוָה; צַדִּיקִים יָבֹאוּ בוֹ.	כ	20. *This is the gate to the Lord; the righteous will enter it.*

כא אוֹדְךָ כִּי עֲנִיתָנִי; וַתְּהִי
לִי לִישׁוּעָה.

21. *I will thank You for You have
made me suffer; and for me You
were a salvation.*

כב אֶבֶן מָאֲסוּ הַבּוֹנִים הָיְתָה
לְרֹאשׁ פִּנָּה.

22. *The stone despised by the
builders has become the chief
cornerstone.*

כג מֵאֵת יְהֹוָה הָיְתָה זֹּאת;
הִיא נִפְלָאת בְּעֵינֵינוּ.

23. *This has emerged from the
Lord; it is wondrous in our
eyes.*

כד זֶה הַיּוֹם עָשָׂה יְהֹוָה;
נָגִילָה וְנִשְׂמְחָה בוֹ.

24. *This is the day that the Lord
has made; we will rejoice and
delight in it.*

כה אָנָּא יְהֹוָה, הוֹשִׁיעָה נָּא;
אָנָּא יְהֹוָה, הַצְלִיחָה נָּא.

25. *Please, O Lord, please save;
Please, O Lord, please bring
success.*

כו בָּרוּךְ הַבָּא בְּשֵׁם יְהֹוָה;
בֵּרַכְנוּכֶם מִבֵּית יְהֹוָה.

26. *Blessed is the one who comes
in the name of the Lord; we
have blessed you from the
house of the Lord.*

כז אֵל יְהֹוָה וַיָּאֶר לָנוּ:
אִסְרוּ חַג בַּעֲבֹתִים עַד קַרְנוֹת
הַמִּזְבֵּחַ.

27. *The Lord is All-powerful God
and He has given us light; bind
the festive offering with cords
unto the corners of the altar.*

כח אֵלִי אַתָּה וְאוֹדֶךָּ; אֱלֹהַי
אֲרוֹמְמֶךָּ.

28. *You are my All-powerful God
and I will thank you; my God,
and I will exalt You.*

כט הוֹדוּ לַיהֹוָה כִּי טוֹב: כִּי
לְעוֹלָם חַסְדּוֹ.

29. *Give thanks to the Lord for
He is good; for His kindness is
eternal.*

118:1-4 *For His Kindness is Eternal*

*Give thanks to the Lord for He is
good; for His kindness is eternal.
Say, now, O Israel; for His
kindness is eternal.
Say, now, O house of Aaron; for
His kindness is eternal.
Say, now, O fearers of the Lord;
for His kindness is eternal.*

At first glance the first four verses of this psalm seem out of place. Immediately following these verses, the psalm continues with an individual story of hardship, prayer, rescue, and worship. The personal singular language in the remainder of this psalm reminds us of Psalm 116.

But look at these four verses. The mention here of the *collective groups - Israel*, the *house of Aaron*, and the *fearers of the Lord*, appears to have no connection to the rest of the psalm.

Problem #1
Why does Psalm 118 mention <u>Israel</u>, <u>the House of Aaron</u>, and the <u>fearers of the Lord</u> before telling a personal story about an individual?

What's more, these verses seem much more relevant to Psalm 115 than to Psalm 118. Recall that verses 9 through 13 of Psalm 115 introduced these specific groups in this exact order.

Israel, trust in the Lord; He is their helper and their shield.
House of Aaron, trust in the Lord; He is their helper and their shield.
Fearers of the Lord trust in the Lord; He is their helper and their shield.
The Lord who remembered us will bless; He will bless the house of *Israel*; He will bless the *house of Aaron*.
He will bless the *fearers of the Lord*; the young with the old. (115:9-13)

The close connection between these verses in 115 and the opening four verses of our psalm is clear. Obviously, if these two psalms – 115 and 118 - were consecutive we would not have seen anything amiss. But they aren't. Psalms 116 and 117 interrupt them.

Problem #2
The opening four verses of Psalm 118 appear more connected to Psalm 115 than to Psalm 116, 117 which come right before it.

To sum up the problem: The first four verses of Psalm 118 seem out of place for two reasons.

- First, they don't appear to have anything to do rest of the verses of the psalm.
- Secondly, they are clearly more connected to Psalm 115 which is separated from them by Psalms 116 and 117.

As I discussed at length in the commentary to Psalm 116, that psalm stands in dramatic contrast to the psalms that precede it. Whereas Psalms 113 through 115 clearly spoke in the *plural* voice of the entire collective, - *Who is like our God;… Not to us;* etc. - Psalm 116 is written in the *singular* and vividly describes an *individual* experience of personal suffering, salvation, and praise.

> *I* love; because the Lord will hear *my* voice; *my* supplication.
> For He has inclined His ear to *me*; and in *my* days *I* call out.
> The cords of death have encompassed *me* and the constrictions
> of the grave found *me*; suffering and anguish have *I* found.
> (116:1-3)

With careful observation we will discover that, of course, the first four verses of Psalm 118 are not out of place at all. When we gain a better understanding we will see that they actually are the key to understanding how all four psalms, 115, 116, 117, and 118 are connected. By drawing us back to the language of Psalm 115 right at the beginning of Psalm 118, these verses alert us to the fact that all of these psalms are linked. Rather than confusing us, these verses reveal *the deeper meaning of the entirety of these four psalms together*.

Are you confused? Let's sum up.

- Psalm 115 is about the collective mission of God's people to defeat idolatry and spread knowledge of God.
- In describing this mission, Psalm 115 twice refers to the three groups: *Israel, House of Aaron, and fearers of the Lord*.
- Psalm 116 is about how an individual moves from his own personal relationship with God into the responsibility to spread God's glory to others.
- Psalm 117 describes of all nations and all peoples joining in praise of God.
- Psalm 118 will retell the personal story of Psalm 116…. But….
- … Psalm 118 begins with direct reference to *Israel, House of Aaron, and fearers of the Lord* – *thereby linking Psalm 118 back to Psalm 115*.
- *By linking Psalms 115 and 118, these opening verses tell us that all four of these Psalms are connected.*

Here's a good rule for studying Scripture. If a phrase or a series of phrases repeats in two separate places, it probably means that these two texts are connected. In other words, when reading these psalms in order, what is supposed to happen is this: I read Psalm 115. I then read Psalms 116 and 117 as well. I may not see any direct connection between them. I then begin to read Psalm 118 and I notice the words *Israel, House of Aaron, and fearers of the Lord* and say to myself, "Hey. Where have I seen that before? Are all these psalms actually connected?"

But in order to understand this connection we first must take notice of another shift that happens right at the beginning of Psalm 118.

222 | *Cup of Salvation*

Introducing Thanks

After no fewer than ten references to the verb *praise* in the five psalms that we have studied up to this point, the opening of Psalm 118 calls upon us to *give thanks*. In fact, the word *praise* does not occur even once in this psalm. This is a dramatic change. In the previous five psalms – 113 – 117 - there is only one reference to *giving thanks*.

> To You I shall offer a *sacrifice of thanksgiving*; and I will call out in the name of the Lord. (Ps. 116:17)

A Striking Parallel

This reference to a *sacrifice of thanksgiving* is particularly interesting in light of the following passage in Jeremiah which also makes reference to the bringing of a thanksgiving offering:

> So says the Lord: 'There will yet be heard in this place about which you say, "It is a desolate waste, without people or animals" - in the towns of Judah and the streets of Jerusalem that are deserted, inhabited by neither people nor animals - the sounds of joy and gladness, the voices of bride and bridegroom, and voices saying,
>
> "*Give thanks* to the Lord of Hosts, *for the Lord is good; for His kindness is eternal.*"
>
> *As they bring a thanksgiving offering to the house of the Lord*; For I will restore the returnees of the land as they were before,' says the Lord. (Jeremiah 33:10-11)

Now look at 116:17 – the promise to bring the sacrifice - in context.

> To You I shall offer a *sacrifice of thanksgiving*; and I will call out in the name of the Lord. I will fulfill my vows to the Lord; now in the presence of all His people. In the courtyards of *the house of the Lord*— in your midst, Jerusalem. Praise the Lord. (116:17-19)

Look at the passage from Jeremiah again. Now look again at our psalms. In our psalms we have a commitment to bring a *thanksgiving sacrifice* (116:17). Then, in the first verse here at the beginning of Psalm 118 we see a phrase identical to that which was said by one bringing a thanksgiving sacrifice, as quoted in Jeremiah 33: *Give thanks to the Lord for He is good; for His kindness is eternal.*

Jeremiah 33	*Psalms 116-118*
• "*Give thanks* to the Lord of Hosts, *for the Lord is good; for His kindness is eternal.*"	• *Give thanks to the Lord for He is good; for His kindness is eternal* (118:1)
• *As they bring a thanksgiving offering*	• To You I shall offer a *sacrifice of thanksgiving;* (116:17)
• *to the house of the Lord;*	• In the courtyards of *the house of the Lord* (116:18)

The parallel between our psalms and the verses in Jeremiah suggests that these words *Give thanks to the Lord for He is good; for His kindness is eternal* comprised the standard declaration when bringing a thanksgiving offering to the temple.

In other words, now that we have seen the verses in Jeremiah 33 we have a better understanding of the connection between Psalm 116 - *To You I shall offer a sacrifice of thanksgiving;* - and the beginning of Psalm 118 - *Give thanks to the Lord for He is good; for His kindness is eternal.*

I would like to suggest that, in fact, Psalm 118 is a continuation of the ideas set forth in Psalm 116. More to the point, the vow of the psalmist to bring a sacrifice of thanksgiving stated in 116:17 is now being fulfilled in Psalm 118. This is indicated by the opening declaration, *Give thanks to the Lord for He is good; for His kindness is eternal,* which, as we saw in Jeremiah, was declared upon bringing such an offering.

Jeremiah demonstrates that one bringing a Thanksgiving offering in the temple would declare:

Give thanks to the Lord for He is good; for His kindness is eternal,

These are the opening words of Psalm 118.

Therefore we see that **Psalm 118 describes a scene in which someone is bringing a Thanksgiving offering**.

From Personal Salvation to Universal Redemption

So why does the psalmist mention *Israel, the house of Aaron*, and *the fearers of the Lord*? Herein lies the message of this entire series of psalms.

Gratitude is, by its nature, very personal. But here we are taught that when we experience the love and kindness of God in our personal lives we must ask ourselves, as the psalmist did, *what can I give back to the Lord?* (116:12) How can I transform my personal sense of gratitude into a public display of praise and worship for the glory of God? Look at those verses in Jeremiah. What is more personal than the joy experienced by a *bride* and *groom*? Jeremiah's choice of the image of the joy of a bride and groom, illustrates this point perfectly. While their joy is intensely personal, they invite the wider community to join them as they celebrate. Jeremiah's message – and the message of our psalms – is that our private blessings must lead us to a public display of gratitude to God. God's kindness to us must be publicized to others. *Israel, the house of Aaron*, and *the fearers of the Lord* all represent the community; the nation, the leadership, those who guide and inspire us.

If we look more carefully at these verses – both in Jeremiah 33 and here in Psalms - we will discover something amazing. As you'll recall, Psalm 116 describes an individual who is experiencing personal hardship. He calls out to the Lord and experiences personal redemption. But His praise of God does not end with his personal feelings of gratitude. He commits himself to bring a *sacrifice of thanksgiving* and to *call out the name of the Lord in the presence of all of His people in Jerusalem.* Personal redemption leads him to collective praise and worship in the temple. His private redemption is the catalyst for the redemption of others.

In Jeremiah the message is the same. The joyous voices of bride and groom culminate first in an offering of thanksgiving in the temple in Jerusalem and ultimately in the return of God's people from exile to the promised land. Once again, the personal rejoicing in God's blessings is placed into the context of collective redemption.

The fullest expression of our gratitude for God's blessings in our personal lives is in publicizing our praise and thanks.

This way, our private redemption enables the redemption of others.

for His kindness is eternal

All four of the verses here at the beginning of Psalm 118 end with the same words, *for His kindness is eternal.* They are clearly being singled out as the focus of the declaration of thanksgiving. Let's take a deeper look at these words.

As I mentioned based on Jeremiah 33, the words *for His kindness is eternal* appear to be the standard statement made by one who brings a thanksgiving offering to the temple.

Truth be told, if we look through the entirety of Scripture we will discover that the connection between the words *for His kindness is eternal* and the temple is actually quite significant.

The phrase *for His kindness is eternal* appears forty-one times in Scripture. Thirty-three of these are in the book of Psalms. This makes sense. Psalms is entirely a book of praises of God. Many of these Psalms were, in fact, recited as part of the temple service.

All about the Temple

Of the eight instances of *for His kindness is eternal* in the rest of the Bible outside of Psalms, seven are in direct reference to the temple in Jerusalem. In addition to the verses from Jeremiah 33 discussed above, I will cite two more examples.

In the description of the dedication of King Solomon's temple:

> When all the Israelites saw the fire coming down and the glory of the Lord above the temple, they knelt on the pavement with

their faces to the ground, and they worshiped and gave thanks to the Lord, saying,

"For He is good; *for His kindness is eternal.*"

Then the king and all the people offered sacrifices before the Lord. (II Chonicles 7:3; see also v.6)

Similarly, in the story of the construction of the second temple in the days of Ezra:

And the builders laid the foundation of the temple of the Lord, the priests in their vestments and with trumpets, and the Levites (the sons of Asaph) with cymbals, took their places to praise the Lord, as prescribed by David king of Israel. With praise and thanksgiving they sang to the Lord:

"For He is good; *for His kindness is eternal* upon Israel"

And all the people gave a great shout of praise to the Lord because the foundation of the house of the Lord was laid. (Ezra 3:10-11; see also I Chronicles 16:34,41; II Chronicles 5:13)

The One Exception

There is only one occurrence of this phrase which is *not explicitly related to temple worship.* II Chronicles describes a war in which the armies of Ammon, Moab, and Seir are threatening the Israelites who are led by Jehoshaphat. After gathering the people and praying to the Lord for salvation from the three enemy armies, Jehoshaphat receives the prophetic message that the Israelites are destined to be saved from harm. Even before the battle begins, Jehoshaphat instructs his men to sing songs of praise and thanks to God for the victory.

After consulting the people, Jehoshaphat appointed men to sing to the Lord and to praise Him for the splendor of His holiness as they went out at the head of the army, saying:

"Give thanks to the Lord, *for His kindness is eternal*."

As they began to sing and praise, the Lord set ambushes against the men of Ammon and Moab and Mount Seir who were invading Judah, and they were defeated. (II Chronicles 20:21-22)

As I mentioned, this is the only example of the words *for His kindness is eternal* that is not in the context of the temple. However, let's take a look at the verses at the end of the scene, after the enemies of Israel have been defeated.

Then, led by Jehoshaphat, all the men of Judah and Jerusalem returned joyfully to Jerusalem, for the Lord had given them cause to rejoice over their enemies. *They entered Jerusalem and went to the temple of the Lord* with harps and lyres and trumpets. (II Chronicles 20:27-28)

In other words, even this one exception that seemed to *not be about the temple* ended up directly related to it! Although they thanked God using these words before the battle, when it was over they brought this celebration of thanks *to the temple*. Clearly, the phrase *for His kindness is eternal* is to be understood as a declaration thanksgiving made in the context of temple worship.

With this in mind, the thematic progression from Psalm 116 through the beginning of our psalm is clearly understood. After personally experiencing God's kindness, (116:1-11) the psalmist commits himself to repay the Lord by offering a sacrifice of thanksgiving, thereby publicly sharing his gratitude and declaring the praises of God to all. (116:12-19)

Then in the two verses of Psalm 117, he expands the scope of his public praise by inviting all peoples and nations of the earth to join him.

I would like to suggest that this is exactly what Psalm 118 is describing. It is the Psalm of praise that accompanies the thanksgiving offering promised in 116:17.

Remember how I explained in my comments to 116:17 that the thanksgiving offering was designed to be publicly shared with many others? Now, in Psalm 118 we are present at the event that the psalmist spoke about before.

Picture yourself at this event. We are present at his feast where he is offering his thanksgiving sacrifice to the Lord. We are sitting in the temple courtyard. Gathered among us are priests of the temple of the House of Aaron, fearers of the Lord, and all God's people of all nations who share in His praises. The host is about to tell his story of God's kindness that led to this joyous gathering.

Before he begins to speak, the formal declaration is made:
Give thanks to the Lord for He is good; for His kindness is eternal!

In other words: *Welcome to the Offering of Thanksgiving to the Lord!*

The Relevance of Psalm 115

One question remains. After opening with the appropriate verse for the thanksgiving offering, what is the purpose of the next three verses? Why specifically mention *Israel, the house of Aaron,* and *the fearers of the Lord* in this context? Furthermore, considering that these verses are obviously an intentional reference back to Psalm 115, we have to ask what connects these two psalms? They appear to be dealing with completely different topics. Psalm 115 described the futility and falsehood of pagan gods followed by a description of God's blessings upon the various groups of people whose collective mission it is to glorify Him on this earth. There is no mention of suffering, prayer, or redemption; the themes of both 116 and 117. If not for these three verses at the beginning of Psalm 118, why would we ever connect these psalms at all?

Individual vs Collective Feelings

I believe that the answer to this question speaks directly to the very definition of our identities as people of faith.

This may be stating the obvious, but think about it. A collective does not have feelings. It does not feel fear, happiness, or relief. In actuality, a collective does not even really exist as a thing. A collective is, of course, nothing more than a group of individual people. Individual people feel things. If I say that a group of people are happy, I obviously am not referring to some large collective nervous system. What I mean is that all of the individuals in the group are happy. To be precise, I probably mean that they are all happy about the same thing. Nevertheless, the emotions themselves are only felt by the individual people. They are the components of the collective. Like I said, this is probably stating the obvious.

My point is that we actually never feel any emotion as a group. Nevertheless, when we are frightened, sad, or joyous together with other people who *feel the same way we do for the same reasons* we experience a sense of collective emotion.

In other words, what determines whether or not our emotions are perceived to be part of a shared collective is our own consciousness; our attitude. To use a common and simple example, I can experience the joy of my sports team winning a championship as a private joy. I rooted for them for many years. I longed for victory. And now that they have won I personally feel that happiness. Other people may strongly feel the collective sense of shared feelings that they are experiencing simultaneously with all of the other fans of the team. Someone who feels this way may even feel compelled to seek out other fans to celebrate with them. The feeling of collective experience is powerful.

To sum up this important point, any sense of collective emotion or collective purpose that we feel in our lives is the result of *a choice that we make*. When we choose to identify collectively, our own personal emotions are experienced in a collective manner. On the other hand, if we choose to keep our emotions private and individual, then that is where our emotions remain.

Even You are not about You

Psalm 115 described the shared mission of all those who trust in the Lord; Israel, the house of Aaron, the fearers of God among all peoples.

That psalm ended with a collective declaration of intent to praise and glorify God.

> And *we* will bless the Lord from now and until eternity; Halleluyah. (115:18)

But how do we get to this sense of collective purpose? As I just pointed out, life is not lived and experienced by collectives; but by individuals. And individuals are concerned with, first and foremost, their own private needs. How can I grow from the natural focus on my private concerns to a feeling of shared mission?

This is why Psalm 116 follows immediately after Psalm 115. Psalm 116 describes a journey that begins with personal private fear and ends with a commitment to use the joy and gratitude for God's salvation as a springboard for the broadest possible public display of collective praise of God. *Praise the Lord all nations; exalt Him all peoples!*

All are participants in the praise of the Lord at the sacrifice of thanksgiving in the temple – *the house of prayer for all nations.* (Isaiah 56:7)

So rather than being out of place, the opening verses of Psalm 118 - precisely because they force us to think back to the second half of Psalm 115 - teach us the powerful lesson of this entire set of Psalms.

As Psalm 115 began, *Not to us.* It is not about us. It is about God. Even the blessings and salvation of the Lord that we experience in our personal lives are not about us; they are not an end in and of themselves. Rather, the feelings of gratitude that we feel to Him are intended to force us to ask, as the psalmist did, *What can I give back to the Lord?* (116:12) And the answer is always the same.

We repay the Lord for His blessings by sharing stories of His glory with others; by including them. We transform our private joy into a collective experience of God. All are invited; those near us and those farther away; with all peoples and all nations.

This is the secret of these psalms. Our personal private salvation is really only a means to the ultimate redemption of all.

We must choose to use our personal gratitude to the Lord as a catalyst for the redemption and salvation of others; and ultimately the entire world.

118:5 *Knowing that there is a Plan*

From the narrow place I called out "Lord" [Yah]; He answered me with the wide open space; Lord [Yah].

My translation of this verse is unique. Specifically, there are three choices that I made that I did not see in any other translation.

1. In the first half of the verse I did not write that the psalmist called out *to* the Lord. Instead, contrary to every other translation I wrote that he called out, "Lord". In other words, "Lord" is what the psalmist said as he cried out.
2. In the second half of the verse I wrote *He answered* and then ended the verse with a second reference to *the Lord*. All translations either do not mention the Lord by name at all or mention the Lord at the beginning of the phrase; e.g. *the Lord answered me in…*
3. I ended with the words *with the wide open space; Lord*. I did not see this in any other translation.
4. In addition to these three translation issues, you probably noticed that I wrote the word *Yah* in brackets after both times that the verse says *the Lord*.

Let's look at these points one at a time.

Calling "Lord" vs. Calling to the Lord
    If I am speaking English and I say the sentence, "I called Dad" there are two possible meanings of what I said.

1. I might mean that I called my Dad on the phone or by yelling to him.
2. I might mean that I called out the word "Dad." "I called 'Dad!'" Like the boy who cried "wolf". "Wolf" is the word that he called out, not who he was calling to.

The first of these two possibilities really means, "I called *to* my Dad." The English language allows us to skip the word *to* in this context as well as many others. For example, "I gave you a present" really means that I gave a present *to* you. What happened to the word *to*? English allows us to drop it. So "I called my Dad on the phone" really means "I called *to* my Dad on the phone."

Hebrew never skips the word *to*. If there is no word or prefix meaning *to*, then the word that follows is what is being said, not who is being called to. In other words, "I called Dad" in Hebrew would always mean I called out the word "Dad."

The opening words of our verse do not say *From the narrow place I called out to the Lord*. The word *to* simply does not appear. According to the rules of Hebrew grammar, the psalmist is saying that he called out "Lord!" Now obviously he called this out *to* the Lord. Who else was he calling to? Nevertheless, this distinction has profound meaning in this verse. But in order to appreciate this meaning we first need to look at another issue that I raised.

The meaning of YaH

The name for God used in this verse is *YaH*. As you can see, it appears twice. However, the fact that this name for God is used is impossible to know from the English translations. Almost every one uses the name *the Lord*. This is misleading because *the Lord* is always the English as a translation of the four letter name of God, *YHVH*.

I explained the meaning of the name *YaH* in my comments to the final verse of Psalm 115. Here are a few key points from what I wrote there:

*   The translators write *the Lord* for YaH because this name is made up of the first two letters of YHVH which is always translated as *the Lord*.

- As a Hebrew word, the divine name YHVH is an impossible mix of past, present, and future tenses of the verb *to be*. YHVH essentially means "the cause of all existence past, present, and future." Pretty good name for God, right?
- Different parts of the four letters of YHVH are grammatical elements of these three different tenses.
- The name YaH or YH is the *future* part of God's name. In other words, it represents God's *will*; *His plan before we see it*. That's what all of existence and all of history is *before it happens*. It is part of *God's will and plan*.

The Comfort in Knowing God's Plan

So what does all of this mean for our verse? If *YaH* refers to that aspect of God that is unavailable to us - *God's will before it happens* – what is our verse saying? I should point out that the name *YaH* appears in a total of 23 verses in all of Scripture. 5 of those verses – *more than one fifth of the total uses of this name for God* – are right here in Psalm 118. In other words, the meaning of *YaH*, i.e. God's unknowable will as it is manifest in His long-term plan for the future, is central to this particular psalm.

Our psalmist is telling the story of his trials and pain; of how he called out to God, was saved, and ultimately found great meaning and inspiration from all that he went through.

From the narrow place I called out "Lord" [Yah]; - When I was suffering and could not see past the pain of the moment I prayed that I would be granted the clarity of vision to understand what God had in mind for me.

He answered me with the wide open space; [Yah] – The Lord responded by broadening my vision; by allowing me to see the big picture. *He answered me by bringing me to the wide open space;* - the broader perspective - of *YaH*. Awareness of the goodness of God's long term plan gave meaning to my suffering and granted me the strength to endure.

When we experience hardship and suffering, it is natural to find ourselves wondering why this is happening? We struggle to see meaning in what we are experiencing. We want to know God's plan. What is this for?

How long will it last? Where is this difficulty supposed to lead us? We are seeking to understand Yah – the will of God that we are not yet able to see. When we are granted a glimpse of the long term plan that the Lord has in mind for us, we find the strength to persevere. We understand the vision. We share in it. Rather than being constricted by the narrow vision of the present moment, we are brought to the wide open understanding of God's plan.

Sometimes God's answer to suffering is not ending the pain but the gift of a broader vision which gives us the strength to endure it.

In moments of struggle we feel a limited sense of vision. There is comfort and strength in knowing that God has a long term plan for us.

118:6 *The Lord is for me*

The Lord is for me, I will not fear; what can man do to me?

The Lord is for me I will not fear.

Faith and *fear* have an interesting relationship. For many of us, our most intimate moments with God - those times when we feel His presence most in our personal lives - are bound up with frightening experiences. I know that in my own life I have felt the strength of God's presence come to the fore at my most trying times. It's probably safe to say that for most people, the experience of dealing with fear of immediate danger is the most common cause of intense moments of faith. We think about God when we are afraid. We want to know that He is with us; that He will protect us and have our best interests in mind.

But is this what our verse is describing? At first glance, our verse immediately reminds us of a similar verse from earlier in the Book of Psalms:

Even though I walk through the valley of the shadow of death,
I will fear no evil, for You are with me; (Psalm 23:5)

Seemingly, these two verses are expressing the identical idea. The Lord is there. There is nothing to fear. But look a little closer. There is a difference. Here in our verse the psalmist says that *the Lord is <u>for</u> me*. In Psalm 23 *the Lord is <u>with</u> me*.

With me = Protection

There are a number of other verses in Scripture which describe God as *with* someone. For example:

> Then Jacob made a vow, saying, "If God will be *with* me and will watch over me on this journey I am taking and will give me food to eat and clothes to wear" (Genesis 28:20; see also Genesis 31:5, 35:3)

Jacob is praying to God for protection. In fact, every time that God is described as *with* someone the context is the same. Protection from danger. Our verse here in Psalm 118 seems no different. So, is there a difference between the Lord is *for* me and the Lord is *with* me? There is a difference; and I believe that the difference is quite significant.

For me = Partnership

Look at the next verse in our psalm.

The Lord is for me as my helper; I will triumph over those who hate me. Here, the psalmist elaborates on the way in which the Lord is *for* him. *The Lord is for me as my <u>helper</u>.* The word for *helper* here is EZeR. I explained the precise meaning of this word in my commentary to Psalm 115 verse 9. Here's what I wrote there:

> EZeR – does not usually connote help in the sense of being saved from danger. More often than not it implies sharing in a task. The first time this word appears is in the well-known scene describing the creation of the first woman. God says,

> It is not good for Man to be alone. I will make for him a *helper* –
> EzeR – matching him. (Genesis 2:18)

There are many other examples in Scripture of this connotation of the word EZeR meaning a partner sharing in a joint task. In other words, while our psalmist certainly does feel protected by the Lord's presence, what he is describing goes beyond protection. *God is his partner*.

I'd like to suggest that this is the difference between God being *with* someone and God being *for* someone. *God is with me* implies that He is protecting and guarding me. *God is for me* takes it a step further. He is acting on my behalf. *He is a partner in my mission*.

Being _For_ God

Here's an interesting example to help prove my point. In Exodus, after the Children of Israel committed the terrible sin of the Golden Calf, Moses makes a call to all those who are willing to join him in punishing the people responsible for leading the nation to sin.

> Moses saw that the people were running wild; that Aaron had let them get out of control and so become a laughingstock to their enemies. Moses stood at the entrance to the camp and said,
>
> "Whoever is *for the Lord*, come to me." And all the Levites gathered to him. (Exodus 32:25-26)

Whoever is for the Lord. Obviously, these people were not going to be protecting the Lord from harm. To be *for the Lord* means that they would be acting *on the Lord's behalf*; doing His work for Him. Now we can fully appreciate the message of our verse. The psalmist recognizes that he and God are on the same team. They share the same goals. The Lord's mission is his mission.

The Lord is for me; I will not fear - He and I are working together. I am doing what I am called by God to do. Therefore, there is no reason to be afraid. As God's partner I am living my life as it is meant to be lived. God has showed me *the wide open space of YaH* - broader picture of my purpose on this earth (see previous verse). Temporal human concerns are rendered insignificant in the face of my partnership with the Lord.

What can man do to me? - May all of us identify so strongly with the Lord's plan that we share His will as if it is our own. May we all strive to be the Lord's partners.

Any fears that I may harbor in my life fade into insignificance compared to the mission that I share with the Lord, because even my own life is less important than that shared mission. When I believe this with complete faith, what can man possibly do to me?

118:7 *God's Messengers*

> *The Lord is for me in those who help me; and I will perceive my enemies.*

God comes to our aid in many different ways. The problem is that quite often we don't recognize that it was God who helped us and not some other worldly force. More to the point, if we are rescued from imminent danger by some timely coincidence that did not involve any other human being we are likely to see the hand of the Almighty. On the other hand, if another person was involved – when a friend stepped in at just the right moment to help us accomplish our goals – God's involvement in our lives often goes unnoticed. Our natural reaction is to attribute the help to the free will choice of the person who came to our aid, not necessarily to God as well.

It's an axiom of faith in God that everything that happens has a purpose. This is not a new idea to anyone reading this book. For people who live by faith, this is a fact. While we know this to be true, it seems that we only really think about it with regard to the big things. For example, if someone that we know becomes gravely ill, we will readily acknowledge that there is a purpose to this illness even as we struggle to know what that purpose is.

But do we use the same thinking with regard to *the fact that we know* that the person is ill? Think about it. If everything that happens has a purpose before God, then this is not only true regarding this person being sick. There is also a purpose to *the fact that I was made aware* of the illness. *My knowing about it* is also something that happened. The illness to this person could have happened without my knowledge. God decided that I would find out.

My point is that if we truly believe that everything that happens has a Divine purpose, then we must extend that belief to the reactions that we and others have when we become aware of someone in need. Going back to our example, I must ask myself, *Why did I find out about this illness?*

Those who help me were sent by God

This is the message of the first half of our verse.

Recall that the previous verse ended with the words, *What can man do to me?* The psalmist recognized that it really is God who is in complete control and that human enemies have no real power over him. Okay, so what about those humans who are not enemies? What about the righteous people who come to my aide? Do they have power?

The Lord is for me in those who help me – I recognize that part of the way that God works in my life is *through* the righteous people who He sends my way to share in my struggle and mission.

Even my enemies are part of God's plan

At first glance, the first half of the verse - *The Lord is for me in those who help me;* - seems unrelated to the second half - *and I will perceive my enemies.* However, in light of the theological point that we have just discussed, I believe that the end of the verse is a natural extension of the beginning.

The words *and I will perceive my enemies* in Hebrew are:

VaANI	and I
ER'EH	will see / will perceive
BESON'AI	(in) my enemies

The third word – BESON'AI – is made up of the word SON'AI – *my enemies* – with the prefix BE attached to the beginning of the word. This prefix usually means *in, within,* or *with.* In this verse it is difficult to translate literally. What does *I will see in my enemies* mean? Almost all translations include the word *triumph* or *defeat* into this phrase. A typical rendering is - *and I will look on in triumph over those who hate me.*

The verb *to see* appears some 1300 times in Scripture. On 40 occasions this verb is followed by the prefix BE. That's only three percent of the time. While our verse is not the only place where the implication is one of looking on in triumph, (see Proverbs 29:16) this meaning is certainly not the most common meaning of the word. Without going through all 40 examples here, I will summarize by saying that *seeing* "BE" – *in* implies *to experience* (Psalm 27:13, Psalm 128:5) or *to understand well* (I Samuel 1:11, Ecclesiastes 3:22). In other words, *to see in*, Biblically speaking, means more than a mere visual experience. It refers to a deeper understanding or an experience that affects the one who *sees* in some significant way.

> The unusual Biblical form **"seeing in"** means
> **"Gaining a deeper understanding of"**
> rather than
> merely seeing with one's eyes.

Now we can understand our verse. In the previous verse the psalmist declared his faith that God is in control of everything that happens to him; that humans have no real power to affect him in any way. In light of this complete faith in God, he sees both his friends and his enemies in a new light. He sees "BE" – *in* them. He understands them in a new and deeper way.

The Lord is for me in those who help me; - Since God alone is the cause of all that happens to me, I recognize His hand acting through those who are on my side.

and I will perceive my enemies. – My adversaries as well are not independent actors. They come against me for a Divine purpose. I see them clearly for who and what they are. They, like my friends, are instruments of the Lord.

Both those who assist us as well as those who are sent as adversaries, are sent to us by the Lord for a purpose. They, too, are part of His plan.

118:8 *Trust vs. Shelter*

It is better to take refuge in the Lord than to trust in humanity.

God is more dependable than man. Is there a more obvious statement to be found in all of Scripture? Theologically speaking, probably not. However, the psalmist in our verse is not addressing our abstract theological or philosophical belief system. He is speaking to our experiences; to our emotions in time of crisis; to our hearts.

The words *refuge* and *trust* are used almost interchangeably throughout Scripture. Both appear many times in the book of Psalms. In context, the two seem to be exact synonyms. Here are a few examples among many:

Trust

But I have *trusted* in Your lovingkindness; My heart shall rejoice in Your salvation. (Psalm 13:6)

In You, Lord my God, I put my *trust*. (Psalm 25:2)

In God, whose word I praise— in God I *trust* and am not afraid. What can mere mortals do to me? (Psalm 56:5)

Shelter

Lord my God, I *take refuge* in You; save and deliver me from all who pursue me, (Psalm 7:2)

Keep me safe, my God, for in You I *take refuge*. (Psalm 16:2)

In You, Lord, I *have taken refuge*; let me never be put to shame. (Psalm 71:1)

So is there a difference between them? There is, and it is quite significant. Think about it. *Trust* is an emotional state. It is a state of mind. I feel secure and have reason to believe that everything will be alright. *Refuge* is more than that. *Refuge* is not merely something that is believed or felt. *Refuge* is the actual experience of safety. It describes *the fact that I am protected*. It exists. It's tangible.

Nothing more real than God

And this is the point of our verse. People are tangible. We see them; touch them; experience them in the material world. God, on the other hand, is beyond our perception. We experience Him in faith; in our hearts.

Our verse tells us not to be fooled. We have it backward. People seem solid and reliable? God is experienced only in our hearts and our faith? Incorrect. Despite what our senses may tell us it is God that is real. Promises of help that come from physical human sources may appear to exist with greater reality than does God's help but that is only an illusion.

Trust in humanity can never be more than that; *trust*. Nothing that man promises is certain. God's protection is a different matter. In the words of Isaiah:

The grass withers and the flowers fall, *but the word of our God endures forever*. (Isaiah 40:8)

God's promises are fact. They are more real even than man's most tangible actions. As I mentioned, to know this as a theological truth is one thing. But our verse teaches us to move beyond philosophical abstraction. Even people of faith must remind ourselves that no matter how secure we feel in the physical safeguards that we see with our eyes, there is only one guardian whose refuge is absolutely certain.

It is better to take refuge in the Lord than to trust in humanity.
God is real. His promises and protection are more real than the phys-ical reality of material protections that are tangible around us.

118:9 *Whom do we look to?*

It is better to take refuge in the
Lord than to trust in nobles.

Admiring vs. idolizing

Human beings from most ancient times down to today have shown a natural tendency to revere people with power. But it's not just people with power. We are inspired by great people. The extremely righteous or wise are just as likely to be idolized. To a great extent this is a good thing. Great and successful people are admirable and worthy of our respect and emulation. However, this becomes a problem when we begin to see these people as independently powerful in their own right; as something more than human; as not quite like the rest of us.

Unfortunately, there is no shortage of examples of people thinking this way about individuals who embody traits that are to be admired. From the ancient god-kings to modern people attributing powers and wisdom to great people that are actually beyond their capabilities; we make this mistake over and over again. The modern expression says it all; we *idolize* them.

Does Scripture repeat itself?

The most noticeable thing about verse 9 is that it is almost an exact repetition of verse 8.

8.   *It is better to take refuge in the Lord than to trust in <u>humanity</u>*
9.   *It is better to take refuge in the Lord than to trust in <u>nobles</u>*

Is verse 9 really necessary? Aren't nobles included in the category of *humanity*? Why would I think that trusting in them is any different? If the two verses are saying the same thing does this mean that Scripture is simply repeating itself?

We encountered the word *nobles* – NeDIVIM – back in Psalm 113, verse 8. In my comments there I explained that the root NDV has the following connotations:

- *generous* (Proverbs 19:6, Exodus 35:5)
- *people of power* (Numbers 21:18, Job 21:28)
- *righteous wisdom* as opposed to foolish wickedness (Isaiah 32:5)
- *a free-will offering* (Leviticus 7:16) is called NeDaVa from this same root.

As I wrote there, "If I was forced to give one single definition for the word NADIV – *noble* - , I would suggest that a NADIV is one who is completely free to use his God given powers – be they money, power, or intelligence – for generous and good purposes."

The lesson of our verse

So a NADIV – noble – is obviously a very capable and righteous person. Nevertheless, the question that I raised earlier still stands. After stating that *it is better to take refuge in the Lord than to trust in <u>humanity</u>,* why wouldn't I know that the same is true of *nobles*?

In my comments to the previous verse I wrote that the psalmist here is not addressing our abstract theological belief system. He is speaking to our experiences; to our emotions in time of crisis; to our hearts. The same is true in our verse. The psalmist is not referring to what we *know*, but to what we *feel*.

Even if we internalize the message of verse 8, that man's promises are not certain in comparison to God's, our experiences in the tangible physical world still deceive us. As people of faith we justifiably see righteous people with the ability and inclination to help us and do the right thing as messengers of the Almighty One. That was the message of verse 7: *The Lord is for me in those who help me*. Where we are mistaken is when we start to see those righteous people as independently responsible for the assistance that they provide.

There is a natural tendency to revere people with power. This is especially true when it comes to righteous and *noble* people. Ironically, the dependability and generosity of these great souls can often lead to a subtle undermining of our faith in God. When we benefit from the kindness of others more wise, powerful, and capable than us, many people begin to see these human beings as Godly – as not quite human.

So while it is true that as a theological statement there is no difference whatsoever between our verse and the one that precedes it, experientially and emotionally they address two separate human tendencies.

Verse 8 taught us that the non-physical God that we can't see is actually more real and reliable than the tangible human forces that seem more real to our senses. Now in verse 9 we are taught the full meaning of the fact that *The Lord is for me in those who help me* (verse 7); that those generous, wise, and righteous people; the *nobles* who come to our aid are only instruments of God. Any power that they have rests with the Lord alone.

The unfortunate human tendency to attribute super-human Godly status to great human beings must be kept in check. Yes, these are great and righteous people. They have made choices to use their God-given abilities for the greater good. While we must respect them and learn from them, we must guard ourselves from attributing to them powers that rest with Almighty God and with no one else.

We must guard ourselves against excessively idolizing and revering great people as this often leads to the attribution of powers that rest with God alone.

118:10 *Cutting Off Evil*

All nations surrounded me; it was in the name of the Lord that I cut them down.

Anyone who finds themselves under attack, yearns for the defeat of their enemies. At the very least, we hope to see them fail in their attempts to destroy us. If we are surrounded, threatened, and fearing for our lives our number one priority is to be saved from the immediate danger that we face.

But while we are in the moment of crisis we usually don't have the ability to see the larger context. "Why am I being attacked in the first place?" "How does my ultimate victory serve to make the world a better place?" "What purpose does this entire experience of danger and salvation serve?" These are questions that can not be addressed while we are still fighting for our lives. Only with the benefit of perspective; when I am no longer in danger, do I have the luxury of thinking about the broader meaning of what I went through.

In this verse, the psalmist is praising God for saving him from danger. His enemies attacked. He prayed. The Lord gave him the help and strength that he needed to prevail. But he knows that God did not only *save him* from danger. *God put him in danger in the first place.* Why? What purpose did it serve?

Defeating Evil in the Name of God

It is a basic axiom of Biblical faith that we are responsible to defeat evil. Those who rise up to attack God's people are His enemies as well as ours. When we defeat them we bring glory to God – provided that we choose to do so; provided that we *call out the name of the Lord* in response to the victory.

> We will rejoice in your salvation, and *in the name of our God* we will set up banners! ... Some with chariots, and some with horses; but *we will recall the name of the Lord our God*. They have bowed down and fallen; but we have risen and stand upright. (Psalm 20:5-8)

But why must we destroy our enemies? To use the language of our verse, why do we have to *cut them down*? Wouldn't it be better if they changed their ways without a fight?

> 'As I live,' says the Lord God, 'I have no pleasure in the death of the wicked, but that the wicked turn from his way and live.' (Ezekiel 33:11)

Of course it would be better if they repented. However, there is an unusual choice of words in our verse that teaches us a very important lesson regarding the battle against evil.

An Unusual Word for "Cut Off"

The Hebrew word that is used here for *I cut them down* is AMILaM. This verb, which means *to cut off*, appears only 35 times in the Bible. But there is another verb that means *to cut off* - KaRaT – that appears approximately 300 times; meaning that our psalmist chose the far less common word for *cut off*. Why did the psalmist choose this unusual word?

The answer to this question contains a powerful and relevant theological message about the defeat of our enemies. As I said, the Hebrew root *to cut off* that is used here appears a total of 35 times in Scripture. Three of those are in our verse and in the two verses that follow. Incredibly, in *every single one* of the remaining 32 instances of this verb it means *to circumcise*. 28 of them are in Genesis, Exodus, Leviticus, and Joshua in reference to various people being circumcised or the commandment to do so. The remaining 4 instances of this verb root appear in Deuteronomy (10:16, 30:6) and Jeremiah (9:24, 4:4) in reference to the "circumcision of the heart" using actual circumcision as a metaphor for spiritual development.

These verses in Psalm 118 are the *only times in the entire Bible* that this verb is used to mean simply *cutting off*. And it is this peculiar choice of words that provides the powerful message of these three verses.

What is circumcision? Well, technically speaking, it is the removal of the foreskin. Metaphorically, as it is used in Deuteronomy and Jeremiah, *circumcision* refers to the removal of barriers that stand in the way of the relationship with God. The foreskin in this imagery represents that flesh that prevents the spiritual potential from being fully realized. God created man with a foreskin. So too, He created human beings with natural barriers of flesh that hinder their relationship with the Divine. God created man imperfect and gave him the responsibility to perfect himself; *to remove the foreskin*; to remove the barriers of imperfection that stand in the way of his spiritual actualization.

This is the meaning of our verse. Just as God created man with flesh that must be painfully removed; so too, He created the world with evil that stands in the way of humanity's relationship with God.

I form the light and create darkness, I make peace and create evil; I, the Lord, do *all these things.* (Isaiah 45:7)

God created evil for the same reason that He created man with a foreskin; in order to enter into a covenant with him. *A covenant means that we have a partnership with God.* God created a world with imperfections and gave us the responsibility to perfect them; *to remove the foreskin.*

And this is precisely what verses 10 through 13 of our psalm describe. *All nations surrounded me; -* our enemies surround us. They attack us: *it was in the name of the Lord that I cut them down –* to serve the ultimate purpose of all of creation – the revelation of the name of the Lord – *I cut them down;* as a circumcision. Painful as it may be, removal of the evil barriers to our relationship with God is our covenantal responsibility to all humanity.

By cutting off evil, I not only save myself from danger, I allow the revelation of good in God's kingdom here on earth.

118:11 *The Lesson of Perpetual Struggle*

> *They encircled me - indeed they surrounded me; it was in the name of the Lord that I cut them down.*

As I mentioned in my comments to verse 7 of this psalm, one basic principle of a life of faith is the belief that everything happens for a reason. Because we believe that the Lord directs the events in our lives we look for meaning in those events. We believe that whatever the Almighty has thrown our way must have a purpose. Knowing that this is the case leads us to ask important questions. "Why did this happen to me?" "What is God trying to tell me?"

Event vs. Theme

But even though every event in our lives may lead us to ask these questions, when a situation repeats itself the effect is even greater. The questions – and answers - are different. "Why did this happen?" becomes "Why does this *keep happening*?" To put it in simple terms, if something happens once it is an *event*. If it happens repeatedly it becomes a *theme*.

Let's take this idea a bit further. For example, think about the difference between a brief medical issue and a chronic one. Besides the obvious difference between them – that a chronic issue does not go away – they have a different effect on the identity of the person who is sick. Simply put, a brief illness is something that *I have*. It's something that I deal with and then I go on with my life. A chronic illness, on the other hand, becomes part of my lifestyle. To some extent, it is part of *who I am*.

This distinction impacts the theological questions that are raised by the two situations. A brief or temporary crisis raises the question, "Why is this happening?" A chronic or recurring problem becomes an ongoing theme which raises different questions.

Beyond the questions, the effects on us are different as well. When a temporary crisis is done and I move on with my life, I am not necessarily permanently transformed by the experience. New traits have not necessarily taken root in my personality. Surely, lessons were learned, but with time the effects of those lessons will likely fade. But when a problem is recurring and lessons are learned repeatedly the attitudes and traits that are developed through dealing with the challenge are no longer mere temporary coping mechanisms. A prolonged or permanent struggle transforms the character of a person who goes through it. It inevitably produces deeply ingrained personality traits. It becomes part of one's *identity* rather than merely being part of one's *experience*.

A prolonged or permanent struggle inevitably produces deeply ingrained personality traits.

It becomes part of one's identity.

What happened vs Who we are

Which brings us to the meaning of our verse. On the surface, it appears to be purely repetitious, adding nothing new to the verse that came before it.

10. *All nations surrounded me; it was in the name of the Lord that I cut them down.*
11. *They encircled me - indeed they surrounded me; it was in the name of the Lord that I cut them down.*

In my commentary to verse 10 I suggested that the unusual choice of word for *I cut them down* – AMILAM – indicates that the goal of destroying our enemies is not merely to save ourselves from danger. To be saved from danger would not necessarily require that the enemies by destroyed. More to the point, If God wanted us safe from harm He could have prevented us from being in danger in the first place. Rather, the reason that we are in danger is so that we will *cut down* our enemies *in the name of the Lord*. It is our God given task to destroy evil. As I pointed out there, AMILAM means *to circumcise*. Circumcision refers to the removal of earthly barriers that stand in the way of growth to a higher spiritual state of being. We remove the imperfections in order to enter into a covenantal relationship with the Lord. This is what circumcision is all about; *and it is what the destruction of our enemies is all about.*

In our verse, a new dimension is added to this lesson. This higher purpose of cutting down our enemies – the *circumcision* of evil – is not something that happens once and then is over. *It is an ongoing and continuing battle.* We are God's agents here on earth charged with the covenantal responsibility to remove the imperfections that act as barriers to the revelation of God; *to circumcise the world.*

After already stating in verse 10 that *All nations surrounded me*, verse 11 then tells us *They encircled me - indeed they surrounded me*. The attacks on God's people continue unabated. The fact that God orchestrates things so that His people are constantly under attack tells us that there is a greater purpose to this pattern. The repeating of the attacks tells us that they are not isolated *events*; they repeat because they are part of *who we are*.

Thinking back to what I wrote a few paragraphs ago, the fact that we get attacked over and over again is God's way of telling us that the destruction of evil is not only something that *we do* to save ourselves from this or that specific crisis. Rather, the *definition of our identity* and ongoing mission is the never-ending battle against the forces of evil in the world.

The circumcision of humanity by destroying the imperfections that stand in the way of our collective relationship with God is not merely something we do. It is who we are.

118:12 *Bees and Thorns*

They encircled me like bees;
they were extinguished like
the fire of thorns; it was in the
name of the Lord that I cut
them down.

The previous two verses described the perpetual attacks on God's people. They are surrounded again and again. Now, in verse 12, after again mentioning the *encircling* attackers - this time with the imagery of *bees* - the psalmist graphically describes the destruction of his enemies as similar to the burning of *thorns by fire*.

As I explained in my comments to the preceding verses, the theme of these three verses 10, 11, and 12, is that there is a divine purpose in the continuing attacks by our enemies. That purpose is so that we will *cut them down in the name of the Lord*. The full revelation of God's goodness and glory in the world requires the destruction of evil; the barrier to that revelation. Take a look at what I wrote explaining the two verses before this one.

Bees and Thorns... OUCH!

But why *bees* and *thorns*? These are two very specific images. Both of them conjure up similar fears of being stung or poked sharply. Nobody wants to get stuck in a thicket of thorns or happen upon a swarm of bees. Both of these uncomfortable images make us think, "Ouch!" But there is something else that bees and thorns have in common. Neither of them is very dangerous. Sure, they can both be painful. But notice that the psalmist doesn't describe the enemy attackers using imagery of swords, arrows, or other instruments of war.

In other words, in our verse the psalmist now describes his enemies as a nuisance that is temporarily painful but not really to be feared.

Who is being attacked?

We can better understand this choice of imagery by looking at a difference between the first two phrases of the verse

They encircled me like bees;   describes the *attack by* the enemies.

*they were extinguished
    like the fire of thorns;*   describes the *destruction of* the enemies.

Now let's look at our verse together with the two verses that came before it.

10. All nations surrounded me; it was in the name of the Lord that I cut them down.
11. They encircled me - indeed they surrounded me; it was in the name of the Lord that I cut them down.
12. They encircled me like bees; they were extinguished like the fire of thorns; it was in the name of the Lord that I cut them down.

Each verse ends with the same exact phrase, *it was in the name of the Lord that I cut them down.* But look closely at the first half of each verse.

All nations surrounded me;	*describes attack by enemies*
They encircled me	*describes attack by enemies*
indeed they surrounded me;	*describes attack by enemies*
They encircled me like bees;	*describes attack by enemies*
they were extinguished	***describes destruction***
like the fire of thorns;	***of enemies***

Why does the transition from describing *their attacks on us* to *our attacks on them* happen in the middle of a verse?

I'd like to suggest that it actually doesn't.

The Wicked as Bees

It is a well known fact that bees are themselves harmed by stinging. Honey bees actually die as a result of stinging someone. Other bees that don't die from stinging are still weakened and are easier to swat and kill as a result. Perhaps the choice of bees to describe the surrounding enemies contains a multi-layered message.

My enemies surround me (v.10). They continually attack and pursue God's people (v.11). We understand that the purpose of this is so that we can defeat evil and build God's kingdom (see comments to previous verses). With this perspective we understand that:

1. Just like bee stings, our enemies are not as dangerous as swords and spears. They do not pose mortal danger. God's people can never be destroyed.
2. Every attack by our enemies and our subsequent survival and victory over them makes them weaker and closer to death; just like bees when they sting.

In other words, our verse's description of the enemies as bees is not only a description of their attack on us; *it is also a description of their defeat*.

The Wicked as Thorns

Thorns, like bees, don't pose a mortal danger. They cause pain but not much more. Beyond being a painful annoyance, in Scripture *thorns* are the paradigm of the plant that does not bear fruit. The first mention of thorns is in God's punishment of Adam after the sin of the Tree of Knowledge of Good and Evil.

> Both thorns and thistles it shall bring forth for you, And you shall eat the herb of the field. (Genesis 3:18)

It's quite fitting that the wicked, a purely destructive force in the world, are likened to thorns – introduced by God in Genesis in response to Adam's sin. Thorns epitomize fruitless growth. They do not serve a positive purpose. There's really only one thing to do with them. Burn them. By removing the thorns we allow more productive, pleasant, and beautiful growths to flourish in their place.

In contrast, the righteous are likened to trees that bear nourishing fruit.

> The righteous shall flourish like a palm tree, He shall grow like a cedar in Lebanon. Those who are planted in the house of the Lord Shall flourish in the courts of our God. They shall still bear fruit in old age; They shall be fresh and flourishing, (Psalm 92:13-15)

The enemies of God's purposes do not pose a true danger to those who fight to defeat evil. They are weakened by their own attacks. They are fruitless and bound for destruction.

118:13 *Pushed to the Brink*

> *You have surely pushed me to the point of falling; but the Lord has assisted me.*

Throughout history there have been many attempts to destroy God's chosen people. The forces of evil are relentless. But of course all of these attempts ultimately fail. God's nation perseveres and is reborn again and again.

In the comments to the previous three verses we explored the idea that the purpose of these repeated attacks is the eventual revelation of God's goodness when the wicked are defeated. Victory by the good and the cutting off of the wicked reveal God's glory.

But here in our verse there is no mention of the destruction of our enemies. This verse is not about victory. It's about survival.

You have surely pushed me to the point of falling;

The implication is that the pushing was sufficient to cause me to fall. In other words, by all logic, left on my own, and by the natural rules of cause and effect, *I should have fallen.*

The miracle of Jewish survival is undeniable to any student of history. In the words of the great American author, Mark Twain:

> If statistics are right, the Jews constitute but one percent of the human race. …
>
> The Egyptian, the Babylonian, and the Persian rose, filled the planet with sound and splendor, then faded to dream-stuff and passed away; the Greek and the Roman followed; and made a vast noise, and they are gone; other people have sprung up and held their torch high for a time, but it burned out, and they sit in twilight now, or have vanished. The Jew saw them all, beat them all, and is now what he always was, exhibiting no decadence, no infirmities of age, no weakening of his parts, no slowing of his energies, no dulling of his alert and aggressive mind. All things are mortal but the Jew; all other forces pass, but he remains. What is the secret of his immortality? (Mark Twain, *Concerning The Jews*, Harper's Magazine, 1899)

All of the other nations mentioned in this quote tried to destroy the people of Israel. Considering their strength and numbers in comparison to the Jews, this fact is, naturally speaking, incomprehensible.

What is the secret of his immortality?

Our verse answers Mark Twain's question. Despite being pushed *to the point of falling;* i.e. to the point at which it only makes sense to fall, we did not fall. We survived. The secret of our immortality is, of course, no secret at all; *the Lord has assisted me.*

The incomprehensible and illogical survival of the Jewish people is itself a revelation of God. If it made sense it would not be so clearly a miracle. Were we not pushed *to the point of falling,* our perseverance and rebirth would not make it so obvious that the only way we made it through is because *the Lord has assisted* us.

This is the deeper meaning of our verse. After stating in the previous verses that the destruction of our enemies reveals God in the world, the psalmist now takes this message a step further. Not only is God's providence and goodness revealed when we are victorious. Even when all that we do is *survive*, the hand of the Almighty is clearly seen.

When we are *pushed to the point of falling* and survive, we cause the Mark Twains of the world to ask the question "What is the secret of their survival?" This leads to the only possible answer – *the Lord has assisted us.* Nothing else makes sense of our survival. Nothing else gives so much meaning to our suffering.

Naturally speaking, the Jewish people should not have survived. It is by the miraculous hand of God that they persevere throughout history. *******This commentary was written on the morning of Holocaust Remembrance Day in Israel April 24, 2017.*

118:14 *Quoting Exodus*

> *My bold strength and the song*
> *of praise of the Lord; for me*
> *was a salvation.*

What is most striking about this verse is that it is an exact quote from the Song at the Sea in the book of Exodus.

> Then Moses and the People of Israel sang this song to the Lord, and said, "I will sing to the Lord, for He is highly exalted; horse and its rider He has hurled into the sea. *My bold strength and the song of praise of the Lord; for me was a salvation.* This is my God, and I will praise Him; my father's God, and I will exalt Him." (Exodus 15:1-2)

The psalmist is clearly connecting Psalm 118 back to the splitting of the sea from the Exodus story. To fully understand this connection, let's go back to the scene at the Reed Sea.

God's Trap

What was the purpose of the splitting of the Reed Sea? In the most immediate sense, it was to save the People of Israel. The Egyptian army was approaching with its army of chariots. There was nowhere to run or hide. Splitting the sea allowed the Israelites to escape mortal danger. But if we take a closer look at events that led up to the splitting of the sea we'll see that it's not so simple.

The splitting of the Reed Sea took place one week after the People of Israel actually left Egypt. For the first three days of travel from away from Egypt, Pharaoh and his army did not chase after Israel. The People of Israel were free. It was only after more than three days that Pharaoh decided to travel out to the desert to attack Israel. "Okay," one could argue, "even if it took a few days, the People of Israel were still in danger when God split the sea." But were they? Here are the verses just before the splitting of the sea.

> Then the Lord said to Moses, "Tell the Israelites to *turn back and encamp* near Pi Hahiroth, between Migdol and the sea. They are to encamp by the sea, directly opposite Baal Zephon. Pharaoh will think, 'The Israelites are wandering around the land in confusion, hemmed in by the desert.' And I will harden Pharaoh's heart, and he will pursue them. But I will

gain glory for myself through Pharaoh and all his army, and the Egyptians will know that I am the Lord." So the Israelites did this. (Exodus 14:1-4)

Israel was free. The Egyptian army was not chasing them. They were in no danger. Then God told them to *turn back*; *to go back the way they came* and then stop traveling and set up camp. As expressed in these verses, the purpose of this was to deceive Pharaoh into thinking that the Israelites were lost and confused in the desert. This would give Pharaoh the false sense of security that he could defeat them. That's the reason that Pharaoh brought his army out to attack Israel. In other words, this was a trap designed by God to lure the Egyptian army out into the desert in order to teach them a final lesson at the sea.

So, were the People of Israel in danger? Well, they certainly *thought* that they were.

As Pharaoh approached, the Israelites looked up, and there were the Egyptians, marching after them. They were terrified and cried out to the Lord. (Exodus 14:10)

But just because Israel felt like they were in danger doesn't mean that they actually were. God had already stated His plan. After tricking the Egyptians into mobilizing *I will gain glory for myself through Pharaoh and all his army, and the Egyptians will know that I am the Lord.*

Enemies Attack so that God is Revealed

The shared message of the splitting of the Reed Sea and Psalm 118 is this. Sometimes, when God allows the enemies of His people to attack, He allows it to happen – *or He even orchestrates the attack* - only to set them up for their eventual defeat. This defeat brings with it the revelation of God's glory. That is what the splitting of the sea was all about.

As I pointed out, our verse here in Psalm 118 is an exact quote from Exodus 15. Look again at the context of each one. Here's Exodus:

I will sing to the Lord, for He is highly exalted; *horse and its rider He has hurled into the sea.* My bold strength and the song of praise of the Lord; for me was a salvation.

The previous verse describes the destruction of Egyptian military power; *horse and its rider He has hurled into the sea.* And here in Psalm 118 the message is the same:

All nations surrounded me; *it was in the name of the Lord that I cut them down.*

They encircled me - indeed they surrounded me; *it was in the name of the Lord that I cut them down.*

They encircled me like bees; *they were extinguished like the fire of thorns; it was in the name of the Lord that I cut them down.*

My bold strength and the song of praise of the Lord; for me was a salvation.

Just as in the Song at the Sea, here too the primary focus is not on our salvation but on their destruction; *it was in the name of the Lord that I cut them down.*

By quoting the Song at the Sea our psalmist is teaching us an important historical lesson. Even when we feel that we are in mortal danger; that the forces of evil that attack God's people look like they are going to win; in reality we are just like Israel in Exodus 14 when the Egyptian army was approaching. As frightening as it is at the time, God sends enemies against His people *in order to destroy them.* It was true when Israel left Egypt and it is true throughout history as well.

From Egypt to the End of Days

It's all too fitting that there is one more verse in Scripture which quotes this verse almost exactly.

In that day you will say: "I will praise you, Lord. Although You were angry with me, Your anger has turned away and You have comforted me. Surely God is my salvation; I will trust and not be afraid. *For My bold strength and the song of praise of the Lord, the Lord; for me was a salvation.*" (Isaiah 12:1-2)

In this End Times prophecy, immediately after describing the destruction of Israel's enemies (see Isaiah 11:13-15) Isaiah invokes this same verse that appears in Exodus 15 and in Psalm 118. Isaiah is connecting the ultimate redemption at the end of times with the message of the Splitting of the Sea – and with Psalm 118.

While we are grateful when God saves us from our attacking enemies, we must understand that the reason that God allows them to attack us in the first place and the reason we are saved is to bring glory to God. As Isaiah continues:

Give praise to the Lord, proclaim His name; make known among the nations what He has done, and proclaim that His name is exalted. (Isaiah 12:4)

The destruction of the enemies of God's people is critical to the ultimate redemption of the world and the building of His kingdom, just as it was vital to the Exodus from Egypt.

118:15 *Redemption Song*

There is a voice of joyful singing and salvation in the tents of the righteous; the right hand of the Lord acts valiantly.

What is Special about Singing?

What makes people *sing*? Why not simply cry out with joy? Why doesn't the verse simply read: *There is joy and salvation in the tents of the righteous*?

The simplest answer is that *singing* is not only an expression of joy. It is also a way of praising God. But we could then ask a follow up question; what is the difference between *praise* and *songs of praise*? Why is it better to *sing*?

One interesting characteristic of *singing* is that it is often done as a group. In fact, when a large group of people is singing together it can be a beautiful and very powerful experience. If you have ever been a part of a large crowd that is singing in unison you know what this feels like. There is a unique emotional bond that we feel when we sing as part of a group.

Group singing is so powerful not only because of how it sounds. Think about the difference between speaking and singing. Both when we speak and when we sing we are expressing ourselves verbally. But when multiple people speak simultaneously, it makes it harder to hear what any of them is saying. On the other hand, when multiple people sing together not only does it sound even better, we actually feel that what we are expressing is even more powerfully expressed than if were singing alone.

The more collective the singing; the greater the power of the expression.

Another Connection to the Song of the Sea

The first mention of singing in the Bible is the song that Moses and Israel sang in praise to God for splitting the Reed Sea and destroying Egypt. In my comments to the previous verse I pointed out the connection between our psalm and that event in Exodus. Now, in our verse and in the verse that follows this connection is deepened.

Notice the reference to *the right hand of the Lord* in both of these verses. This expression originates in the Song of the Sea as well.

Your *right hand*, Lord, was majestic in power. Your *right hand*, Lord, shattered the enemy. (Exodus 15:6)

You stretch out your *right hand*, and the earth swallows your enemies. (Exodus 15:12)

In light of the clear and deliberate connection between the Song of the Sea and our psalm it is interesting to note an important linguistic detail in our verse.

After the previous verse recalled the Song of the Sea in Exodus by quoting it directly,
 our psalm now continues the connection by referring to
 the right hand of the Lord;
 a biblical image that originates in the Song of the Sea as well.

Two Types of Song
The Hebrew word for *song* in our verse is RINAH. The Hebrew word for *song* in Exodus 15 verse 1 – the introductory verse of the Song of the Sea - is SHIRAH. So what is the difference between these two Hebrew words for *song*?

Like many synonyms, in many contexts it appears that these words have exactly the same meaning. That said, careful attention to a number of specific examples reveals an important distinction between the two.

Besides the Song of the Sea, the word SHIRAH appears 12 additional times in the Bible. Half of these – 6 of 12 – occur in Deuteronomy 31 and 32.

"Now write down this *song* – SHIRAH - and teach it to the Israelites and have them *sing* it, so that this *song* – SHIRAH - may be a witness for me against them. When I have brought them into the land flowing with milk and honey, the land I promised on oath to their ancestors, and when they eat their fill and thrive, they will turn to other gods and worship them, rejecting me and breaking my covenant. And when many disasters and calamities come on them, this *song* - SHIRAH - will testify against them, because it will not be forgotten by their descendants. I know what they are disposed to do, even before I bring them into the land I promised them on oath." So

Moses wrote down this *song* – SHIRAH - that day and taught it to the Israelites. (Deuteronomy 31:19-22)

"Assemble before me all the elders of your tribes and all your officials, so that I can speak these words in their hearing and call the heavens and the earth to testify against them. For I know that after my death you are sure to become utterly corrupt and to turn from the way I have commanded you. In days to come, disaster will fall on you because you will do evil in the sight of the Lord and arouse his anger by what your hands have made." And Moses recited the words of this *song* – SHIRAH - from beginning to end in the hearing of the whole assembly of Israel. (Deuteronomy 31:28-30; see also Deuteronomy 32:44)

Here, the point of the *song* is not to praise and thank the Lord for His salvation. Rather, the purpose is to record God's message for future generations. Songs are an effective way to set down a message that is meant to be remembered in the future. Songs are easier to memorize and pass on than regular prose writing.

From this context and from others (e.g. Numbers 21:17, II Samuel 22:1) I would like to suggest that SHIRAH is used for a song that is meant to *commemorate an event in order to record it for posterity*. It can certainly be used as praise of the Lord for His hand in the event, but praise and thanks to the Lord do not *define* the concept of SHIRAH – song. They do not describe its primary purpose.

Now look at the uses of RINAH in Scripture:

When the Lord restored the captives of Zion, we were like dreamers. Our mouths were filled with laughter, our tongues with *joyful singing* - RINAH. Then it was said among the nations, "The Lord has done great things for them." (Psalm 126:1-2; see also verses 5 & 6)

and those the Lord has rescued will return; they will enter Zion with *joyful singing* - RINAH; (Isaiah 35:10 & 51:11)

> Leave Babylon, flee from the Babylonians! Announce this with *joyful singing* – RINAH - and proclaim it. Send it out to the ends of the earth; say, "The Lord has redeemed his servant Jacob." (Isaiah 48:20)

There are more than twenty occurrences of RINAH in Scripture. Like the three examples here, almost all of them refer directly to the redemption of Israel and their return to their land. Here's a notable exception.

> When righteous people prosper, a city is glad. When wicked people die, there is *joyful singing* - RINAH. (Proverbs 11:10)

Based on what we have seen I would like to suggest that RINAH refers to a specific kind of *joyful singing*. Whether it is the restoration of Israel to Zion or the destruction of the wicked, the celebration is the same. Good has triumphed over evil. God's plan is coming to fruition. The world is being restored to the way it is meant to be. This is the essence of redemption.

To sum up the difference in connotation between the two words for song:

- SHIRAH is a song that records a past event for posterity. Sometimes this is done as praise of God; sometimes it serves as an easy to remember warning to future generations.
- RINAH is the expression of joy at the realization of God's plan; for example, the restoration of His people or the triumph of good over evil.

At the Song of the Sea in Exodus the word is SHIRAH. Here in Psalm 118 it is RINAH.

To strengthen this point even further, it is worth noting that the Hebrew words translated here as *a voice of joyful singing* are KOL RINAH. This two word phrase appears in only four places in Scripture; Isaiah 48:20, Psalms 42:5, Psalms 47:2, and our verse. In all four of these instances KOL RINAH refers to group singing. It never describes the song of an individual.

What do the Righteous Sing About?

As I mentioned before, the verses leading up to ours in this psalm describe both redemption and the destruction of the wicked. These are the themes that are associated with RINAH – *joyous singing*.

Now we can better understand our verse.

There is a voice of joyful singing and salvation in the tents of the righteous. Every person, righteous or not, rejoices when they are *personally* saved from danger. But our psalm is about much more. What makes the righteous sing songs of joy and salvation? The righteous do not rejoice only because they themselves were redeemed by God. As servants of the Almighty, their greatest joy is reserved for the Kingdom of God - the realization of God's plan for the world, the destruction of evil, and the restoration of His people to their land.

This is the essence of RINAH – *the joyous singing of redemption.*

We must rejoice when we see evidence of God's plan for the world unfolding. When evil is defeated and the righteous are redeemed, we must join together and sing His praises.

118:16 *The Right Hand of the Lord*

The right hand of the Lord is most high; the right hand of the Lord acts valiantly.

The right hand of the Lord

Many times throughout the Bible there is mention of God's *right hand.* The right hand obviously connotes power and control. This is what the right hand is for people. It's the stronger hand; the hand that is more skilled. Obviously, God has no physical body. So when we refer to His right hand we are referring to the characteristics that are represented by this concept; power and control.

Looking at the many places where God's *right hand* appears, we see that there is a variety of ways in which this concept is used.

Right Hand as Judgment

One of the most common is when judgment is being carried out upon the wicked. The *right hand of the Lord* is invoked. Here are a few examples.

> Your *right hand*, Lord, was majestic in power. Your *right hand*, Lord, shattered the enemy. (Exodus 15:6 Song of the Sea)

> Your hand will lay hold on all Your enemies; Your *right hand* will seize Your foes. (Psalm 21:9)

> The cup from *the Lord's right hand* is coming around to you, and disgrace will cover your glory. The violence you have done to Lebanon will overwhelm you, and the destruction of animals will terrify you. (Habakuk 2:16-17)

> How long will the enemy mock You, God? Will the foe revile Your name forever? Why do You hold back Your hand, *Your right hand*? Take it from the folds of Your garment and destroy them! (Psalm 74:10-11)

From all of these examples we would assume that the *right hand* of God connotes the power of God's judgment on His enemies expressed in military might.

Right Hand as Protection

And yet, the second most common use of the *right hand* of God in Scripture has a completely different connotation.

So do not fear, for I am with you; do not be dismayed, for I am your God. I will strengthen you and help you; I will uphold you with my righteous *right hand*. (Isaiah 41:10)

Save us and help us with *Your right hand*; that those You love may be delivered. (Psalm 60:7 & 108:7)

Because You are my help, I sing in the shadow of Your wings. I cling to You; *Your right hand* supports me. (Psalm 63:9)

In these and numerous other verses we see the *right hand of the Lord* as a symbol of God's kindness and protection. So which is it? Does the right hand describe God's fierce judgment on the wicked or His compassionate protection of the righteous?

What does <u>The Right Hand of the Lord</u> mean?

Judgment upon the wicked   *e.g. Exodus 15, Habakuk 2, Psalm 21, Psalm 74*
Protection of the righteous   *e.g. Isaiah 41, Psalm 60, Psalm 63, Psalm 108*

Splitting of the Sea: Judgment and Compassion
The answer is found, once again, in the Song of the Sea. I mentioned in my comments to the previous verse that *the right hand of the Lord* makes its first appearance – the first *three* appearances, actually – in Exodus 15 in the song that Moses and Israel sang at the splitting of the sea.

Was the miracle of splitting of the Reed Sea a mighty act of judgment on the wicked or a loving act of compassion and protection for the righteous? It was both. Most miracles in the Bible fit in to one category or the other. Either they are acts of punishment and justice, like the ten plagues or they are acts of divine mercy like the miracle of the multiplication of the widow's oil in II Kings chapter 4.

It should be noted that in the ancient polytheistic pagan mindset it makes no sense for a single miracle to be an expression of both harsh justice and loving mercy simultaneously. It is all too fitting that the final destruction of Egypt came through just such a miracle.

Judgment + Compassion = Kingship

Only the ruler of all of heaven and earth, Lord of all powers and forces of nature, is capable of expressing justice and mercy through the very same miracle. I would like to suggest that this explains another textual first that appears in the Song of the Sea.

The Lord will be *king* forever and ever! (Exodus 15:18)

The very first time in all of Scripture that God is referred to as *King* is in the closing line of the Song of the Sea. The combination of justice and mercy is unique to the king. Only the king has the power to override the rules, to mete out justice, and show compassion all at the same time. This brings us to one last notable mention of the right hand of God in Scripture.

As for the likeness of their faces, they had the face of a man; and they four had *the face of a lion on the right side*; and they four had the face of an ox on the left side; they four had also the face of an eagle. (Ezekiel 1:10)

In Ezekiel's vision of God we see the lion associated with the right side of the throne. The lion is the universal symbol of *kingship*. Lions are feared by all their enemies for their power *and* they are extremely protective of their own. This combination is the essence of Kingship. This is the right hand of the Lord. Now, look back at the two different meanings of *the right hand of the Lord*. Put them together and they mean that the Lord is King.

The dual role of protector of His own and destroyer of His enemies has been the theme of the praises of God that we have seen in the last few verses of our psalm.

- Verses 8 and 9 described the trust in the *protection* of the Lord.
- Verses 9, 10 and 11 described the *destruction of the wicked* attackers of God's people.

Now, in verses 14, 15, and 16, by once again connecting our psalm to the themes of the splitting of the Reed Sea in Exodus, the psalmist emphasizes a lesson for all who serve the Lord and fight His battles.

God's protection of us and His destruction of our enemies are not to be separated. Both elements are necessary for the kingdom of God on this earth.

God's compassion for those devoted to Him and His judgment on those who reject Him do not represent different aspects of who He is. He is King.

118:17 *Personal vs. Collective Identities*

I will not die for I shall live
and I will recount the acts
of the Lord.

I will not die

One thing that can be said with absolute certainty is that everybody eventually dies. Obviously our psalmist does not mean that he, as an individual, will never die. The most straightforward understanding of the verse is *I will not die as a result of this current suffering; I will survive this*.

"I" means Israel

But there is another way to see these words. If we look back at the previous verses we see that although the psalmist is speaking as an individual in the singular, he is actually speaking *on behalf of the entire people of Israel*. Consider verse 10 where he wrote,

All nations surrounded me; it was in the name of the Lord that I cut them down.

All nations surrounded me? Clearly he does not mean to say that he, as an individual, was surrounded by all the nations of the world. Rather, the simple meaning of the verse is that he is speaking on behalf of Israel as a collective.

Sometimes "I" means "I"

A psalm that is written in the first person singular on behalf of the entire people of Israel is especially interesting in light of the many psalms that speak in the plural when referring to the nation as a whole. Generally, this is the difference between those psalms that are written in the singular and those that are written in the plural. In other words, the standard practice is for psalms that refer to the collective experience of Israel to be written in the plural. The examples are too numerous to mention.

On the other hand, psalms that are written in the singular usually refer to a more personal experience. Here, too, there are too many examples to list, such as:

A special psalm and a prayer by David when he was in the cave: *I pray to You, Lord; I beg for mercy.* (Psalm 142:1-2)

To sum up:

- Psalms about the *collective of Israel* are generally written in the *plural*.
- Psalms that express *individual* experiences and prayers are generally written in the *singular*.
- Psalm 118 is clearly about the *collective of Israel* BUT is written in the *singular*.

Personification or Identification

As we have said, the author of our psalm chose to write in the singular language as though speaking on behalf of the entire people of Israel. I would like to offer two different ways of understanding the meaning behind this choice.

One way to understand this is to see the psalm as poetically *personifying* the entire people as a single entity. In this psalm, as though a single person, the People of Israel speaks. It expresses its fears. It cries out to God. It fights its enemies. It praises and thanks the Lord for its salvation. The message is profound and easy to understand. *Israel is one*. It is one body; *one person*; with a single collective relationship to the Lord.

This is a beautiful explanation of the singular language of our psalm. But then what do we do with the many psalms that speak of Israel in the plural? Surely, those psalms are not implying a lack of unity in Israel?

I'd like to suggest another way of looking at it.

Perhaps the psalmist is not using imagery of a singular personification of the collective of Israel at all. Rather, this psalm is describing a single person speaking. However, he is speaking from the perspective of *his own identification with his people*. Allow me to explain.

Personal vs. Collective Identity

Identification with a collective means that I have an identity that is not defined by my individual self. As a part of this entity my primary goals are not personal private goals. My pain, happiness, dreams, and fears are determined and defined by the suffering or success of *the nation*. Anyone who is part of any collective experiences this to some extent. There are many circumstances in life that call upon us to think collectively. If our country is attacked or our town needs volunteers during a crisis we drop our individual concerns and *become* members of the collective.

At the same time, I am also an individual. I have my own private pain, concerns, and dreams. There are situations in life that relate only to our individual selves; e.g. our job situation or our family relationships.

Each and every one of us lives both of these experiences. We are individual private people and at the same time we are part of a nation, a religious group, and a community.

While there are many situations where this choice between individual and collective identification is clear, there are many more in which it is not. In these situations, the extent to which I, as an individual, identify with the collective *is up to me*.

Do I make key choices in life based on *me*? Based on my family? Based on my country? Based on God?

When I read the news do I reserve my concern for those issues that only affect me personally? Or am I also concerned with those that affect my country? What about those issues that affect the entire world?

I'd like to suggest that our psalmist is an individual who *identifies with* the entirety of the People of Israel; the eternal Israel; Israel throughout her history.

This is the meaning of the words *I will not die for I shall live*. To the extent that I identify with the collective of Israel, *I will not die*. Oh, as an *individual* – of course I will die. Every individual dies eventually. *But the nation of Israel does not die*. Because I have chosen to identify with the nation - my suffering, my salvation, my struggles, and my victories all are part of the collective experience of Israel; because my destiny is not about me or my finite time on this earth; because *I* am Israel. *I will not die*.

This is the eternal mission of Israel – to struggle, to survive and to live – and to *recount the acts of the Lord*.

By identifying with broader concerns – my country, my brothers and sisters in faith, or God's plan for the world – I expand my identity. I become part of something larger and more eternal that my finite individual life.

118:18 *Growth from Suffering*

> *The Lord has surely chastised me; and to death He has not delivered me.*

Why do people suffer? There are many approaches to this difficult question.

- Human beings use their free will to perpetrate evil, thereby causing suffering to others. God does not stand in the way of human beings using their free will this way.

- Sometimes, suffering is used by God to test the righteous as in the famous story of Job.
- Suffering can lead one away from frivolous careless behavior. Suffering does this by causing people to focus and refine their goals and values. We saw this in Psalm 116. Recall verses 6 and 7 of that psalm:

> 6. *The Lord protects the unwary; I was brought low; but for me it brings salvation.*
> 7. *Return, my soul, to your restfulness for the Lord has bestowed this upon you*

In my comments to 116:7 I wrote:

The psalmist realizes that sometimes hardship is sent by God to keep him from careless sinful thoughts and behavior. It is not uncommon for people who feel weak and fearing death to find the experience reminding them of higher values that they may have been neglecting in their lives. This happens precisely because suffering is a context that facilitates this kind of thinking. Earthly temporal desires fade into the background. Our psalmist understands that his suffering is itself a form of salvation.

And now in this verse we have yet another purpose of suffering.

The Lord has surely chastised me;

The Hebrew word for *chastise* that is used here is often used as a synonym for *suffering*. But a careful look at the word reveals an important distinction. To be *chastised* implies that one is at fault and deserves to be punished. But *chastisement* is not punishment merely because a price must be paid. The goal of *chastisement* is the correction and improvement of the behavior of the one who was chastised. The Hebrew word for chastise used here in our verse makes this point. YASAR – *chastised* - is actually a causative verb form of the root for *ethics* or *proper behavior* - MUSAR.

In other words, the phrase in our verse *The Lord has surely chastised me* could just as accurately be translated as *The Lord has surely caused me to improve my ways*.

In light of this nuance, we can see that our verse has introduced a new idea to our psalm.

Up until this point Psalm 118 has mentioned suffering as:

- incentive to call out to the Lord (v.5)
- a situation brought on by enemy attackers who are to be destroyed (v.10-13)
- something from which the mighty hand of the Lord saves (v.13-17)

Now, in verse 18, the psalmist introduces a new element; his own responsibility for his suffering.

The psalmist recognizes that the fact that his enemies are evil and destined to be destroyed by God does not absolve him of his share of responsibility for his own suffering. Yes, God's mighty hand saved me from my enemies and I will praise Him for that. Yes, one important product of this crisis was the revelation of God that accompanies the triumph of good and the destruction of evil. At the same time, I dare not miss the *rebuke* inherent in my suffering. While I happily revel in God's miraculous salvation I dare not let my religious ego get the better of me. Yes, God loves me and saved me from harm. *But He also put me in that position in the first place*. And it is my responsibility to ask myself what I did to deserve that. What can I improve about my behavior? What was lacking in my spiritual or ethical life that needed correcting?

As we have seen, the theme of this psalm is the *cutting down of the wicked* (v.10-12) and the *joyous singing of the righteous* (v.15); in other words, *the triumph of good over evil*. The message of our verse is that this triumph is not just about saving the good guys and killing the bad guys. The triumph of good over evil also requires repentance; a change in ways to fix what isn't right about our lives.

The Lord has surely chastised me; and to death He has not delivered me.

God did not punish me simply to exact a price for my wrongdoing like a judge meting out a sentence. For that He could have sent me to my death. But He was not seeking *atonement*. *The Lord chastised me*. He wanted me to *live*; to live differently; to change my ways; to improve; to *repent*.

We dare not be arrogant and forget that God sends us a message by allowing evil to rear its head. We must introspect and look to weed out the evil <u>within</u> even as we celebrate the defeat of the evil <u>without</u>.

118:19 *The Gates of Righteousness*

Open for me the gates of
righteousness. I will enter them;
I will thank the Lord.

What exactly are the *gates of righteousness*? What do they have to do with *thanking the Lord*?

TZEDEK – Justice, Fairness, Honesty

The Hebrew word in our verse for *righteousness* – TZEDEK - is actually more precisely used in Scripture as the word for *justice, fairness*, or *honesty*. Here are just a few well known examples among many throughout the Bible.

> And I commanded your judges at that time saying, "Be attentive to that which is between your brethren and judge with *justice* – TZEDEK, whether the case is between a man and his brother or his foreigner." (Deuteronomy 1:16)

> Judges and officials place for yourselves in every town the Lord your God is giving you, to your tribes; and they shall judge the people with *fairness* – TZEDEK. Do not pervert judgment or show partiality. Do not accept a bribe, for a bribe

blinds the eyes of the wise and twists the words of the innocent. *Justice; justice* alone – TZEDEK TZEDEK, shall you pursue so that you may live and possess the land the Lord your God is giving you. (Deuteronomy 16:18-20)

Use *honest* – TZEDEK - scales and *honest* – TZEDEK - weights, an *honest* – TZEDEK - *ephah* and an *honest* – TZEDEK - *hin*. I am the Lord your God, who brought you out of Egypt (Leviticus 19:36)

So, if TZEDEK actually means *justice*, *honesty*, and *fairness*, what are the *gates of TZEDEK*?

Open for me the Gates of TZEDEK (Psalm 118:19)

TZEDEK	=	*Righteousness*
TZEDEK	=	*Justice*
TZEDEK	=	*Fairness*
TZEDEK	=	*Honesty*

So what exactly are these Gates?

Praise vs. Thanks

In my comments to verse 1 of this psalm I pointed out that in contrast to the previous five psalms which spoke of *praise* of God, Psalm 118 is about *giving thanks* to God. This shift in theme is dramatically indicated by the opening words of the psalm, *Give thanks to the Lord for He is good;* - which are repeated in the closing line of the psalm as well.

There is a big difference between praise and thanks. Most obviously, *giving thanks* means that the one who is doing the thanking personally benefited from the one whom he is thanking. I say *thank you* if I received something. Otherwise, thanking makes no sense. *Praise*, on the other hand, does not imply personal benefit on the part of the one doing the praising.

I thank	=	I personally benefited
I praise	=	regardless of personal benefit

This brings us to another difference between *praise* and *thanks*. Imagine I witness an act of kindness done by someone for someone else. Having seen this, it is certainly appropriate for me to praise the person who did this wonderful thing. But would I *thank* them? Well, I could thank them but doing so would imply that somehow I gained something as well. In fact, if you think about it, if I did thank someone for doing something nice to someone else, I would really be sort of saying – *you helped me too.*

What about the other way around? Imagine a situation where someone did something nice for me and instead of thanking them I just praised them. Like, if I said, "That was a really nice thing you did there," without ever saying *thank you.* Would that be appropriate? No. It would not.

To sum up:

Praise is a compliment or endorsement of an event, without necessarily acknowledging any connection or effect between the one praising and either the event or agent of the event. *Thanks*, on the other hand, admits that one has been affected by the event and is obligated thereby to the agent.

Thank you means *I owe you.* It means I personally am *obligated to thank you* for what you have done *for me.* Praise is freely bestowed. Thanks is a debt; an obligation.

Gates of TZEDEK – Beyond Praise

Now we can understand the meaning of our verse. I have an *obligation* to *give thanks* to the Lord for all that He has done for me. Not to give thanks would be *unjust; unfair; wrong.* It would deny that what He did actually helped me.

When I fully recognize what God did for me; that without His salvation I would have been doomed; my perspective changes. My awareness of the presence of the Lord in my life brings the realization that I *owe a personal debt to Him.*

With this outlook, I enter into a new place in my relationship with the Lord - I enter into the *gates of TZEDEK – justice, fairness; i.e. that which is duly deserved.* This is beyond being only *worthy of my praise*; He is *owed my thanks.*

When we thank God we are telling Him that we recognize that we personally benefited from what He has done; that we are indebted to Him.

118:20 *The Gate to the Lord*

This is the gate to the Lord; the righteous will enter it.

The Gate to the Lord?

The highest goal that every person of faith strives for is to be close to God. There is no doubt that if there is a *gate to the Lord* - a direct path to get closer to Him - we all want to enter it. But what exactly is this gate? Where is it? How do I enter it?

Our verse is obviously making a very important theological state-ment. *This is the gate to the Lord.* But what is *This?* The words of the verse do not make it clear.

"This is the Gate to the Lord"
The meaning of the word <u>This</u> is not clear from context.

One possibility is that *This* refers to the *gates of righteousness* mentioned in the previous verse. It would make sense that the *gates* in two consecutive verses are the same. But this explanation is problematic for a number of reasons.

The righteous are righteous?

First, if the gates in the two verses are the same this would mean that our verse is stating that *the gates of righteousness* are entered by *righteous people.* Righteous people enter the gates of righteousness. Does the verse need to tell me this? Consider the fact that we are not talking about any actual physical gate. The poetry of the psalm is using *gate* to mean a *way*, a *process*, or a *way of approaching*. Why would a verse state that *righteous people enter the gates of righteousness*? Is the verse simply saying that *the righteous* are, in fact, *righteous*?

How many gates?

Second, in the previous verse *gates* is written in the plural whereas our verse *gate* is singular.

12. *Open for me the <u>gates</u> of righteousness. I will enter <u>them</u>; I will thank the Lord.*
13. *<u>This is the gate</u> to the Lord; the righteous will enter <u>it</u>.*

If the *gate* in our verse is the same as the *gates* in verse 19, there is no reason for this change from plural to singular.

I'd like to suggest that this change from plural to singular alerts us to the fact that *<u>This</u> is the gate to the Lord* actually refers to the phrase that immediately precedes it - *I will thank the Lord.* In terms of syntax this makes sense. *This,* under normal circumstances, refers to whatever was just mentioned.

According to my suggestion the five statements in these two verses would be understood like this.

1. Open for me the gates of righteousness.
2. I will enter them.
3. I will thank the Lord.
4. <u>This</u> – *i.e #3* - is the gate to the Lord
5. The righteous will enter it.

Gratitude and Faith

There is a fundamental connection between gratitude and faith. More precisely, one could argue that without a developed sense of gratitude any real relationship with God is impossible.

There are two lines of thinking – even among people who profess belief in God – that undermine our sense of gratitude. There are many people who see the world governed by the natural forces of chance and coincidence. Some of these people will even say that they believe in God. But they will often speak of faith in "a higher power" or "a creator" rather than an all powerful God who is intimately involved in our lives and directs events here on earth. They believe in "God" as some great and distant force, not as concerned with each of us as individuals. For such a person, there is no necessity to feel grateful to God. After all, what we have is not the result of gifts that are knowingly bestowed upon us personally. So why thank Him?

A second line of thinking sees all that I have in my life as largely of my own doing. God has given me great gifts of health or wealth either because I deserve them or because God has allowed me to govern my own life through free will and I have made good choices. What this approach misses is the fact that so many people are denied happiness and health through disease, sudden tragedy, or other circumstances that are clearly our of their control. The fact that God has kept this happy successful person free from trouble is a deliberate choice the Lord has made.

The cure for these faulty ways of thinking is the proper development of a sense of gratitude. As soon as I begin with the question, "Why me? Why do I have the good things that I have?" I am on the road to an intimate personal relationship with God. As long as I realize that I am not entitled to anything; that everything that I have is a gift, the result will always be gratitude to God.

Thanks is the "Gate to the Lord"

This is the meaning of our verse and the verse that came before it

14. *Open for me the <u>gates</u> of righteousness. I will enter <u>them</u>; I will thank the Lord.*

If I am *righteous, just* and *honest,* I will acknowledge that God is owed my thanks. To deny that God is owed my thanks is not only heretical. *It is unjust.* Lack of gratitude displays a lack of *righteousness.*

15. *<u>This is the gate</u> to the Lord; the righteous will enter <u>it</u>.*

This expression of gratitude is the *gate to the Lord. Gratitude is the way forward towards a relationship with Him.*

It is through thanking Him that we fully acknowledge the Lord's involvement in our personal lives. This is how we enter into relationship with Him.

118:21 *Suffering and Higher Meaning*

I will thank You for You have made me suffer; and for me You were a salvation.

* Note: I am employing a radical translation of the Hebrew word ANITANI which I have translated as <u>You have made me suffer</u>. This translation is supported by one classical Jewish commentary which inspired this piece.

How do we make sense of our suffering? Without a doubt, this is the most painful and difficult question that facing all people of faith. For many people it is the greatest challenge to our relationship with God. Yes, it's true that when we emerge from suffering and are saved from it we feel gratitude. However, the questions still remain. After all, it was God who made us suffer – or at least allowed us to suffer – in the first place.

The problem of suffering is dealt with in a number of sections of the Bible; most notably in the book of Job. But in that story no answer is given to Job's questions about why he is suffering. Instead, Job has a revelation of God at the end of the book through which he realizes that he will never understand the ways of God.

Lamentations is another scripture that deals with suffering. There, the answer is found in our sins. The response to suffering according to the text of Lamentations is for those suffering to take responsibility, to introspect, and to mend our ways.

Psalm 118, like Psalm 116 before it, deals with the question of suffering differently from these two other texts. Here, the question that is being answered is not *why am I suffering?*; but *what is the purpose and meaning of my suffering?*

This is a very important point. These are two different questions. The first, the theological question of theodicy, the justification for God allowing undeserved suffering in the world, is not fully satisfied by any answer that Scripture offers. As God tells Job in the final chapters of that story, there is just no way for human beings of limited perspective to understand certain things.

> Then the Lord answered Job out of the whirlwind, and said: "Who is this who darkens counsel by words without knowledge? Now prepare yourself like a man; I will question you, and you shall answer Me. Where were you when I laid the foundations of the earth? Tell Me, if you have understanding." (Job 38:1-4)

In other words, as mere mortals we can not ever understand.

That said, the human inability to understand *why* there is suffering does not prevent us from deriving *meaning from our suffering*.

And that is the point of our psalm. The true reasons for my suffering will never be known to me. But this I know. If not for the suffering that I endured, I would never have experienced the divine hand of salvation in my life. Whether we like it or not, the revelation of God's goodness requires the rise of evil so that it can be defeated.

It is with this perspective that the psalmist expresses his gratitude for what he has gone through.

I will thank You for You have made me suffer; and for me You were a salvation.

Had I been offered the choice I most certainly would have asked not to suffer in the first place. But now that it has happened I am grateful for the new level of revelation of God in my life. And I know, like it or not, that this would have been impossible had I not been in dire straits to begin with.

At the end of my comments to verse 10 of this psalm I wrote:

> *All nations surrounded me;* - our enemies surround us. They attack us:

> *it was in the name of the Lord that I cut them down* – to serve the ultimate purpose of all of creation – the revelation of the name of the Lord – I cut them down; as a circumcision. Painful as it may be, removal of the evil barriers to our relationship with God is our covenantal responsibility to all humanity. By cutting off evil, I not only save myself from danger, I allow the revelation of good in God's kingdom here on earth.

Our psalmist is certainly thanking God for saving him from danger. But that is not his primary goal. The theme of this psalm is that the entirety of the combined experience of danger and redemption is meant to serve the ultimate purpose of all of creation; namely the revelation of God's glory in the world.

And that is the truest salvation of all.

We do not wish any suffering upon ourselves or others. But when we go through such crises we must thank the Lord for our growth in relationship with Him even in those unwanted and trying experiences.

118:22 *Why the Chief Cornerstone?*

The stone despised by the builders has become the chief cornerstone.

Up to this point Psalm 118 has described rescue from attack, defeat of enemies, and escape from harm all done by the hand of the Lord. Now, in our verse, the psalmist introduces a new theme. He has not only been saved from harm; he has risen to a newfound preeminent status in spite of being rejected and disregarded as worthless. The enemies who once despised him now see him as worthy of respect.

Now, it certainly feels nice to prove the naysayers wrong, but it seems that this extra victory pales in comparison to the more fundamental fact that he has been saved from death.

Imagine you are experiencing mortal danger. You are being attacked from all sides. Then, miraculously, the hand of God intervenes and rescues you from harm while defeating your enemies. At the time of crisis, are you also dreaming of a rise to prominence? Is it really important to you at that moment of escape from peril that those who doubted you should now see you as victorious?

A second issue relates to the metaphor of builders. Up to this point, we have described the enemies as attackers who seek to harm. Why are they referred to as builders? What are they building?

Why the Great Wealth?

In God's covenant with Abraham He foretold that there would be exile, slavery, and Exodus from Egypt. In that prophecy of the future redemption, Abraham was promised that his descendents would receive more than just their freedom.

> Then the Lord said to him, "Surely know that your descendants will be foreign in a country not their own and that they will be enslaved and mistreated there for four hundred years. And so too, I will punish the nation they serve as slaves, _and afterward they will emerge with great wealth._" (Genesis 15:13-14)

Here in Genesis, like in our psalm, it's not enough to simply be redeemed from suffering; there is a promise of high status – *great wealth* - as well. Why? Is this some kind of compensation for the suffering? "Look, I'm sorry you had to suffer. Here's some wealth to make up for it."

To ask the question another way, is the promise of great wealth and high status essential to the redemption or is it something that is added on to it? Wouldn't the redemption from Egypt have been complete without the *great wealth*?

The Real Purpose of Redemption

The answer lies in the purpose of redemption. If God's purpose in freeing Israel from slavery in Egypt was simply to make them free men, then no, the wealth is not an essential component of that process. The goal would have been to bring the chosen people to freedom. That purpose would have been fulfilled with or without the added blessing of great wealth.

But that was not the goal. As a critical component of the Abrahamic covenant, the enslavement and subsequent redemption of Israel from Egypt were meant to serve a higher, more universal purpose. The People of Israel were saved from Egypt not merely to be free and to serve God as their own private affair. They were chosen to influence the entire world. Even the miracles of the Exodus were not meant primarily for their own benefit.

> Then I will lay my hand on Egypt and with mighty acts of judgment I will bring out my divisions, my people the Israelites. And *the Egyptians will know that I am the Lord* when I stretch out my hand against Egypt and bring the Israelites out of it. (Exodus 7:4-5)

If the purpose of redemption is only Israel's freedom then why does it matter if the Egyptians *know that I am the Lord*?

Shortly after the Exodus, at the beginning of Exodus 19, the Lord introduces the covenant at Sinai by telling Israel that they are about to become *a kingdom of priests and a holy nation*. (Exodus 19:6) The Hebrew word for *priest* - KOHEN – is not unique to Israel. It is the word that Scripture uses to describe all who serve in a priestly role in any nation. The role of a priest is, simply, to help others – members of the flock – draw closer to the deity; to help them grow spiritually. In other words, a priest is not a priest without a flock. *The job of a priest is to provide spiritual influence and leadership.*

All of this means to say that the primary purpose of Israel's redemption is *actually not Israel*. It is the world. Israel's mission is to bring knowledge of God and Godly values to all of humanity. Israel's purpose is to change the world; to influence it. *To be a priestly kingdom.*

Change and influence can not happen without the ability and power to do so.

The great wealth that God promised Abraham as part of the Exodus was not mere compensation for centuries of suffering. *It was essential to the entire purpose of Israel.* In effect, God told Abraham that his descendants would emerge from Egypt with the resources to carry out their great mission. *Great wealth* is a synonym for the power and status necessary to change things; the means to make things happen.

This exact theme repeats itself in the prophetic description of the ultimate ingathering of Israel at the end of days first described in Deuteronomy.

> He will bring you to the land that belonged to your ancestors, and you will take possession of it. He will make you *more prosperous* and numerous than your ancestors. (Deuteronomy 30:5)

Our verse here in Psalm 118 is making the same point. In the previous verse I explained that the psalmist recognizes that the purpose of the entire process of his suffering and redemption is the eventual revelation of God that results. Now, he takes this point a step further. It is not enough that the one who suffers and is saved recognizes the glory of God in this process. It is not even enough that those who are friendly and on his side share in his joy and praise of the Almighty. Ultimately, the goal of all that he has gone through is the revelation of the glory of God to the world; *especially to those who didn't see it before.* Without that result, the redemption would lose its highest value.

By bringing him respect and new-found status in the eyes of those who despised him, the true goal of his redemption from harm is realized.

On a personal level we ought to think about our individual lives the same way. When we experience the redemptive hand of the Lord we should remind ourselves that He wants us to serve a purpose in the world. When God grants us any measure of wealth, power, or status we must see them for what they are meant to be. These gifts are given to us not as reward or compensation. They are the tools of influence that God puts in our hands to serve Him and bring knowledge of Him to others.

So who are the builders and what are they building?

I have just explained that the theme of this verse – and of this entire psalm – is that the reason that God protects His people from harm is to facilitate His plan for the world. Those who are dedicated to God and serve Him are charged with the mission to carry out His will and create His kingdom here on earth; a perfect world governed by morality, peace, and love of God.

But many people who oppose faith in God also want to create a perfect world. Many people who reject religion are good people. They also speak of world peace and a system of morals and ethics. These secularists see religion as backward looking. For them, faith in God is passé, obsolete, and a hindrance to the progress of human society.

They see themselves as the builders of the future; as the architects of progress. As they see it, the ball and chain of religion should be left behind if we are to build the perfect world. So they despise religion. They do battle against it in their effort to build the future. But they are sorely mistaken. The values of a good and just society; the progress of humanity towards a world of peace; are built on Biblical faith. Without belief in God's timeless word, there is no foundation for the future of humanity. Atheistic morality will at best result in the perpetuation of humanity for its own sake; but it cannot achieve the goal of a redeemed society, a society that has a message for the future beyond mere survival.

Getting back to our original question on this verse, our goal as people of Biblical faith is not only our own salvation. It's the perfection of the world as the kingdom of heaven. We know that peace on earth, the value of every human life, and the triumph of good over evil are only possible *when the earth will be filled with knowledge of God like water covers the sea.* (Isaiah 11:9)

This is the meaning of our verse. As a result of the miraculous redemption that God bestows upon us; as a result of His blessings to His people; the ultimate goal will be realized. All those who sincerely seek a better world will realize the truth. That what they saw as an out of date and irrelevant barrier to progress is actually the cornerstone of all that is good in human society.

I believe that our verse describes the experience of all people of faith in today's world. The derision and attacks that religion endures in today's society are unprecedented. But in the end, as Scripture promises over and over again, the truth of God will win out. Peace will reign supreme. And those who were despised and deemed irrelevant will be the foundation of God's kingdom.

The stone despised by the builders has become the chief cornerstone.

We must see the gifts of wealth, respect, and talent that God gives us as tools to be used to influence the world in a positive way; towards the building of His kingdom.

118:23 *The Wonder of History*

This has emerged from the Lord;
it is wondrous in our eyes.

To immediate questions come to mind:

1. Well, isn't *everything* from the Lord?
2. What exactly is the psalmist referring to with the word *This*?

The answer to the second question will help us to answer the first.

The most straightforward explanation of the word *This* in our verse is that it refers to what immediately preceded it; namely what is described in the previous verse. *The stone despised by the builders has become the chief cornerstone.*

In my comments to that verse I explained that it is not enough for God to redeem His people from danger. It is critical that He give them status, power, and respect in the eyes of others. These added gifts are necessary so that they have the wherewithal to influence the world to bring all of humanity to knowledge of Him.

In our verse the psalmist adds a vital element to this message. To serve its purpose, this rise to prominence must come about in such a way that it is clear that it is a miraculous gift from God. If God's people go from being despised and cast aside to being recognized as a cornerstone of human progress it must happen in such a manner that it is clear to all that it is a divine gift.

If God's people achieve great wealth and status and it appears likely that it came about naturally or through the work of their own hands, then the glory of God is not fully served. In other words, when *the stone that was despised* and left for useless becomes *the chief cornerstone* it has to be perfectly clear that this rise to greatness is a miraculous act of God. The inescapable conclusion must be - *This has emerged from the Lord; it is wondrous in our eyes.*

There is no greater example of this than the story of the Jewish people over the past 100 years. Never was this nation as weak and impoverished as in the wake of the Holocaust. Millions had been murdered. Millions were displaced. When the State of Israel was founded it was an impoverished country with barely any arms to fight to defend itself. Many of the immigrants were penniless refugees.

In only a few decades Israel has become an economic powerhouse, a world leader in technological innovation, and an island of freedom in a tumultuous region of the world. All of this has been accomplished while under constant attack from numerous enemy nations that surround it; not to mention the international diplomatic isolation and criticism that is relentlessly heaped upon the Jewish State.

Imagine if the story of the modern State of Israel had not happened yet and it was written as a work of fiction. Imagine reading such an fullness of God's power over creation. We are no longer living by the rules of nature set out by God during the six days of creation. This is not the day that *God* has made. Rather…

This is the day that <u>the Lord</u> – YHVH - has made.

We must appreciate God as revealed in nature separately from how we experience Him as He is revealed in the supernatural. God chose the natural order as our everyday experience of Him. This way, He allows us the glorious experience of miracles when He chooses to override that natural order.

118:25 *Helping Us to Help Him*

Please, O Lord, please save;
Please, O Lord, please bring
success.

Are we thanking or asking?

Imagine that a great favor has just been done for you. You were in serious trouble and someone came along and bailed you out. You are overjoyed, relieved, and filled with gratitude. You begin to praise and thank this person for what they have done. So far, so good. In the middle of all that praise and thanks, would you start asking for more help? Is this appropriate? Does it make sense to interrupt the expressing of gratitude and appreciation to plead for further assistance?

And yet, this is exactly what our verse seems to be saying. The entirety of this psalm up to this point has been praise and thanks to God. The only cry for help that was mentioned appeared in verse 5 when the psalmist began to tell his story and recalled how in the past he had called out to the Lord for help. But our verse is not telling the story of what God has done in the past. It is simply a plea to the Lord for further help, *"please save… please bring success."*

In my comments to verse 22, I explained that the theme of this psalm is the recognition that the true purpose of our own redemption and salvation is not actually us at all. God assists us in times of trouble and redeems us from our suffering so that we will, in turn, spread knowledge of Him to others. As I wrote in verse 22:

> When we experience the redemptive hand of the Lord we should remind ourselves that He wants us to serve a purpose in the world. When God grants us any measure of wealth, power, or status we must see them for what they are meant to be. These gifts are given to us not as reward or compensation. They are the tools of influence that God puts in our hands to serve Him and bring knowledge of Him to others.

In other words, there are two stages in God's process of calling and empowering us to spread knowledge of Him to others. First he redeems us. We feel His hand in our lives individually and collectively as He saves us from harm and suffering. This is followed by stage two. God grants us gifts, talents, abilities or a measure of wealth. It is then our responsibility to use these resources *for Him.*

With this understanding we can answer our question. Is it really inappropriate to interrupt our praise of God with a plea for more salvation and success? Well, it depends. If our goal is our own benefit; if our cry for help is about *us* and *our needs* then the answer is that it is not appropriate. But here, it's not about us. *It's about Him.* Rather than a seemingly out of context request for our own benefit, our verse is actually a very lofty statement of worship.

In this verse what we are actually saying to God is, "Lord, I understand what You want from me. I understand that You have redeemed me from suffering and granted me success so that I will use the fruits of that success to glorify Your name and build Your kingdom on earth. I recognize what You have done for me and I praise You for it. But Lord, *I want to do more.* **Please, O Lord, please save; Please, O Lord, please bring success.** Give me added measures of redemption; grant me more resources so that I can use these gifts to spread Your Name to all."

When we truly believe that the gifts that the Lord bestows upon us are meant to be used for His glory, our requests for more success are actually only requests for more resources with which to serve Him.

118:26 Who is "we"? and Who is "you"?

> *Blessed is the one who comes in the name of the Lord; we have blessed you from the house of the Lord.*

<u>*We* have blessed *you*</u>?

What just happened? Who is *we* referring to? If we look back at the entire psalm up to this point we see that it is written in the *first person singular*.

> … I called out "Lord" [Yah]; He answered *me* … (v.5) The Lord is for *me*, I will not fear; what can man do to *me*? (v.6) The Lord is for *me* in those who help *me*; and I will perceive *my* enemies. (v.7) All nations surrounded *me*; … I cut them down. (v.10) They encircled *me* … surrounded *me*; … I cut them down. (v.11) They encircled *me* …I cut them down. (v.12) You have surely pushed *me* … but the Lord has assisted *me*. (v.13) *My* bold strength … for *me* was a salvation. (v.14) I will not die for I shall live and I will recount the acts of the Lord. (v.17) The Lord has surely chastised *me*; and to death He has not delivered *me*. (v.18) Open for *me* the gates of righteousness. I will enter them; I will thank the Lord. (v.19) I will thank You for You have made *me* suffer; and for *me* You were a salvation. (v.21)

So why does our verse use the plural word *we*? The truth is that this change from singular to plural took place a few verses ago and it will continue after our verse.

23. This has emerged from the Lord; it is wondrous in <u>our</u> eyes.
24. This is the day that the Lord has made; <u>we</u> will rejoice and delight in it.

The question remains. After twenty two verses in the first person singular, why does the psalmist switch to plural? Who is speaking in these verses? And when our verse states *we have blessed you*, who is the psalmist speaking to? How is it that we have gone from a single individual telling his story of danger and redemption to a group of people addressing somebody else?

<u>We</u> have blessed <u>you</u> from the house of the Lord

* *Who is "we"?*
* *Who is "you"?*
* *Why did the psalmist switch from "I" to "we"?*

Let's recall what led up to Psalm 118.

Psalm 116: The Invitation

Two psalms ago, Psalm 116 described an individual who is enduring personal hardship. He cried out to the Lord and experienced personal redemption. But His praise of God did not end with his personal feelings of gratitude. He committed himself to bring a *sacrifice of thanksgiving* and to *call out the name of the Lord in the presence of all of His people in Jerusalem.* Personal redemption led him to collective praise and worship in the temple; including others in a public celebration of God's kindness to him.

The closing word of that psalm is *Hallelujah*, which literally translates as *Praise the Lord*. With this word, this person who experienced God's hand and vowed to share this with others in the temple in Jerusalem called on those who have joined him to praise the Lord. *Hallelujah*, as would be expected, is written in the second person plural. He is speaking to many others. *Praise* (2nd person plural) the Lord!

The two-verse Psalm 117 expanded this invitation to include *all nations and peoples.*

Which brings us to Psalm 118.

Psalm 118: The Big Event

As I explained in my comments to verse 1, in Psalm 118 we have arrived at the scene of the event of celebration and praise accompanying the offering of thanksgiving in the temple in Jerusalem. After inviting everyone to join him, our grateful host opens the proceedings by calling on all present to *Give thanks to the Lord for He is good* (v.1); stated in the second person plural. He is addressing the crowd that is before him.

After three more verses of introduction he begins to tell his story. *From the narrow place I called out... they encircled me... but the Lord has assisted me... etc.*

I would like to suggest that beginning with verse 23, the psalmist is describing the *reaction of those who are present*. After they have heard the story they declare that they, too, see the greatness of God's salvation described by their host.

This has emerged from the Lord; it is wondrous in <u>our</u> eyes.
This is the day that the Lord has made; <u>we</u> will rejoice and delight in it.

These lines are spoken by the crowd that has assembled as they express their wonder and praise of God for the redemption that they have heard told. Now we understand the change from *I* to *we*.

Now, in our verse, the guests at the thanksgiving offering turn to bless the host. *Blessed is the one who comes <u>in the name of the Lord</u>;* This is a direct reference back to verses 10 through 12.

10. All nations surrounded me; it was *in the name of the Lord* that I cut them down.
11. They encircled me - indeed they surrounded me; it was *in the name of the Lord* that I cut them down.
12. They encircled me like bees; they were extinguished like the fire of thorns; it was *in the name of the Lord* that I cut them down.

To do something *in* someone's *name* means to do it *on their behalf*; to act *for* them. Those who are present at this offering of thanksgiving hear the host declare that his victory over his enemies was *in the name of the Lord*; to add glory to *His name* in the world.

Not everyone who comes to the temple to thank God recognizes this. It is perfectly normal for people to thank God for kindnesses that He has bestowed upon them without realizing that their own salvation must be used *for the Lord's name*. Many very grateful people of faith thank God wholeheartedly for saving them and they leave it at that. Our psalmist takes his gratitude to a higher place. He declares that what God has done for him is actually all for God. *It was in the name of the Lord that I cut them down.* My victory over my enemies was not for my own sake at all.

Hearing this message of total devotion to God, all those present; *Israel, the house of Aaron,* and *the fearers of the Lord* of all peoples and nations bless him.

Blessed is the one who comes in the name of the Lord; we have blessed you from the house of the Lord.

When we hear a tale of God's blessings over someone that we know we ought to bless them for using their experience to increase His glory.

118:27 *Delaying the Celebration*

> **The Lord is All-powerful God**
> **and He has given us light; bind**
> **the festive offering with cords**
> **unto the corners of the altar.**

Layers of meaning in Scripture

What is poetry? The Merriam-Webster dictionary defines poetry as follows:

> Writing that formulates a concentrated imaginative awareness of experience in language chosen and arranged to create a specific emotional response through meaning, sound, and rhythm.

One of the primary ways that language creates a *specific emotional response through meaning* is through the use of words that have multiple meanings and connotations. In numerous earlier passages in this book I have shown examples of this. When a specific word is chosen despite the existence of a more common synonym, I have shown how this choice causes the secondary meaning of the word to add layers of imagery and nuance to that which is explicitly conveyed by the verse. Similarly, when a word is chosen that has definite connotations or symbolism in one place in Scripture, those layers of meaning are often implied beneath the surface by use of that word in other contexts as well.

Unfortunately, for the English reader these layers of meaning are usually lost in translation. One of my goals throughout this book has been to give an opportunity to those who do not have access to the Hebrew to appreciate and be inspired by these nuances.

I say all of this here because our verse includes a number of highly unusual word choices. But before I point them out I'd like to point out the general difficulty that this verses poses.

Should this be two verses?

First, what is the connection of the first half of the verse to the second half? The first half of the verse is a general statement of praise to the Lord Almighty.

The Lord is All-powerful God and He has given us light;

The second half of the verse describes a specific procedure that is done prior to the actual slaughter of the offering.

bind the festive offering with cords unto the corners of the altar.

Problem #1

The first half of the verse has nothing to do with the second half of the verse.

Why mention the binding?

Second, this latter half of the verse is extremely difficult to understand on its own.

We already know that our psalm is describing the offering of a sacrifice of thanksgiving in the temple in Jerusalem. What is the meaning of this particular image in our verse? This verse states that an animal being sacrificed is supposed to be bound with cords before it is slaughtered. But why is this significant enough to be mentioned here? Neither the actual *slaughtering* of the animal, nor the *burning* or *eating* of portions of it is mentioned. Surely these other components of the process are at least as important as the binding of the sacrifice.

Problem #2

Why does the verse mention the <u>binding of the sacrifice</u> in preparation for its sacrifice?
No other parts of the process of the offering are mentioned.

An unusual word for <u>sacrifice</u>

Third, the Hebrew word for festive offering in our verse is ChAG. This word appears sixty-two times in Scripture. *In all but three of them, it does not refer to an offering at all.*

ChAG is the Hebrew word for *festival*. This is the word used for all of the pilgrimage festivals without any reference to the sacrificial offerings that are brought on those days. In other words, the word ChAG simply means *festival*. ChAG also appears in a verb form in sixteen different verses meaning *to celebrate*. Such as:

> The Lord will bring on them the plague he inflicts on the nations that do not go up to *celebrate* the *Festival* of Tabernacles. This will be the punishment of Egypt and the punishment of all the nations that do not go up to *celebrate* the *Festival* of Tabernacles. (Zechariah 14:18-19)

Problem #3

The Hebrew word for "sacrifice" used here – CHAG - is an unusual word for sacrifice.
In fact, it does not even mean "sacrifice" in 59 of 62 times it appears in the Bible, where it means "festival" or "celebration."

Where it means *festival <u>offering</u>* (here, Exodus 23:18, & Malachi 2:3) the meaning is *borrowed* from the fact that offerings are brought to the temple *on the festivals*. These three exceptions do not change the fact that the straightforward and plain meaning of ChAG is *festival* or *celebration*.

The use of ChAG for to describe the offering in our verse is especially strange because, as opposed to Exodus 23:18, there is no indication whatsoever that the sacrifice in our psalm has anything to do with one of the festivals. On the contrary, based on what has led up to this verse, the sacrifice here is a thanksgiving offering brought in response to an event of divine salvation. Why does the psalmist use this specific and unusual word to describe this offering?

Problem #4

In the two other places where CHAG refers to a sacrifice, this is only because it refers to a <u>festival offering</u>.

But our psalm is not about a festival offering. It is about a thanksgiving offering.

Bind: Constrict vs Connect

The phrase *bind the festive offering with cords* is made up of three Hebrew words.

ISRU	*bind*
ChAG	*festive offering*
Ba'AVOTIM	*with cords*

The root of the word ISRU – *bind* – is ASaR, one of two Hebrew words for *tying* or *binding*. The other is KaShaR. Despite the fact that these two words are often synonyms, there is a significant difference in meaning between the two. ASaR, the word used in our verse, also means to *restrict* (e.g. Numbers 30:3) and to *trap* or *imprison*. (e.g. Genesis 42:16,19) In other words, while ASaR means *to bind*, the connotation is more of *restriction* than of *connection*. KaShaR, the other word for *binding*, implies *tying* or *connecting* two things together. As in the description of the emotional bond between David and Jonathan:

> When David had finished speaking to Saul, the soul of Jonathan was *bonded* to the soul of David, and Jonathan loved him as himself. (I Samuel 18:1; see also Genesis 44:30)

To emphasize this point, other than our verse, the word *with cords* appears with the verb ASaR in two other contexts in Scripture.

> They said to him, "We've come *bind you* and hand you over to the Philistines." Samson said, "Swear to me that you won't kill me yourselves." "Agreed," they answered. "We will only *bind you* and hand you over to them. We will not kill you." So they *bound* him with two new *ropes* and led him up from the rock. (Judges 15:12-13; see also ibid 16:11)

And

> And you, son of man, they will *bind* with *ropes*; you will be *bound* so that you cannot go out among the people. I will make your tongue stick to the roof of your mouth so that you will be silent and unable to rebuke them, for they are a rebellious people. (Ezekiel 3:25-26)

Both in the story of Samson and the Philistines as well as in the prophecy of Ezekiel the clear meaning of being *bound* is that of being *constricted* and *limited*.

Confused? Let's kept things simple.

There are two Hebrew words for binding with ropes.

- One is used to emphasize the idea of *connection*; that one thing is being *tied to another*.
- The other refers to the *tying up* of something; that what it tied is *bound, trapped*, and *restricted*.

The word in our verse is the second one.

Bound to the altar?

Lastly, our verse refers to the offering being *bound unto the altar*. This is very strange as there is no sacrifice that was bound to the altar. The thanksgiving offering was slaughtered *in front of the altar*, blood of the animal was sprinkled *on the altar*, and then certain body parts were burned *on top of the altar*. *Nothing was tied to the altar*. To make matters worse, the word for *unto* is actually the Hebrew word AD which means *until*, not *unto* in the way it would be meant in the English.

To review:

We have raised the following questions:

1. What does the first half of the verse which praises God in general terms have to do with the second half of the verse describing the binding of the offering?
2. Why is the binding of the offering mentioned at all?
3. Why is the offering referred to as ChAG – which literally means *festival* or *celebration*?
4. The phrase *bind... with cords* implies restriction. The only other places these words appear imply limiting one's actions or expressions and here the offering is being tied to something.
5. Why does the verse seem to say that the sacrifice was bound to the altar when this was never done?

A multi-layered declaration

I began my comments on this verse by asserting that Scripture often chooses specific words in order to convey multiple layers of meaning. Our verse is a beautiful example of this.

The plain meaning of our verse continues with the words spoken by those assembled for the celebration. After blessing the host in the previous verse, they now praise the Lord and call upon the priests in the temple to proceed with the offering. *"Bind the festive offering unto to corners of the altar! Let the sacrificial service begin!"*

Based on all of the above, perhaps this verse is making a powerful theological statement about how and when we celebrate what God has done for us.

Restrict your celebration until you have sacrificed!
The host has told his story of how God came to his aid and granted him victory over his enemies. He recognizes that he now has a responsibility to use the gifts that he has been given in the service of the Lord. In fact, the entire purpose of this celebration is to inspire others so that they too will praise God and devote their lives and the gifts they have been given to the building of His kingdom.

Now, as the celebratory feast of the thanksgiving offering is about to get underway, our verse declares:

Hold back and restrain the celebration - CHAG - with cords until the corners of the altar.

In other words, *do not dare to begin the festivities until it is obvious to all that this celebration is intrinsically bound up with personal sacrifice and devotion to God. Only when it is clear that the primary purpose is THE ALTAR – that portion of the sacrifice that is given to HIM – can we continue with the celebration with the secure knowledge that our responsibility to Him will not be lost in the joyous festivities.*

To help with what I am suggesting, let's call the actual translation, TRANSLATION and we'll refer to my suggested lesson from the strange word choices, NUANCE.

HEBREW	TRANSLATION	NUANCE
ISRU	*Bind*	*Hold back*
CHAG	*the offering*	*the celebration*
Ba'AVOTIM	*with ropes*	*with restriction and caution*
AD	*unto*	*until*
KARNOT	*the corners of*	
HAMIZBEACH	*the altar*	*proper commitment to serve God has been made*

Now we can understand the connection between the first half of the verse and the second.

The Lord is All-powerful God and He has given us light – we see the great hand of the Lord and our eyes are now open. We see more clearly. Like the pillar of fire for Israel in the desert, God has illuminated the path that we must walk. Therefore, merely thanking God and rejoicing in what He has done for us will not suffice. Before we engage in that celebration we must first declare our dedication to Him and our willingness to *sacrifice* for Him. So we declare,

bind the festive offering with cords – hold back on the festivities

unto the corners of the altar – until our commitments to sacrifice for God are made.

Our celebrations of God's salvation must come after we have secured our commitments to serve Him and to sacrifice for Him.

118:28 *The Personal Relationship Returns*

You are my All-powerful God
and I will thank You; my God,
and I will exalt You.

A personal message to God

There are two particularly striking features of this verse. First, the verse opens with a second person direct reference to God; <u>You</u> *are my all powerful God*. Every other verse in this psalm with the exception of verses 25 and 21 speak of God in the third person. For the most part, psalm 118 is about God; it is not addressed *to God*.

The second notable change in this verse is that it is written in the singular. The five verses leading up to this one were written in the plural, as though spoken by a group of people collectively.

...we have blessed you from the house of the Lord. The Lord is All-powerful God and He has given *us* light...

To understand the important message of this verse we must remind ourselves of the larger context of the verses and psalms that precede it.

From personal to collective

Over the course of my commentary beginning with psalm 116 and up to this point I have emphasized one predominant theme.

After personally experiencing God's kindness, (116:1-11) the psalmist committed himself to repay the Lord by offering a sacrifice of thanksgiving, thereby publicly sharing his gratitude and declaring the praises of God to all. (116:12-19)

Then in the two verses of Psalm 117, he expanded the scope of his public praise by inviting all the nations of the earth to join him.

Psalm 118 then continued with the scene of the gathering for the offering of thanksgiving. The story was told before all those assembled with gratitude and praise of God. In the verses that led up to this one, as the scene comes to a close, all those who are gathered joined together in praise and blessing.

We have seen over and over that the theme of these psalms is that what God does for us in our own personal lives is meant to be shared with others. We begin with personal private needs and end with a commitment to use the private experience as a springboard for the broadest possible public display of collective praise of God. *Praise the Lord all nations; exalt Him all peoples!*

Here's how I summed this up at the end of my comments to Psalm 116: *It's not about me.* ... God answers my personal prayers so that I can make my contribution to His kingdom over all humanity on this earth; to building His temple in Jerusalem.

Too many people of faith think about their faith only as a private relationship with God. As servants of the Lord we are charged with the responsibility to build His kingdom. This means that we must think collectively rather than personally.

Restoring the personal

I have just emphasized how important it is to focus on universal collective concerns. This is an important lesson, but it has a downside. Just as it is important to use our personal relationship with God as a springboard to more collective concerns; it is equally important to strengthen our faith in the Lord as our own private personal God as well. Caring for all of humanity and working to fix the world and build God's kingdom can lead someone to go to the other extreme. One is liable to think only about the big picture and forget that God cares about each and every one of us as individuals as well; that He is involved in our lives for *us personally* and not only as part of the larger plan.

The intensely personal nature of our verse, the second to last verse in this psalm, brings this message into focus.

After sharing his story with others; after fulfilling his duty to use his personal experience as a catalyst to spread knowledge of God to others, the psalmist turns directly to God and says; *You are my God.* Yes, I am using what I have received from You to spread Your glory to others; but that does not mean that I have moved on from our personal relationship. The intimacy with God remains.

Even as we embrace the universal mission to influence others, we must not lose focus on private personal relationship. This is the source of strength in faith that we need to continue to serve Him.

118:29 *Who is the Psalmist?*

Give thanks to the Lord for He is good; for His kindness is eternal.

This final verse of Psalm 118, and the last in the entire series of the *Hallel* psalms of praise, is an exact repetition of verse 1.

For He is good; for His kindness is eternal

In my comments to verse 1 I quoted the following passage from Jeremiah:

So says the Lord: 'There will yet be heard in this place about which you say, "It is a desolate waste, without people or animals" - in the towns of Judah and the streets of Jerusalem that are deserted, inhabited by neither people nor animals - the sounds of joy and gladness, the voices of bride and bridegroom, and voices saying,

"Give thanks to the Lord of Hosts, for the Lord is good; for His kindness is eternal."

As they bring a thanksgiving offering to the house of the Lord; For I will restore the returnees of the land as they were before,' says the Lord. (Jeremiah 33:10-11)

Not including this passage in Jeremiah and our verse here in Psalm 118, these words, *Give thanks to the Lord for he is good; for His kindness is eternal*, appear ten additional times in Scripture. In the majority of these, the context is celebratory worship in the temple by the entire people of Israel. (Ezra 3:11; I Chronicles 16:34,41; II Chronicles 5:13; 7:3,6) The remaining examples all refer to specific situations of the redemption of Israel from either danger or exile. (Psalm 106:1; Psalm 107:1; Psalm 136:1; II Chronicles 20:21) Notice that the verses from Jeremiah that I just cited actually combine both of these themes – *celebratory worship in the temple* and *redemption from exile*.

My point is this:

The words of our verse, *Give thanks to the Lord for he is good; for His kindness is eternal*, appear 12 times in Scripture. The context is *always*:

- Celebratory worship by the entire Israel   (Ezra, I Chronicles, II Chronicles)
- Collective redemption of from exile or danger   (Psalms, II Chronicles)
- *Both*   (Jeremiah)

In other words, the implication of these words – the opening and closing verse of Psalm 118 – is that we are not talking about an *individual*.

So Who is our Psalmist?

As we read Psalm 118 we envision an individual who was suffering, in danger, was then saved by the Lord, and is now sharing this experience in praise and worship by bringing a thanksgiving offering in the temple in Jerusalem. But in truth, Psalm 118 is not about an individual at all. It is about the ultimate redemption of all of God's people.

As I just pointed out, Psalm 118's identical opening and closing verses are words that are reserved for collective praise and thanks to God for his great hand in history. *These words never appear in a private individual context.*

The truth is that there were indications in our psalm that despite all of the singular language the subject was really not an individual at all. For example, in verse 10 we read, *All nations surrounded me; it was in the name of the Lord that I cut them down.* What individual has ever experienced an attack by *all nations*? Obviously, the voice that is speaking in our psalm is not a solitary private person. Rather, it is the single voice of *the people of Israel.*

But the first indication of this was in the transition from Psalm 116 to Psalm 117 that immediately preceded our psalm. After committing himself to *fulfill my vows to the Lord; now in the presence of all His people,* the psalmist continued by inviting *all peoples and all nations* to join in praising God for the kindness He has done *for us.* Who is this individual who has the status and power to invite all peoples and all nations to join him? Again, the individual is no individual at all. It is Israel.

So why is the story of suffering and redemption in Psalms 116 and 118 stated in the singular? If it really is the story of God's people in their difficult exile culminating in being joined by all people of faith in the ultimate redemption, why is it written as though it is one person?

God's Story is My Story too

As I explained in my comments to verses 1 through 4, collective experiences are the sum total of the experiences of individuals who choose to identify with the collective. This identification is the journey of Psalm 116 through 118. Danger, fear, and gratitude are very *private feelings.* Times of personal hardship help us cultivate intense personal feelings of faith. Without that sense of intimacy; the knowledge that God cares for each and every one of us individually; we will never really have faith nor will we acknowledge God's hand in our lives. But here we are taught that when we do experience that intimacy with God in our personal lives we must transform our personal sense of gratitude into a public display of praise and worship for the glory of God?

Furthermore, when the danger, fear, and redemption that I personally experience are part of a *larger historical process,* I have a responsibility to be conscious of this broader perspective. I ought not to be concerned about current events only inasmuch as they affect my own life. In this way I identify myself as part of history; as part of God's plan for the world. By identifying with God's plan I transform myself as well. My concern for how things will turn out is no longer primarily about my own well being. With a God-plan perspective I see history as my own personal story.

This is how personal private concerns can culminate in a commitment to use the private experience as a springboard for the broadest possible public display of collective praise of God. *Praise the Lord all nations; exalt Him all peoples!*

So, is Psalm 118 a personal story or a collective one? The answer is that if I choose to identify with God's plan for the world, then history becomes my own personal story as well.

The more we widen the lens of our concern the more we identify with God's larger plan for the world.

A final thought for Psalm 118

Thinking about history can be overwhelming. I don't know if this was always the case but in the times that we live in, it certainly is. Living in Israel makes history a part of everyday life. When I walk the streets of Jerusalem my mind inevitably wanders to what it must have looked like, 10, 100, 500, or 2000 years ago. The changes in Jerusalem are a lens through which to see the entirety of Jewish History.

When I read history I try very hard to get into the head of someone who lived in the time period that I am reading about. I picture myself there. What would I have felt? What would I have believed? What would someone living through a different time have thought if they could really see the future; if they could see our world?

When the nation of Israel was heading into exile around the time of the destruction of the temple in Jerusalem, what was going through their minds? What did they think when Jeremiah spoke the words that I quoted in my comments to Psalm 118?

> So says the Lord: 'There will yet be heard in this place about which you say, "It is a desolate waste, without people or animals" - in the towns of Judah and the streets of Jerusalem that are deserted, inhabited by neither people nor animals - the sounds of joy and gladness, the voices of bride and bridegroom, and voices saying,
>
> "*Give thanks* to the Lord of Hosts, *for the Lord is good; for His kindness is eternal.*"
>
> *As they bring a thanksgiving offering to the house of the Lord*; For I will restore the returnees of the land as they were before,' says the Lord. (Jeremiah 33:10-11)

Jerusalem really was desolate. It really was devoid of the sounds of joy and gladness. What did people really think of Jeremiah's promise that these joyous sounds would return; that the exiles would be ingathered?

I am a big fan of fine art. In my spare time and on my travels for work I use every opportunity available to see great works of art. I am always in middle of some book about art or art history. There is one particular painting by Rembrandt that is my single favorite work of art. I was fortunate enough to see the original in person once in my life, but you can find it easily on the internet. It's called Jeremiah Lamenting the Destruction of Jerusalem. It depicts Jeremiah sitting with what appears to be a few items salvaged from the temple, his head leaning on his hand, with a look of deep sorrow and contemplation on his face. It is a beautiful painting. It is one of Rembrandt's masterpieces.

When I look at this painting I think about what the thousands of years of exile of Israel must have looked like to someone who knew that they were only just beginning. That is thought that I imagine going through Rembrandt's Jeremiah's mind.

I think about the centuries of Jews who held firm to the hopeful prophecies of a glorious restoration to Jerusalem despite a reality that made this future appear completely impossible. How did they hang on? I am perpetually in awe of their extraordinary faith.

You see, for me it is easy to believe in the Biblical promises of the future. With millions of Jews returned from the four corners of the earth, with sovereignty over the land of Israel restored to the people of Israel – with so many of these prophecies already fulfilled, it is easy to believe that the rest of them will eventually come true as well. But how did they do it? I stand in awe.

The only way I can understand it is that they understood that the word of God is real. It is more real than the reality in which we live at any given moment. They knew that when Jeremiah said that there will be a restoration and that Jerusalem would once again be filled with joy and gladness, this meant that it was a certainty! In the words of Psalm 115, *All that He wills is done!* They depth of their faith is awe inspiring.

With this perspective, one can only imagine what kind of strength they must have drawn every time they read these *Hallel* psalms of praise and thanks.

All nations surrounded me; it was in the name of the Lord that I cut them down.

They encircled me - indeed they surrounded me; it was in the name of the Lord that I cut them down.

They encircled me like bees; they were extinguished like the fire of thorns; it was in the name of the Lord that I cut them down.

You have surely pushed me to the point of falling; but the Lord has assisted me.

Just imagine how these words sounded – *and felt* - through the centuries of exile, persecution, and weakness.

How easy it is for me to praise and thank the Lord. How humbling it is to think about these same words spoken by centuries of Jews whose entire reality was:

All nations surrounded me;

and

You have surely pushed me to the point of falling;.

For us, the impossible dream of Jeremiah is a reality. The streets of Jerusalem are once again filled with joy and gladness; the voices of bride and bridegroom, and of voices saying *Give thanks to the Lord for He is good; for His kindness is forever.*

I wish I could reach back in time and speak to those generations who believed. I wish I could show them our world. I wish I could show them the State of Israel. I wish I could show them Jerusalem filled with the nation of Israel ingathered from all over the world. I wish I could show them the millions among the *peoples* and *nations* who join us in praising and thanking the Lord for all that he has bestowed on *us*! In the words of Psalm 117; *His kindness has overwhelmed us.*

I wish I could call to them across the centuries and say, "Look! We're here! We made it through! We're back! Look at Jerusalem!"

But you know what; they wouldn't be surprised at all. They had real faith. They knew it was coming all along.

A final thought on the study of Scripture.

Have you ever received a love letter? Or a text message from someone that you are yearning to be closer to? Did you find yourself reading it over and over again? Did you cherish certain choices of particular words and turns of phrase? Did you sometimes wonder about possibilities of what could have been written instead?

The reason that you do this to a love letter is simple. You care. When we delve deeply into the words of the Bible we show God that we care. We show Him that we love Him and want to be closer to Him; to better understand exactly what He is trying to tell us. When we pay close attention and work to understand the layers of meaning that He intended for us, we are engaged in a form of worship. Study of the word of God is a form of worship of God.

I pray that I have brought this sentiment to the explorations of Scripture that you have found in this book.

A NOTE ON THE NAMES OF GOD

There are three names of God that appear in the *Hallel* psalms. While I have explained each of them in context where relevant, I thought it would be helpful to include a more thorough explanation of the etymological meanings of these names.

YHVH

God's name, YHVH, also known as the tetragrammaton, appears over 6000 times in the Bible. Throughout most English translations of the Bible this name is translated as "the Lord." But, in actual fact, "the Lord" is not a translation of the tetragrammaton at all as YHVH has no meaning in Hebrew outside of being God's name.

So why is YHVH always translated as "the Lord"?

Jewish practice prohibits explicitly saying the tetragrammaton as written. Due to this prohibition, thousands of years ago a euphemism was introduced to be used as a *replacement* to be said instead of explicit written letters YHVH. That euphemism is "ADON*AI*" – which literally means, "my Lord". The Hebrew word ADON means "lord" or "master" human or otherwise. ADONAI includes the first person possessive suffix – which translates as "my".

So "the Lord" is not a translation of YHVH. It is a translation of the *euphemistic replacement* for YHVH. As I just explained, the actual name YHVH has no English translation as it is not actually any Hebrew word other than God's name.

So what does YHVH actually mean?

The name YHVH, like every name of God, is a Hebrew word. It is a very holy and lofty Hebrew word, but it is a word, nonetheless. Like every Hebrew word, YHVH has a root. The root of YHVH is the verb *to be* or *to exist*. The form or conjugation of this root that is YHVH is an impossible mix of past, present, and future tenses.

We can see where God's name YHVH comes from if we consider three words:

#1	YEHYEH	Will be
#2	HOVEH	Is / Present
#3	HAYAH	Was

I will try to keep this simple. Look at these words. They have some features in common. They have some differences. Each one has an exception that the other two do not have.

- #1 begins with YE
- #2 contains OV in the middle
- #3 ends with AH

#2 & #3 begin with H
#1 & #3 do not.
#1 & #2 end with EH

Look at those three exceptions together. Look familiar?

YE   OV   AH

Let's put it all together. The name of God YHVH is made up of three syllables.

The first syllable   YE is the unique *beginning* of YEHYEH "will be."
The middle syllable   OV is the unique *middle* of HOVEH   "present"
The last syllable   AH is the unique *end* of HAYAH   "was"

So, YHVH, as *a Hebrew word*, is a blend of the words for *future, present*, and *past*. Pretty good name for God, right?

Different parts of the four letters of YHVH contain grammatical elements of these three different tenses. The Y at the beginning indicates future tense. The V in the middle indicates present. The aH sound at the end is for the past tense. *Future, present, past.* Does this seem out of order? Wouldn't it make more sense if the order was *past, present,* and *future*?

Everything in existence first exists in the *future*. Then it becomes part of the *present*. It then slips into the *past*. Before I sat down to write this, my writing was a part of the future. Right now, as I am writing it is in the present. After I am done it will be part of the past. The same is true for every created being and every moment in time. So in actuality, *future, present, past* is the order of existence.

In fact, if you look back at the name YHVH as I just explained it you will see something amazing. A person reading this name would begin by starting the word for "will be". He would then continue in the next syllable by saying the word "present". He would finish the word by saying the final syllable of the word "was." His expression of God's name begins in the future, passes through the present, and ends up in the past!

Again, this name does not actually translate into "the Lord". You see, Jewish law and tradition prohibits the explicit utterance of this holy name as it is written. This should make sense now. After all, the meaning of the name is a concept that human beings can not hold in their consciousness. Past, present, and future all being blended together as they are in God may be a matter of faith, but the human experience within time prevents us from fully grasping this concept. Therefore, in deference to the fact that this name describes an aspect of God that is beyond our comprehension, we express this by the prohibition against saying this name. After all, to express something that I do not actually know is tantamount to falsehood. If I express something, I am giving the impression that it is something that I know. And this name of God is unknowable.

So, as I explained, thousands of years ago we came up with a euphemism that is the standard replacement when we see the name YHVH. That euphemism is ADONAI. The translation into English of ADONAI is "my Lord" which popularly became, "The Lord."

ELOHIM

The second most common name for God in the Bible is ELOHIM. This name is universally translated as "God". It also appears quite often as ELOHEINU.

ELOHEINU – *our God* – is the possessive form of the name ELOHIM – *God*.
This is the only name of God that appears in Genesis 1, the six days of the creation of the world. Unlike YHVH, this name is pronounced as it is written.

Three important points to help us understand this name better:
1. ELOHIM is also the Biblical Hebrew word for "judges" or "courts". One example is Exodus 22:9 "the cause of both parties shall come before the *judges.*"
2. ELOHIM is also used when Scripture speaks of false gods; e.g. in the 10 commandments, "You shall have no other gods before Me."
3. ELOHIM is a plural word, although when referring to God, the verbs that accompany it are always in the singular.

Essentially, the name means "powers". This is why it is the name of God that is associated with the creation story. All the various forces of nature are part of God. He is ALL POWERFUL. In other words, all powers rest with Him. This is the meaning of ELOHIM.

YAH

A third name of God that appears in the *Hallel* psalms is YAH.
This name of God is often written as Jah in English. This is the name that makes up the last syllable of the word *Halleluyah*, or *praise the Lord.*

Most translators write *the Lord* for YaH because this name is, in fact, made up of the first two letters of YHVH which, as I mentioned, is always translated as *the Lord*. So just as they translate YHVH as *the Lord*, they translate YAH as *the Lord* as well.

While this is an understandable choice, the result is that readers of Scripture in English are unaware when the name in use is the much more rarely used YAH instead of YHVH.

In addition, by translating them identically, any unique purpose and meaning of the name YaH is completely lost in translation.

The name YaH or YH – the beginning of YHVH - is the *future* part of God's name. In other words, it represents *God's will*; His plan *before* we see it. That is where all of existence and all of history *is* before it happens. It is part of the *future*; still part of God's will and plan.

When we see events unfolding and believe and declare that we see *God's plan*, what we mean is that we believe that God thought of this and willed it before it happened. That from the beginning of time, all the events that we experience already existed in the future tense.

There are many other names of God used throughout Scripture. Each of these names, like the three here, are actual Hebrew words. They are descriptions of traits, modes of behavior that God employs in His interactions with His creation.